BLACK GOLD IN TEXAS

OIL AND GAS HISTORY FROM THE SOUTHWESTERN HISTORICAL QUARTERLY

Edited by Richard B. McCaslin

Introduction by Jason P. Theriot

TSHA
Texas State Historical Association
An Independent Nonprofit Since 1897
AUSTIN, TEXAS

© 2025 Texas State Historical Association
All rights reserved. Printed in the U.S.A.

LIBRARY OF CONGRESS CATALOGING-IN-PUBLICATION DATA
Library of Congress Cataloging-in-Publication Data

Names: McCaslin, Richard B. editor | Theriot, Jason P., 1975– writer of introduction
Title: Black Gold in Texas: Oil and Gas History from the Southwestern Historical Quarterly / Richard B. McCaslin, ed.; introduction by Jason P. Theriot.
Publisher: Texas State Historical Association, [2025]
Identifiers: LCCN 2025044332 (print) | LCCN 2025044333 (ebook) | ISBN 9781625110947 (paperback) | ISBN 9781625110954 (ebook)
Subjects: LCSH: Petroleum industry and trade—Texas—History | Gas industry—Texas—History | Oil fields—Press coverage—Texas | Texas—Economic conditions
Classification: LCC HD9567.T3 B53 2025 (print) | LCC HD9567.T3 (ebook) | DDC 338.2/728209764—dc23/eng/20250924
LC record available at https://lccn.loc.gov/2025044332
LC ebook record available at https://lccn.loc.gov/2025044333

Design by Neil Ferguson

Texas State Historical Association
P.O. Box 5428
Austin, Texas 78763
(512) 471-2600
www.tshaonline.org

"Every citizen of Texas is engaged either directly or indirectly in the oil industry or is affected by it. The words oil, gas, and Texas are truly synonymous."

—CHARLES A. WARNER

Southwestern Historical Quarterly

Contents

- vii — Editor's Preface: Black Gold in the *Southwestern Historical Quarterly,* RICHARD B. McCASLIN
- xi — Introduction: From Gushers to Fractures: A Historiographical Survey of Texas Oil and Gas, JASON P. THERIOT
- 1 — Oil, the Courts, and the Texas Railroad Commission, JAMES P. HART (*January 1941*)
- 20 — Texas Collection, H. BAILEY CARROLL (*July 1944*)
- 24 — A Plea for More Business in History, EUGENE C. BARKER (*July 1944*)
- 28 — The Spirit of Santa Rita, GEORGE A. HILL JR. (*July 1944*)
- 38 — Electra, A Texas Oil Town, ABBY W. COOPER (*July 1946*)
- 46 — Spindletop, BOYCE HOUSE (*July 1946*)
- 58 — Reminiscences of Sour Lake, CHARLIE JEFFRIES (*July 1946*)
- 72 — Texas and the Oil Industry, CHARLES A. WARNER (*July 1946*)
- 100 — The Oil Industry in Texas Since Pearl Harbor, CHARLES A. WARNER (*January 1958*)
- 116 — Texas Petroleum History: A Selective Annotated Bibliography, WALTER RUNDELL JR. (*October 1963*)
- 136 — Chaos in the East Texas Oil Field, 1930-1935, ROBERT D. BOYLE (*January 1966*)
- 150 — The Texas Railroad Commission and the Elimination of the Flaring of Natural Gas, 1930-1949, DAVID F. PRINDLE (*January 1981*)
- 168 — Oil and the Permanent University Fund: The Early Years, DAVID F. PRINDLE (*October 1982*)
- 192 — The Failed Promise of Wartime Opportunity for Mexicans in the Texas Oil Industry, EMILIO ZAMORA (*January 1992*)
- 220 — Creating Company Culture: Oil Company Camps in the Southwest, 1920–1960, DIANA D. HINTON (*April 2008*)
- 242 — "I'm a Tool Pusher from Snyder:" Slim Willet's Oil Patch Songs, JOE W. SPECHT (*January 2010*)
- 260 — Risky Business: Oil Well Shooters in the Southwestern Oil Fields, DAVID F. DIXON (*July 2010*)
- 285 — Authors
- 289 — Notes

Spindletop in January 1901 by Francis J. "Frank" Trost.
Courtesy of Portal to Texas History

EDITOR'S PREFACE

Black Gold in the *Southwestern Historical Quarterly*

RICHARD B. McCASLIN

O IL REDEFINED TEXAS during the twentieth century. Texans had won their independence from Mexico in 1836, joined fellow Southerners in losing the Civil War in 1865, and made a great economic recovery with cattle and cotton as the nineteenth century came to a close. All of that provided more than enough history to give Texas a distinct image in the eyes of many outside observers, even as Texans debated which of those backstories truly defined them. Then Spindletop exploded in 1901, flooding the surrounding landscape with barrels of black gold. Other drillers found glory and profit in other parts of the Lone Star State, and by 1927 Texas led the United States in oil production, a distinction it still retains. Texans also profited greatly from natural gas, refining, pipelines, petrochemicals, and many other oil-related enterprises, all of which contributed to redefining not just the Texas economy, but also its politics and society.

Historians arguably were slow in realizing the impact that oil had on Texas, but they have made important contributions. This can clearly be seen in the articles that have appeared in the *Southwestern Historical Quarterly*, the oldest continuously published academic journal in the United States and the only one among those operating for more than a century that focuses almost exclusively on Texas. It was not until 1941, four decades after Spindletop erupted, that the first article on oil appeared in the *Quarterly*. Three years later, the former director of the Texas State Historical Association, Eugene C. Barker, lamented the lack of business history in a speech published in the *Quarterly*. The Association had already produced its first book on an oil-related topic, a history of Santa Rita No. 1, the West Texas oil well that made the University of Texas one of the wealthiest schools in the world. The Association published the *Quarterly*, so Barker's challenge bore fruit in its pages. In 1946, in the first issue of the *Quarterly's* fiftieth anniversary year, four articles on Texas oil appeared. But it was another twelve years before the *Quarterly* staff printed the next piece on oil history, the first of a trio published between 1958 and 1966. Similarly, sets of three articles have been printed again from 1981 to 1992 and 2008 to 2010, bringing the total number of oil-related essays in the *Quarterly*, including Barker's speech, to seventeen.

The *Quarterly* articles included here provide an interesting and useful perspective on the history of the oil industry and related enterprises in Texas. The first articles, produced during the World War II era when Barker called for more business history, focus naturally on the early years, especially Santa Rita No. 1 and the struggles of the Texas Railroad Commission to expand its authority over oil production. The four that appeared in 1946 include articles on Spindletop and an overview of the Texas oil industry through the eve of World War II, but there are also some of the first community-level studies. The three that appeared twenty years later include a survey of the oil industry after Pearl Harbor, the first historiographical essay on Texas oil enterprises, and a look at the East Texas oilfields during the turmoil of the Great Depression. Since then, there have been more articles on the Commission and Santa Rita, but historians have also provided insightful studies on oil towns, employment, technology, and even music.

In 1995 and 1996, Larry S. Milner published a two-part bibliography of academic sources concerning the history of Texas business. In the preface to the list concerning oil, he wrote, "To the rest of the nation, Texas and oil are synonymous terms." And yet, after almost a century of highly profitable oil and gas production, titles on that business (112) were still outnumbered by works on agriculture (145). Both categories greatly outdistanced other topics such as commerce (17), finance (28), manufacturing (31), mining (12), railroads (61), shipping (38), timber (13), and transport (9). Too, a handful of works on oil and gas could be found in other categories, such as biographies. But clearly the influence of the oil industry and related enterprises had been overlooked by Texas historians.[1] Perhaps this publication will spur more historical research on oil?

Today, the Association provides a tremendous amount of information on Texas oil and related industries in a variety of formats. There are hundreds of articles on the subject in the *Handbook of Texas,* which first appeared in 1953 and is now maintained online and regularly updated by the Association. More articles and statistics for the oil industry and related enterprises can be found in the *Texas Almanac,* first published in 1857 and produced since 2010 by the Association. And this is the sixth book on such topics published by the Association.

This compilation presents the original articles much as they first appeared. All of the text and pictures have been retained, while some new images have been added. Typographical and grammatical errors have been corrected, and the footnotes, if necessary, have been updated in format. Last but not least, Jason P. Theriot has provided a fine new essay to bring the historiographical commentary up to date. In the years to come, this anthology should prove to be just one of many new historical studies of oil and gas in Texas.

Oil Rig in the Permian Basin during the 1950s.
Courtesy of Portal to Texas History

INTRODUCTION

From Gushers to Fractures: A Historiographical Survey of Texas Oil and Gas

JASON P. THERIOT

THIS ESSAY UPDATES earlier historiographic surveys of the Texas oil and gas industry—a subject closely tied to the state's economic development, political power, and cultural identity. The title, "From Gushers to Fractures" is a play on words that signals both a long-term technological evolution and a shift in how historians have approached the subject. Early narratives glorified the gusher—a powerful symbol of discovery and destiny. Later works fractured that popular storyline, breaking it apart to reveal the deeper human, institutional, and cultural layers of the Texas oil economy. Historical literature has moved from mythmaking to critical interpretation, from celebration to scrutiny. Each phase reflects a shift not only in perspectives but in methods—from corporate memoir and biography to oral history and community studies rooted in archival sources.

Using a three-part framework, this overview surveys historical literature by eras of study that closely align with phases of industrial growth. The first phase, dominant through the mid-twentieth century, has been defined by celebratory accounts that cast oilmen as pioneers and painted the industry—and the oil gusher—as a symbol of Texas pride and bravado. The second phase, beginning around the 1980s, marked a shift towards critical inquiry, as historians turned their attention to labor conditions, regulatory structures, and the social costs of boom-and-bust cycles. The final phase, still taking shape, reflects the twenty-first-century shale revolution and the rise of contested issues such as landowner disputes, water management, and rural environmental risks. These subjects remain largely unexplored in the literature but will likely define the next wave of Texas oil and gas history.

This essay also acknowledges the long-standing role of the *Southwestern Historical Quarterly* in documenting Texas oil history. Several of the field's leading scholars—whose books are surveyed here—also contributed to the journal over the decades, dating back to the 1940s. The *Quarterly* has served as a key forum for publishing research on the state's petroleum past and has played a key role in shaping the broader historiography of Texas oil. Its pages reflect the field's evolution, offering insight into how interpretations of oil and its influence have developed over time.

The earliest phase of Texas oil and gas historiography documents the discovery, enterprise, and expansion of the petroleum industry with a tone of admiration and confidence. These works, largely written in the mid-twentieth century, reflect a celebratory view of petroleum development focused on the thrill of discovery, the rise of corporate power, and the transformative impact of oil on Texas's economy and identity. Industry figures are cast as visionary pioneers, while oil itself is portrayed as a near-miraculous force of progress. Absent are critical considerations of labor, community impacts, or environmental consequences. These elements would not enter the scholarly conversation until decades later.

Charles A. Warner's *Texas Oil & Gas Since 1543* stands as the first comprehensive historical treatment of oil in Texas, so it is a pioneering text in the literature of petroleum history.[1] Published in 1939, it presents an ambitious, encyclopedic narrative that traces the evolution of Texas's mineral wealth from Spanish exploration to the emergence of the oil industry in the early twentieth century.

Warner's chronological sweep is his most distinctive legacy. He begins with early European encounters with natural oil seeps in the sixteenth century and proceeds through the salt dome discoveries of the Gulf Coast, the gusher at Spindletop, and the rise of major oil centers like Beaumont and Houston. His work documents the birth of industry regulation, early conservation laws, and the legal frameworks surrounding oil and gas production. In doing so, he laid a foundation for generations of historians, legal scholars, and industry analysts.

Although Warner's approach is largely celebratory and rooted in the Progressive Era ideal that natural resources could be rationally managed for public good, he also pays close attention to economic, legal, and political aspects of Texas oil production. His account of the Texas Railroad Commission's rise to power and the challenges of proration and overproduction in the 1930s provides an early window into the mechanics of government oversight. In many ways, Warner set the stage for the mythmaking tradition in oil history by portraying Texas oilmen as visionaries and the oil patch as a proving ground of American grit and ingenuity.

The book reads more like an institutional or policy chronicle than a narrative history. At over 700 pages, it is densely packed with names, dates, and technical details, yet it lacks the human context found in later memoirs and oral history compilations. Still, Warner's synthesis of legal statutes, field development reports, and geological surveys remains impressive in scope. Later scholarship challenged this early approach for overlooking the social consequences of oil development, particularly the workers, landowners, and communities affected by oilfield expansion. Warner's narrative is top-down and industry-focused, but it provides a baseline for understanding how the Texas oil story was first published.

In sum, *Texas Oil & Gas Since 1543* should be recognized as the seminal scholarly work of Texas oil historiography, a cornerstone upon which later writers would build. For anyone serious about tracing the intellectual arc of Texas oil and gas history, it begins with Warner.

Martin W. Schwettmann's *Santa Rita: The University of Texas Oil Discovery* is a short but significant contribution to early Texas oil literature.[2] Published in a limited edition by the Texas State Historical Association in 1943, and since reprinted several times, this book commemorates the 1923 discovery of the Santa Rita No. 1 well in Reagan County. Schwettmann, a master's student working under the direction of Walter Prescott Webb, then director of the Association and a member of the history faculty at the University, frames this well not merely as a petroleum triumph but as the financial savior of the University. Illustrated by Tom Lea, rich with institutional reverence, the volume tells the story of how a group of Catholic women, owners of the Texon Oil and Land Company, secured the lease, brought in drillers like Carl Cromwell, and transformed the University's land holdings in West Texas into a permanent mineral endowment. While it lacks scholarly intent and offers no broader historical analysis of the Permian Basin, Schwettmann's account is valuable as an institutional narrative—one that framed oil as not just a natural resource but also an economic and moral cornerstone for public higher education in Texas. In contrast to Warner's encyclopedic scope, *Santa Rita* focuses on one field and one event, but its cultural and symbolic significance looms large in Texas oil mythology. It marks a bridge between the sweeping early state histories and the more localized memoirs and regional studies that would follow in the postwar years.

James A. Clark and Michel T. Halbouty's *Spindletop: The True Story of the Oil Discovery That Changed the World* stands as one of the most iconic early narratives in Texas oil historiography.[3] Published in 1952 to commemorate the fiftieth anniversary of the famed "Lucas Gusher," the book serves as both a dramatic retelling and a commemorative tribute to the event that ignited the Texas oil boom and launched the modern petroleum age. Co-authored by a veteran oil journalist (Clark) and a Beaumont native turned geologist and wildcatter (Halbouty), the narrative is steeped in pride, reverence, and regional mythmaking. Though celebratory in tone, it also delivers a level of technical detail, historical scope, and narrative drama that helped define the genre of mid-century petroleum literature in Texas.

The authors cast the discovery as nothing short of a global economic turning point: "It was the beginning of the liquid fuel age that inaugurated the rise of America to dominant world power and its people to an abundant life." Spindletop, as the authors acknowledge, not only fueled a transportation revolution, "It completely cracked the Standard Oil monopoly on the petroleum industry," thus opening the floodgates for a new generation of independent oil companies.[4] From its muddy crater near Beaumont emerged some of the most powerful corporate giants in twentieth-century energy history, including Gulf, Shell, Texaco, and Sun Oil. Edgar Pew of Sun Oil, for example, was among the pioneering industrialists who recognized the commercial scale of the discovery and quickly built the region's first integrated transportation network—complete with storage tanks, pipelines, and tanker-loading docks—to bring Spindletop crude to market.[5] In doing so, Pew and others helped accelerate the decline of coal as a popular transportation fuel, ushering in a profound global energy transition.

In addition to Pew, *Spindletop* celebrates other "captains" of the boom—men like Anthony F. Lucas, the Austrian-born engineer whose persistence and salt-dome theory drove the project forward; Patillo Higgins, the self-taught geologist who first believed in the dome's resource potential; Joseph S. Cullinan, who founded Texaco; Al and Curt Hamill, the Pennsylvania drillers who brought the gusher in; and John Henry Kirby, the East Texas lumber baron who pivoted to oil investment and infrastructure. Also recognized is Frank Yount, a pivotal figure in Spindletop's second boom during the 1920s, who quietly consolidated leases and reworked depleted wells using modern techniques, laying the groundwork for secondary recovery and sustained field development. Clark and Halbouty's narrative is not only biographical but regional, linking the rise of the Beaumont-Port Arthur refining corridor to the birth of petrochemical manufacturing in the United States. The book traces how Spindletop's supply of high-volume, low-cost crude oil catalyzed the refining boom in Southeast Texas, creating one of the largest refining and export complexes in the world by midcentury.[6]

Importantly, *Spindletop* also situates the historic event within a broader geological and scientific context. The authors credit the discovery with proving the hydrocarbon potential of Gulf Coast salt domes, which would shape exploration strategies across the region for decades to come. This theory quickly bore fruit: just a year later, oil was discovered at the Jennings field in South Louisiana, about 100 miles to the east, ushering in that state's oil era. The book's technical appendix provides one of the most accessible early descriptions of salt dome formation, helping bridge the gap between geologic theory and applied fieldwork for both engineers and lay readers.

While *Spindletop* avoids critical engagement with labor, land use, or social disruption—concerns that defined later scholarship—it succeeds as an informative account of risk, grit, and transformation. Though celebratory and selective, *Spindletop* remains a keystone text in the historical imagination of Texas oil, offering a timeless narrative of the oil well that changed the world.

Clark and Halbouty returned to the Texas oil story in 1972 with *The Last Boom*, a companion volume to their earlier work on Spindletop. This time the focus was East Texas.[7] The discovery of the East Texas oilfield in 1930—still the largest in the lower 48—marked the next great chapter in the state's petroleum history. Once again, the authors cast the key players as larger-than-life figures: Columbus "Dad" Joiner, the failed wildcatter with more guts than cash; and A. D. "Doc" Lloyd, the self-taught geologist whose unconventional theories proved right. The book delivers a familiar blend of geological insight, narrative flair, and regional pride. It celebrates the East Texas field not just as a resource boon, but as a turning point that disrupted global markets, crashed oil prices, and forced the hand of state regulators to institute modern prorationing policies to curb production. Like their earlier Spindletop volume, *The Last Boom* steers clear of labor or community impacts and sticks to the high drama of discovery and development. But in doing so, it extends the mythic arc of Texas oil from the salt domes of Beaumont to the piney woods of Kilgore—securing its place as a cornerstone of mid-century oil historiography.

Published nearly a century after the Lucas gusher erupted at Spindletop, Paul N. Spellman's *Spindletop Boom Days* provides a ground-level social history of the Texas oil boom's earliest and most chaotic chapter.[8] Drawing heavily on newspapers, oral histories, and trade publications, Spellman reconstructs the volatile years between 1901 and 1905 with an eye for the rougher edges of oilfield life. His focus is not on the wealthy titans of industry, but on the roughnecks, speculators, landmen, and townspeople who descended on Beaumont and its nearby boomtowns like Sour Lake and Batson. He captures the chaos and danger of the early fields where hastily constructed derricks stood shoulder to shoulder, law enforcement struggled to keep pace, and lives were often ruined overnight.

Spellman's narrative is steeped in the drama of daily life—fires, blowouts, bar fights, and backroom deals—but it avoids romanticizing the era. Instead, it underscores the disorder and instability that defined the early oil patch, offering a corrective to midcentury works that celebrated the era's breakthroughs without reckoning with its costs. While the book does not rely on manuscript collections or personal diaries, it is rooted in contemporary reporting and firsthand newspaper accounts, providing a unique perspective of an emerging industrial society in flux. As such, *Spindletop Boom Days* stands as a regional, people-centered complement to the more industrial or corporate accounts of the same period.

Casting an eye out west, Clarence C. Pope's *An Oil Scout in the Permian Basin* is a lively, firsthand account of life in the oilfields of West Texas, told through the eyes of a man whose job it was to gather intelligence in the most competitive corner of the oil patch.⁹ Written in the classic booster style of midcentury oil memoirs, Pope's story is less about corporate titans and more about the unsung field hands who gathered and traded vital information—well logs, production figures, leasing activity—often before the data reached the official record.

Pope's narrative spans his long career from the early 1920s through the postwar boom of the 1950s, an era when the Permian Basin transformed from a remote frontier to one of the most prolific oil provinces in the world. His complex role as a scout—part spy, part salesman, part geologist—was critical before digital databases and regulatory transparency. He paints vivid scenes of long drives across dusty ranch roads, backroom deals in Midland coffee shops, and the camaraderie (and competition) among fellow scouts trying to stay one step ahead of the drilling crews. "There was no textbook," Pope wrote. "You learned to scout the hard way—by getting beat, and learning from it."¹⁰

From a historiographical perspective, Pope's narrative fits squarely within the early tradition of oil industry storytelling—first-person accounts that romanticize the rough nature of the business. Like other midcentury memoirs, it offers little critical analysis but plenty of color and insight. It is particularly valuable for what it reveals about the unwritten rules of the oil business—the networks of knowledge, rumor, and reconnaissance that shaped decisions in the field long before they showed up in corporate reports or regulatory filings. Pope's story is less about strategy and more about survival, where instinct and experience often mattered more than formal training.

From the oil scout to the oil giant, John O. King's *Joseph Stephen Cullinan: A Study of Leadership in the Texas Petroleum Industry, 1897–1937* adds a biographical dimension to a transitional period in Texas oil history.¹¹ Written in the style of a "great man" business history, King's study focuses on Cullinan's role in shaping the modern oil industry, from his early success in Corsicana and Spindletop to his leadership in founding the Texas Company. King portrays Cullinan as a visionary entrepreneur who brought industrial organization, infrastructure investment, and national reach to the chaotic Texas oilfields. This work provides a useful contrast to any roughneck memoirs by focusing on the corporate architect rather than the field-level grunt. While the tone remains complimentary towards Cullinan as a leader and visionary, King's biography provides a detailed account of diversification in the industry, such as pipeline development, refinery siting, and early corporate strategy. These key themes resurfaced in sponsored institutional histories that followed.

Marquis James's *The Texaco Story: The First Fifty Years* and Henrietta M. Larson and Kenneth W. Porter's *History of Humble Oil & Refining Company* mark a shift in Texas oil historiography from field memoirs and mythic discovery tales to polished, institutional retrospectives underwritten by the subject companies.[12] Both works were written in the early postwar era amid a surge of commemorative literature that followed the fiftieth anniversary of the Lucas Gusher. While they differ in tone—James's being more narrative-driven and Larson and Porter's more academic—each offers a carefully crafted origin story that links the chaos of the early boomtowns to the rise of disciplined, vertically integrated oil giants.

James's opening chapters focus on the "pioneering period" from 1901 to 1913, during which Cullinan led the formation of the Texas Company out of the early Spindletop supply glut. In just over thirty pages, James recounts how Cullinan and his partners moved quickly to build tank farms, acquire leases, and construct a major refinery at Port Arthur, positioning the Texas Company—later rebranded Texaco—as a serious competitor in a rapidly growing petroleum market. The remainder of the book shifts northward to the company's New York headquarters and outward to global ventures, portraying Texaco as a modern international corporation.

Larson and Porter's tome, though more scholarly in approach (and over 700 pages), follows a similar trajectory. The book begins with Humble's roots in the aftermath of Spindletop and traces its steady rise through the Texas oilfields before entering into partnership with Standard Oil of New Jersey in 1919. From there, the authors trace Humble's transformation into a national energy powerhouse, chronicling the expansion of its refining and marketing operations and its critical role in wartime production. Larson, a pioneer in business history, emphasizes the intellectual and technical challenges of oil exploration. As she writes in the book's opening pages: "This has meant pitting man's skill against nature's obduracy and applying human intelligence to solving the riddle of where oil and gas are stored in the recesses of the earth... [T]he riddle is solved only by finding one reservoir after another."[13] This metaphor of oil discovery as a scientific quest runs throughout the text, distinguishing it from the colorful personal accounts that characterized earlier works.

Together, these three above-mentioned works represent a turn in Texas oil writing—away from the individualistic ethos of the oil wildcatter and towards the institutional legitimacy of modern energy firms. They are light on labor, environmental, and regulatory critique, but provide a window into how oil companies sought to shape public memory during the postwar era. These corporate histories serve as a bridge between the frontier boosterism of *Spindletop* and *Santa Rita* and the more critical, analytical treatments that emerged in the late twentieth century. They also underscore the lasting symbolic power of the Spindletop discovery, which these narratives continued to invoke as the moment when chaos gave way to order—and when Texas oil became a national enterprise.

Samuel D. Myres's two-volume history—*Era of Discovery* and *Era of Advancement*—offers one of the most detailed industrial accounts of West Texas oil development.[14] The first volume (708 pages) traces the rise of the Permian Basin from the early 1920s through the Depression, while the second (624 pages) follows its growth into a dominant petroleum region through the postwar years. Myres structures the narrative geographically and chronologically, documenting discoveries, drilling techniques, corporate expansion, and infrastructure development with meticulous attention to detail.

Myres's volumes read more like an industrial encyclopedia than a traditional history narrative, drawing from engineering reports, production data, and maps to chart the evolution of one of the most productive oil regions in the world. The pair contains little social or political analysis, but they serve as essential reference works for understanding how the Texas oil machine was built field by field, pipeline by pipeline. Myres's reference style complements the earlier biographies and corporate histories by grounding the mythology of the oil boom in the practical realities of field development. His work captures the scale, complexity, and engineering prowess that turned the Permian into the heart of America's petroleum empire.

Walter Rundell Jr.'s *Early Texas Oil: A Photographic History, 1866–1936* offers a compelling visual archive of Texas's formative petroleum years, spanning from the first wells in the 1860s through the 1930s.[15] This 260-page volume includes more than 300 archival photographs—many previously unpublished—that document early oil development across the state. From Spindletop and Corsicana to Burkburnett and the Permian, Rundell captures the people, places, and machines that shaped the industry's rapid rise.

More than a picture book, *Early Texas Oil* is a key reference for visualizing the "gusher age." Each image is paired with detailed captions and commentary compiled from trade journals, company archives, and local newspapers. The author's lens reveals both the ambition and chaos of boomtown life—rotary rigs, blowouts, mule teams hauling pipe, and the early construction of refineries and tank farms. Rundell—an accomplished historian and former research director for the American Petroleum Institute—brings a scholar's eye to the visual record of this first period of development in Texas oil history.

James Presley's *A Saga of Wealth: The Rise of the Texas Oilmen* marks a turning point in how the story of Texas oil was told.[16] Rather than focusing on discoveries or technological breakthroughs, Presley points to the men behind the fortunes such as H. L. Hunt, Sid W. Richardson, Clint W. Murchison, and others who turned Texas oil into an empire. Drawing from newspaper accounts and interviews, the author traces the rise of these icons through a mix of ambition, risk-taking, and political savvy. The tone is neither critical nor overly admiring. These are character studies—sharp, revealing, and often messy. Presley's storytelling is more journalistic than academic, but it reflects a shift in emphasis from the mythic wildcatter to the more complicated oil tycoon. Published at the height of the energy crisis of the 1970s, *A Saga of Wealth* bridges the gap between the boosterism of earlier oil histories and the more analytical studies that followed.

By the 1980s, a new wave of Texas oil scholarship began to challenge earlier celebratory accounts of the industry's rise. No longer content with tales of heroic wildcatters and profitable expansion, this emerging body of work shifted the focus to social structures, politics, regulatory frameworks, and labor dynamics that shaped development. Historians began to examine how oil wealth was distributed, how class shaped access to opportunity, and how state institutions—from the Texas Railroad Commission to local zoning boards—tried to mediate the boom-and-bust cycles of the oil economy.[17]

Diana D. Olien [Hinton] and Roger M. Olien, *Oil in Texas: The Gusher Age, 1895–1945,* marks the dawn of a new historiographical era—one in which the romanticism of the gusher age gives way to a more critical, analytical interpretation of petroleum's place in modern Texas.[18] Co-authored by Hinton, professor of history at the University of Texas–Permian Basin, and Olien, also a longtime history professor at the same institution, this volume reflects the scholarly maturity of two historians who helped reframe Texas oil as more than just a story of gushers and heroic discoveries. Drawing on archival research and oral histories, Hinton and Olien shift the focus away from larger-than-life wildcatters and company mythology to explore how oil reshaped Texas's economy, society, and political institutions.

Structured around three themes—discovery, infrastructure, and regulation—the book by Hinton and Olien traces how speculative investors and evolving technology fueled booms, how refining and transportation systems emerged to handle supply gluts, and how the state provided oversight. The authors frame Spindletop not simply as a miraculous discovery, but as a disruptive force that demanded new forms of governance and public involvement. This intervention, they argue, signaled the beginnings of institutional control over an industry that had long been defined by individualism and sporadic compliance with lax laws and orders.

What sets *Oil in Texas* apart from its midcentury predecessors is the authors' willingness to show the hidden costs of progress. They examine the rise of labor disputes, growing tension between majors and independents, and the uneven distribution of oil wealth across class and region. They note how oil money flowed into universities and public infrastructure, even as its extraction often left behind pollution and dislocation. The book's tension—between pride in innovation and awareness of its consequences—makes it a pivotal contribution to Texas oil historiography.

In tone and structure, *Oil in Texas* links the celebratory works of the mid-twentieth century with the critical scholarship that came the wake of the energy crises of the 1970s and 1980s. As one of several collaborations between Hinton and Olien over the decades, this volume reflects their shared legacy as leading figures in late twentieth-century oil historiography.

In the first book project from Hinton and Olien, *Oil Booms: Social Change in Five Texas Towns*, the authors signaled a turning point in Texas oil history by reframing the industry's story as one of volatile community transformation rather than corporate heroism.[19] They examined five towns—Ranger, Mexia, Wink, Kilgore, and Odessa—whose histories were shaped by the cyclical nature of the oil economy. Relying upon archival research and sociological methods, the two authors explored how social structures based on race, class, gender, and civic organization adapted (or collapsed) through booms and busts. Rather than glorifying prosperity, the book exposes the unevenness of oil's benefits and the unforeseen consequences of rapid growth. *Oil Booms* was one of the first historical studies to put regular people, rather than executives or wildcatters, at the center of the oil story. Its approach foreshadowed broader trends in community-based social history, establishing Hinton and Olien as key figures in the emerging literature of petroleum studies.

At the same time, Olien's *Easy Money: Oil Promoters and Investors in the Jazz Age* offered a parallel critique of the financial and cultural machinery that fueled early oil development.[20] Focusing on the speculative frenzy of the 1910s and 1920s, Olien documented how oil became a magnet for fast-talking promoters, questionable financial schemes, and small-time investors chasing dreams of instant wealth. Through advertising records, mail-order promotions, and regulatory hearings, the book reveals how oil was sold not just as a fuel but as a fantasy. Olien argues that this speculative culture democratized risk but also magnified fraud and market volatility. Far from a sideshow to production, the world of promotion and capital raising was essential to the Texas oil narrative. *Easy Money* exposed the myth of the self-made gusher baron and replaced it with a muddy picture of financial manipulation and mass persuasion—an early foray into the political economy of oil.

With *Wildcatters: Independent Oilmen as Producers and as a Cultural Phenomenon*, authors Hinton and Olien turned their focus to the mythic figure at the center of Texas oil folklore—the independent producer.[21] Rather than reinforce the rugged individualist stereotype, the authors deconstructed it, showing how wildcatters were shaped by social norms, institutional barriers, and economic systems beyond their control. Based on interviews, trade publications, and memoirs, the book portrays wildcatters as diverse and complex, entrepreneurial but vulnerable, revered but often unstable. The authors suggest that the wildcatter persona functioned as a cultural construct—one that celebrated independence while obscuring the institutional realities of the oil and gas business. *Wildcatters* offered one of the earliest serious treatments of oilmen as social actors embedded in regional and class-based networks. In doing so, it humanized the petroleum entrepreneur without romanticizing him, and it also deepened the scholarly critique of Texas oil dominance.

Bobby D. Weaver's *Oilfield Trash* brings a ground-level, steel-toed perspective to the Permian oil patch.[22] Weaver, a former roughneck with a doctoral degree and years of experience as a museum administrator, uses an extensive oral history collection to chronicle the experiences of rig hands, shooters, tool pushers, and roustabouts. The book lays out the customs, labor hierarchies, and day-to-day risks of oilfield life, painting a vivid and downright grimy portrait of the hard work that powered Texas petroleum booms. By centering the voices of everyday field hands, *Oilfield Trash* fills a historiographical gap and deepens the postmodern turn to social history in oil studies. Weaver revisited many of his earlier themes in *Reinventing Texas: The Legacy of Santa Rita No. 1*, which expanded upon the history provided by Schwettmann in his book on the iconic well by exploring its impact on the Permian Basin and its people.[23]

In *Boom or Bust: Narrative, Life, and Culture from the West Texas Oil Patch*, editors Sheena B. Stief, Kristen L. Figgins, and Rebecca Day Babcock present selections from oral history, creative nonfiction, and cultural critique to explore how the volatile rhythms of the oil economy shape life in the Permian Basin.[24] Drawing from a National Endowment for the Humanities–funded project, the editors gathered firsthand accounts from educators, engineers, truck drivers, and community members living through the boom–bust cycle. The result is a bottom-up portrait of the oil patch—one that moves beyond economics and geology to capture the emotional and cultural toll of energy dependency. *Boom or Bust* marks a shift in oil historiography to storytelling and lived experience, documenting the human side of the Texas oil legacy.

The twenty-first century introduced new players, methods, and concerns in the historical study of the oil and gas industry. The shale revolution brought renewed national attention to Texas as an energy powerhouse, but the scholarly literature has struggled to keep pace. Much of what has been published on this important new topic centers around journalistic profiles, commemorative volumes, or business biographies, rather than critical academic assessments. Still, these works reveal important shifts in the narrative: from mythmaking to memory, from wildcatters to technocrats, from boomtown glory to environmental unease. The centennial of Spindletop sparked a wave of public history projects similar to *Boom or Bust* that also revisited the foundational moment but added a broader cultural appeal. Other narratives focused on the shale boom underscore how technological innovation and entrepreneurial risk reshaped the industry. At the same time, a new genre of popular books emerged that explored "old oil money," cultural legacy, and the personal costs of energy capitalism. While this recent literature varies in scope and depth, it reflects a new effort to discuss Texas oil not just as a resource, but as a story still unfolding—marked by volatility, reinvention, and a lingering tension between past triumphs and future uncertainty.

Published on the centennial anniversary of the Lucas gusher, Judith Linsley, Ellen Walker Rienstra, and Jo Ann Stiles's *Giant Under the Hill: A History of the Spindletop Oil Discovery at Beaumont, Texas, in 1901* revisits the founding moment of the Texas oil industry with the benefit of a century's hindsight.[25] This volume offers an entertaining and well-researched account of Spindletop's discovery, impact, and legacy. While grounded in the same booster tradition as Clark and Halbouty's *Spindletop*, this more modern book diverges by drawing on new archival materials, local perspectives, and updated interpretations that challenge earlier heroic portrayals.

The authors—three Beaumont-area historians—draw particular attention to the collaborative and often chaotic reality behind the gusher myth. They elevate the technical prowess of the Hamill brothers, explore Pattillo Higgins's erratic but pivotal role, and place Anthony Lucas within a larger context of shifting capital, wild speculation, and entrepreneurial ambition. The book captures not just the pivotal event itself, but the messy buildup and the explosive aftermath in Beaumont's streets, courts, and oilfields. Although the tone remains celebratory at times, *Giant Under the Hill* reflects a more grounded public history—one that corrects the factual errors, widens the cast of characters, and deepens the plot of the Spindletop saga.

Gregory Zuckerman's *The Frackers: The Outrageous Inside Story of the New Billionaire Wildcatters* moves readers forward one century to the dawn of a new oil and gas revolution, offering one of the boldest narratives of the shale boom's entrepreneurial frontier.[26] Written in a fast-paced business-journalism style (Zuckerman was a reporter for the *Wall Street Journal*), the book chronicles the rise of a new generation of oilmen—George Mitchell, Harold Hamm, Aubrey McClendon—who defied conventional geology and capital markets to unlock vast unconventional reserves through hydraulic fracturing and horizontal drilling. Zuckerman centers most of his narrative in Texas, particularly the Barnett and Eagle Ford shale plays, capturing the raw ambition, financial risk, and technological experimentation that has defined this transformational epoch in oil history. Though the book largely sidesteps environmental critique, it documents a seismic shift in American energy production and revisits the familiar themes of the Texas maverick wildcatter. "These men ignored conventional wisdom and bet everything they had on a hunch," Zuckerman writes, adding, "And in doing so, they reshaped the energy industry and, arguably, the world."[27] While not an academic history, *The Frackers* delivers a compelling account of how Texas, through relentless innovation and risk, reasserted itself in the global energy spectrum.

One of the main characters in *The Frackers* is Mitchell, the founder of Mitchell Energy, who is considered one of the pioneers of the shale revolution. Loren C. Steffy's *George P. Mitchell: Fracking, Sustainability, and an Unorthodox Quest to Save the Planet* offers a rare, full-length biography of one of the most consequential figures in this new storyline.[28] Drawing from interviews, archival sources, and Mitchell's reflections, Steffy traces the life of the Texas wildcatter turned visionary, whose relentless pursuit of hydraulic fracturing technology unlocked vast shale reserves and reshaped global energy markets. But Mitchell's legacy, as Steffy shows, extends beyond oil and gas. The book explores his philanthropic investments in urban planning (The Woodlands), sustainability, and climate research. In this process, Steffy reveals a complex figure who linked the frontier ethos of Texas oil with a dedication to environmental stewardship.

While Zuckerman's reporting and Mitchell's biography represent the cutting edge of historical studies on the shale boom, another set of modern narratives turns the lens backward, toward the old dynasties funded by the first great oil fortunes. Bryan Burrough's *The Big Rich*, Harry Hurt III's *Texas Rich*, and Jerome Tuccille's *Kingdom* chart the rise and fall of iconic Texas families such as the Hunts, the Murchisons, and the Bass brothers.[29] Blending biography with regional drama, these popular works explore how Texas oilmen accumulated enormous wealth, reshaped politics, and cultivated larger-than-life personas that loomed over the state's cultural and economic landscape. Burrough's account, the most polished of the three, connects oil wealth to Cold War influence, philanthropic empires, and the slow unraveling of family dynasties under the weight of excess. These books are not academic histories, but they serve a valuable purpose, capturing the personalities of Texas oil capitalists in all their glory and gluttony. In contrast to the wildcatters of the early twentieth century or the modern tech-driven shale pioneers, these stories of oil family dynasties offer a bridge between eras, reminding readers that oil in Texas has always been more than a commodity. It has been a way of life, a measure of success, and a lasting symbol of power, privilege, and political intrigue.

In conclusion, the historiography of Texas oil and gas has matured alongside the industry itself—evolving from early tales of triumph and transformation to more critical accounts that include labor, regulation, and social issues. The most recent works reflect a period of resurgence driven by shale technology and entrepreneurial revival. Yet even as Texas reasserts itself as a global energy leader, the historical literature has not fully caught up with the implications of this latest boom.

Few scholarly works have explored the legal, environmental, and property-rights tensions that shape the current realities of oil and gas development in rural Texas. Long standing issues of groundwater access, water disposal, and orphaned wells remain largely outside the published record despite their central role in shaping public discourse and policy in this new energy era. Recent court cases and legislation point to vital changes in the Lone Star oil story, shifting landowner sovereignty and resource management from secondary concerns into central questions for the future.

These shifts offer an opening and a challenge for the next generation of historians. As the narrative fractures again, scholars will be tasked with not only chronicling more innovation and expansion but with interpreting the relationship between economic opportunity, environmental risk, and community resilience. The story of black gold in Texas is far from over. In many ways, it is just entering its next frontier.

Beaumont Oilfield in 1901 by Francis J. "Frank" Trost.
Courtesy of Portal to Texas History

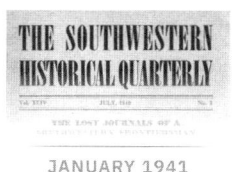

JANUARY 1941

Oil, the Courts, and the Railroad Commission

JAMES P. HART

AT THE BEGINNING of the history of this State, the owner of the surface did not have any ownership rights in the oil and gas beneath the surface of his land. Under the civil law, which was in force while Texas was under the rule of Spain and Mexico, all minerals belonged to the sovereign, and they did not pass by the ordinary grant of the land without express words of designation. When Texas became an independent republic, many of the rules of the civil law were changed, but by an early act of the Texas Congress all rights in minerals were reserved to the Republic. By the Act of June 3, 1837,[1] it was provided "that no lands granted by this Government shall be located on salt springs, gold or silver mines, copper or lead, or other minerals, or on any island of the Republic." Again, by the Act of January 20, 1840,[2] adopting the common law and repealing certain Mexican laws, it was expressly provided that the repealing act should not apply to "the reservation of islands and lands, and also of salt lakes, licks and salt springs, mines and minerals of every description."

1

There was thus manifested in the very beginning of the State's history, at the very outset of its career, a fixed purpose and established policy to reserve its minerals from the appropriation of the land, evincing, as Judge Wheeler said in *Cowan v. Hardeman* (26 Tex. 217) "the solicitude of the Legislature to guard the interest of the State" in them.[3]

The general policy of the State to retain the title to the minerals within the State was not changed until immediately after the Civil War. By an ordinance which was adopted by the Constitutional Convention in 1866 (and which was effective without being ratified by a vote of the people) it was provided "that the State of Texas hereby releases to the owner of the soil all mines and mineral substances that may be on the same, subject to such uniform rate of taxation as the Legislature may impose."[4]

It may be interesting to point out the background of this reversal of the policy of the State, as related in the opinion of Judge Nelson Phillips in the case of *Cox v. Robison*.[5] It seems that the primary purpose of the adoption of the ordinance quoted above was to validate the title of private owners in a salt lake in Hidalgo County, and the ordinance was in fact titled, "an ordinance relative to the salt lake known as El Sal del Rey."

"From an early time there has existed in Hidalgo County the famous salt lake called 'El Sal del Rey.' It was of large extent and regarded as of great value. Public historic accounts are to the effect that its salt was comparatively pure as dug from its bed and apparently inexhaustible. For many years it was the source of supply for people on both sides of the lower Rio Grande, and during the Civil War it furnished salt for a large portion of Southern Texas."[6] A patent to the lake had been issued by the State in 1847. This patent was confirmed by an act of the Third Legislature in 1850[7] in which the State relinquished all of its rights. However, when the salt lake became of more importance to the State during the Civil War, by a joint resolution approved January 10, 1862,[8] the Legislature asserted title of the State to the lake, and required the Governor to take possession of it and to detail troops to maintain such possession, and required the agent of the State to sell the salt from the lake at the customary rate.

At the Constitutional Convention in 1866, a committee was appointed "relative to the salt lake 'El Sal del Rey.'" On March 17, 1866, the committee made its report recommending the passage of an ordinance containing the provision quoted above, whereby the State released to the owners of the soil all mines and minerals beneath their lands, subject to the right of the Legislature to impose taxes thereon, and this ordinance was adopted by the convention and later included in and printed as a general provision of the Constitution. Thus, by an ordinance designed primarily to confirm the title of private owners in a salt lake in Hidalgo County, the State gave away the ownership of all minerals under lands which had theretofore been patented by the State.

By successive constitutional provisions and legislative acts since 1866, the State has relinquished its claim to minerals in land which has been patented by the State. Article X, Section 9, of the Constitution of 1869, contains substantially the same language as that quoted above from the Constitution of 1866. In 1876, when the Constitution now in force was adopted, it was provided by Article XIV, Section 7, of that Constitution:

> The State of Texas hereby releases to the owner or owners of the soil all mines and minerals that may be on the same, subject to taxation as other property.

Similar provisions were contained in the Revised Civil Statutes of 1879,[9] and also in the Revised Civil Statutes of 1895.[10] By these laws, the State has relinquished to the owners of lands patented prior to those dates the title to oil and gas, as well as other minerals under the land.

These constitutional provisions and statutory provisions have been interpreted by the courts as being only retrospective in effect, and not prospective. That is, these provisions have been held not to apply to lands which had not been patented prior to the effective date of these provisions.[11] Under the laws which have been in effect since 1895, the State, in general, has reserved at least a portion of the minerals under the mineral lands which it has patented,[12] and, of course, retains the title to oil and gas in vacant or unpatented lands.

Assuming that a person "owns" the legal title to a tract of land, including all mineral rights, the question for the courts to determine was what specific powers and rights went with such ownership. The chief handicap under which the courts labored in the early days was that there was no exact scientific knowledge as to the characteristics or behavior of oil and gas in their subterranean reservoirs. The location and extent of oil and gas fields were largely matters of guesswork. In evolving applicable legal rules, the courts groped for analogies in settled rules of law applicable to other forms of property. The fact that oil and gas are contained within the land evoked the analogy of solid minerals, such as coal, where the doctrine of ownership in place is well established. The further facts that oil and gas are not fixed in their location, but are fluid, and therefore "fugitive" or "vagrant" when pressure is applied to them, called to mind the analogies of subterranean waters and wild animals, where complete ownership does not vest until the property is reduced to possession. Finally, the courts of this State have settled upon a sort of compromise, which recognizes the right of ownership of oil and gas in place, but at the same time recognizes the so-called rule of capture, or the right of any landowner to keep as his own any oil which may be produced from a well on his land, no matter where this oil may have come from. These two logically inconsistent but practically defensible rules have been restated by the Supreme Court in the case of *Brown v. Humble Oil & Refining Co.*,[13] as follows:

> The rule in Texas recognizes the ownership of oil and gas in place, and gives to the lessee a determinable fee therein. [Cases cited.]
>
> Owing to the peculiar characteristics of oil and gas, the foregoing rule of ownership of oil and gas in place should be considered in connection with the law of capture. This rule gives the right to produce all of the oil and gas that will flow out of the well on one's

land; and this is a property right. And it is limited only by the physical possibility of the adjoining landowner diminishing the oil and gas under one's land by the exercise of the same right of capture.

While the first oil well was brought in in Texas as early as 1866,[14] oil did not become of any substantial commercial importance in this State until the end of the nineteenth century. The discovery and development of the Corsicana and the Spindle Top fields, together with the haphazard and wasteful method of their development and production, emphasized in the public mind the necessity of passing conservation measures for the preservation of what was, for the first time, regarded as an important public resource. Beginning in 1899,[15] the Legislature passed statutes which had as their purpose purely the prevention of the physical waste of oil and gas by regulating the manner of the drilling for and production of oil and gas, and other mechanical features of the oil and gas industry. For example, it was provided that oil and gas wells should be cased off so as to prevent the intrusion of water into the oil sand or oil and gas into fresh water sands, that abandoned wells should be plugged, that gas should not be burned in flambeau lights, and that gas from the gas wells should not be permitted to escape into the open air.

Until 1917, the Legislature undertook to provide by statutes such regulation as was thought to be necessary for the production of oil and gas. In 1917, however, the Legislature first passed a statute conferring upon the Railroad Commission of Texas the power to act as the governmental agency to administer the conservation laws relating to oil and gas, and to promulgate and enforce the necessary regulations.[16] In 1917, also, the Constitution of the State was amended so as to declare that the conservation and development of all of the natural resources of the State are public rights and duties, and that the Legislature shall pass all such laws as may be appropriate thereto.[17]

At the time the Legislature first vested the Railroad Commission with the power to regulate the oil and gas industry, there was no overproduction of oil and gas, and the only substantial public concern was that the oil and gas should not be wastefully produced or used so as to deprive present and future generations of the full benefit of these natural resources. The Railroad Commission was evidently designated as the agency for the administration of the conservation statutes, because the Railroad Commission had performed acceptably the duties which had been imposed upon it to regulate the railroads in the State and the Railroad Commission then enjoyed general public confidence.

The idea of exercising control through an administrative body over an industry having a widespread and vital influence over the life of the people of the State as a whole, was not new, since the Railroad Commission itself had for many years been exercising control over the operation of the railroads within the State. The necessity of some form of regulation of the oil industry by a public agency was then accepted, as it is still accepted, because of the importance of the petroleum industry in the lives of all of the people within the State and the inability of the industry itself to prevent wasteful practices.

Aside from the question of the advisability of placing the regulation of the oil and gas industry in the hands of the Railroad Commission of Texas when that body already had other important duties to discharge, the reasons for delegating the duties of formulating and enforcing regulations governing the production of oil and gas to some administrative body were fairly obvious. Although these reasons have almost become platitudinous, it may be helpful to restate them, in view of the recurrent attacks which are made upon the regulation of oil and gas production by the Railroad Commission of Texas.

One of the prime reasons for delegating the duties of regulation and supervision to the Railroad Commission was a desire to have these problems handled by an agency which at least had had the opportunity by continuous and extensive experience and study to become experts and specialists with reference to the needs and demands of the industry. It was obviously impossible to expect the Legislature, in view of the multitude of its other duties, to make a study of the oil industry or to provide detailed regulations with reference to the manner in which different oil and gas fields in the State should be produced and developed. On the other hand, the Railroad Commission of Texas, or at least its employees who were assigned to oil and gas work, had every opportunity to specialize and become experts in the problems relating to oil and gas. For the purpose of efficiency, therefore, it was advisable to have the Legislature only indicate the broad outlines of the policies to be followed by the administrative body, leaving all matters of detail to those who make a specialty of the study of the problems involved.

Not only does the Railroad Commission have the advantage of specialization, but it also has the advantage of a continuity of action. The Legislature convenes only intermittently, and its membership changes to a large extent with each session. There is no assurance that the Legislature will be in session when any pressing problems in the oil and gas industry arise, or that the governor can be prevailed upon to call a special session to meet the emergency. On the other hand, the Railroad Commission is a continuing body, with the power to exercise a constant supervision over the oil industry at all times, meeting such unforeseen situations as may arise with expedition that could never be expected of the Legislature.

Not only was the duty of formulating rules and regulations delegated to the Railroad Commission, but it was also given the primary duty of enforcing the statutes and regulations passed by it pertaining to the conservation of oil and gas. Its members and employees, by keeping in constant touch with the oil industry, are not only able to pass immediately such new rules or amendments to old rules as become necessary, but they also are in a position to acquire first-hand knowledge of the violations of any statutes or regulations, and, because of their knowledge of the industry, can ascertain with the greatest promptness the means which should be adopted to stop or to prevent violations.

As has already been pointed out, the statutes and regulations first adopted by the Legislature and the Railroad Commission pertained purely to the mechanics of the production of oil and gas, and had as their sole object the prevention of physical waste. Such regulations encountered practically no opposition. There was no difference of expert opinion as to their necessity. Furthermore, they applied to all alike, and they did not have the effect of depriving one person or group of certain rights or privileges to the advantage of others.

Of a somewhat different nature was the spacing rule, known as Rule 37, which was first adopted by the Railroad Commission in 1919. This rule provided in substance that no well could be drilled closer than 150 feet to another producing oil well or closer than 300 feet to a lease line, except that the Railroad Commission upon application therefor could grant permits to drill at closer distances to prevent waste or to protect vested rights. Prior to the promulgation of this rule, each operator was permitted to drill as many wells as he pleased, and to produce each well to capacity. The incentive was apparent for an operator to drill as many wells as quickly as possible, in order to get as much oil as possible before it could be produced by other operators. By fixing the general pattern for the drilling of wells at certain distances from lease lines or from other wells, the Railroad Commission not only directly limited the number of wells which could be drilled, but also, to a certain extent, limited the amount of oil which could be produced from any particular tract. That is to say, while all wells could still be produced to capacity, an operator with ten wells could generally expect to get about twice as much oil as his neighbor with only five wells.

Rule 37 was generally endorsed by those operators who had large tracts, and who wished to produce their oil from such tracts at a minimum expense in the drilling of wells. On the other hand, Rule 37 was at first opposed by those persons who had small tracts, or tracts which were narrow or irregularly shaped, and who, by the application of Rule 37, were deprived of the opportunity to drill as many wells as they wished.

In view of the prevailing rule of capture, it was argued by those operators who attacked the validity of Rule 37 that each operator was entitled to exercise as much diligence as he desired in drilling and producing his wells, thereby recovering for himself as large a portion of the total field recovery as possible, and that all other operators had a correlative right to drill offset wells on their property, and thereby recover for themselves oil approximately in direct proportion to their diligence. However, the courts rejected all arguments against the validity of Rule 37 and sustained it as a conservation measure. The exact ground for sustaining Rule 37 is still a matter which is debated, some arguing that it is sustained on the theory that the dense drilling of wells causes waste and that the Railroad Commission by requiring drilling at greater distances prevents waste, while others argue with support in the Supreme Court's decision in the case of *Gulf Land Co. v. Atlantic Refining* Co.[18] that the sole purpose of the rule was to confer upon the Railroad Commission the right to regulate the drilling of wells so as to attain a reasonably uniform pattern of drilling, regardless of whether or not drilling in a dense pattern leads to a waste of recoverable oil. At any rate, there was not any very serious objection to Rule 37, even by the independent operators, because at that time, the Railroad Commission did not undertake to limit directly the production of oil from any field or well, and, by exceptions, the Railroad Commission generally granted permits as exceptions to Rule 37 where any substantial hardship would have resulted from a strict enforcement of the rules. In fact, of the approximately 26,000 wells drilled in the East Texas field, about 65 per cent have been drilled as exceptions to Rule 37.

The situation changed radically, however, beginning in 1930. The general depression and the discovery of the East Texas oilfield coincided to create a very serious situation in the oil industry. Even prior to that time, the industry had accumulated great above-ground stores of oil and its products, and it was obvious that production would have to be limited in some manner or there would be a serious breakdown in the price structure. When a vast new reserve of oil was discovered in the East Texas field, it was regarded as absolutely imperative that the production of oil and gas be restricted. There can be little question but what the primary desire of the advocates of governmental restriction on production was to achieve stabilization or in plainer words, to keep the price of oil up. The fact that restriction of production also in fact prevents physical waste was a fortunate coincidence for the proponents of restriction.

Since by far the greater part of the litigation relating to the regulatory orders of the Railroad Commission has had to do with the East Texas field, it is well to state here some of the outstanding facts as to the discovery, development and general characteristics of the field.

The East Texas field was discovered when a well was brought in by "Dad" Joiner on Mrs. Daisy Bradford's farm in Rusk County on October 9, 1930.[19] Prior to this time, all of the geologists for the major oil companies had rejected the possibility of the existence of an oilfield in this vicinity. Even after the Joiner well was brought in, the existence of a major field was not suspected, because the discovery well was drilled toward the eastern edge of the field and therefore was not a big producer. In December 1930, however, when the BatemanCrim No. 1 was drilled almost ten miles north of the Joiner well, some idea of the size of the field was indicated. Development was extended rapidly, until by July 1931, the approximate limits of the field were fairly well defined.

Figures as to the size of the East Texas field are so big that it is hard to understand their significance except by comparison with other fields. The East Texas field is about 40 miles in length and from 4 to 12 miles wide, and it has a producing area of about 133,000 acres. Within its borders could be comfortably fitted the eight well-known fields of Kettleman Hills in California, Oklahoma City and Seminole in Oklahoma, Hobbs in New Mexico, and Yates, Hendrick and Hastings in Texas. The estimated total ultimate recovery from this field is about five billion barrels, and it has already produced during its ten years' life to date a total of about 1,400,000,000 barrels. At the peak of its production, it produced about three-fifths of the Texas production, three-eighths of the United States production, and twenty-two per cent of the entire world's crude oil output.

From the viewpoint of regulation, there are certain other characteristics of the East Texas field, aside from its bigness, that are worthy of note. The land lying within the field was composed mainly of small farms, town lots, school lots and church lots, and other small tracts of land. No major oil company became seriously interested in the field until development was well under way, with the result that this is one of the very few fields where independent operators own about as many wells as the major oil companies. Compulsory or voluntary unit operation of the field was not even seriously thought of until the field was thoroughly developed, and today, as applied to this particular field, it has become a practical impossibility.

It is also important to give a brief statement of the general physical characteristics of the field. The oil is confined in the Woodbine sand formation at a depth of about 3,600 feet below the surface. The principal source of energy is the water drive, which is furnished by the water pressing upward against the oil in the western half of the field. In cross-section, the field is triangular in shape, the thin sands being in the western and eastern edges, and the thickest sands of about 100 feet being in the center of the field. There is communication between all sections of the field, with the result that, generally speaking, the field is one big reservoir. As oil is produced, the water gradually encroaches on the western edge, forcing wells here to be abandoned. In the portions of the field where water has not encroached, all oil that is produced is replaced by other oil from the west, except in those portions of the field which are not sufficiently permeable to permit the rapid passage of the oil. The eastern portion of the field is relatively impermeable, with the result that wells are being abandoned there, not because of water encroachment, but because of lack of pressure. The portion of the field having the longest producing life will probably be the eastern portion of the center or "fairway."

The first serious question as to the right of the Railroad Commission to limit the production of oil in order to make the production conform to the market demand was whether such restriction was authorized by the Texas statutes, and if so, whether such restriction would be constitutional. Here the question was not as to the method of the allocation of the allowable production among the various producers, but of whether limitation of production as such was legal. In this encounter over proration, the line-up of the opposing forces was the major oil companies for the Railroad Commission and for proration, and the independent producers against the Railroad Commission and against proration. Obviously, the economic interests of the parties affected governed the stands which they took upon proration. The major oil companies, with vast reserves above ground and in fields which they already owned and controlled, desired production to be limited so that the value of their assets would not be destroyed. The independent operators, on the other hand, had in general no assets except their leases in the East Texas oilfield, and they desired to enjoy them immediately to the fullest extent. While they also wished to have a good price for their products, they were willing generally to accept a much lower price than the major oil companies, because they did not have their investments tied up in other fields or in reserves above ground, which had been produced or purchased at higher prices.

While the federal courts regarded proration with a coldly suspicious eye,[20] the Austin Court of Civil Appeals in March 1932, in the Danciger case,[21] finally sustained the power of the Railroad Commission of Texas to limit and prorate the production of oil. The ground for the court's holding, which was amply supported by the evidence, was that by limiting the total daily production, the Railroad Commission prevented the waste of oil resulting from rapid reduction of pressure and trapping of oil in the reservoir, and also prevented overground waste resulting from production in excess of market demand. The same conclusion was reached by the Supreme Court of the United States, which upheld the Oklahoma proration statute in the Champlin case.[22]

It must have been obvious even then, however, that with the tie-up between the spacing rules and proration, the Railroad Commission was in effect vested with the power to partition the production of oil within any common reservoir, such as the East Texas field. Under the common law, any operator could drill as many wells upon his land as he wished, and produce each well to its maximum capacity, if he desired to do so. He was free to drain not only the oil beneath his land, but the oil beneath other tracts surrounding him as far as possible, and any oil which he brought to the surface was his without any question.

With the introduction of Rule 37, the right to drill as you please was removed, but the right to produce as much as you please still remained. When proration also went into effect, however, an operator could no longer either drill as many wells as he pleased or produce as much oil as he wished from any one of his wells. The result was that the Railroad Commission, by fixing the number of wells which could be drilled upon any tract, and by limiting the production from each well, could in effect decide how much oil could be produced by any operator from any particular tract. The drilling permits granted and the proration formulas adopted by the Railroad Commission therefore became of acute concern to every operator in every field in the State of Texas.

In Rule 37 cases and in proration cases, the attitudes taken by the various producers are unquestionably dictated by their economic interests, and the talk of experts for the various affected parties, with reference to conservation, is largely a rationalization in an effort to justify a stand which is dictated primarily by far different considerations. In Rule 37 cases, it is obviously to the advantage of the major oil companies who own the big leases and who have large reserves above ground and in fields scattered throughout the United States to limit as far as possible the drilling of wells, in order to keep down their total drilling costs and maintain the value of their assets in other states, some of which, such as California and Illinois, have unlimited production. These companies evidently feel that they can produce more economically by drilling fewer wells, and they desire that their neighbors be required to produce their properties in the same way. The so-called independent operators, on the other hand, have generally small tracts and no other investments in oil reserves, above ground or in other fields, and they are generally operating on borrowed money. They therefore feel that if they can drill and produce at a rapid rate, they will be able to make sufficient profits to stay in business, whereas if they are limited in the number of wells which they can drill, or if their production is restricted unduly, their investment will be destroyed.

The East Texas field offers the best illustration of the workings of the conflicting interests in any oilfield. Here, the Railroad Commission is torn between the antagonistic interests of the various operators. Major oil companies are almost always found opposing the granting of exceptions to Rule 37, because when such permits are granted, the companies are faced with the alternatives of either having their share in the total field allowable reduced, or of going to the expense of drilling additional wells and thereby increasing their producing costs. Each applicant for a permit, on the other hand, hopes by obtaining such permit to increase his percentage of recovery in the field as a whole, and he is of course indifferent to the effect that such recovery may have upon other operators.

The anxiety of the major oil companies to keep down the number of wells drilled has resulted in the situation in the East Texas field where, speaking on the average, the major oil companies' leases are less densely drilled than the leases of the so-called independents. This, of course, has directly affected the attitude which the major oil companies and the independents have taken toward the various formulas of proration. It is with reference to the method of allocation that proration litigation has been concerned during the past eight years.

Many possibilities are offered to the Railroad Commission as bases for allocation of the allowable production. The first method that suggests itself is to give each well the same allowable. This is objected to, however, on the ground that it ignores the differences between the productive capacities of the various wells. For example, some wells in the East Texas field are capable of producing only about twenty barrels per day, or even less, while others could produce in excess of twenty-five thousand barrels per day. It also ignores the fact that wells may be drilled on large or small tracts, with thick or thin sands, with wide variations in the amount of recoverable oil beneath different tracts of land. Various proration formulas have been suggested, most of which include a base per-well allowable, with additional factors such as acreage, the potential capacity of each well, the thickness of the sand, and the bottomhole pressure in each well.

The various operators in the field demand different forms of proration, depending on which method will give them the largest current and ultimate recovery. An operator with a densely drilled lease wishes to have the allowable distributed almost wholly on the flat per-well basis, or, if this operator has leases in the center of the field, where the highest well potentials are found, he would like to have the added factor of well potential. Operators of leases which are not densely drilled would like to have the acreage of each lease considered, for in this way, by drilling few wells, they can recover the same amount of oil as their neighbor who has made heavier investments in drilling costs. Operators whose leases are not very densely drilled and whose leases are located wholly or principally in the fairway, would like to have the field prorated on the basis of acre feet of sand beneath such lease, or what amounts to practically the same thing, on the basis of current reserves. Operators of leases in the western portion of the field want to have some factor, such as bottom-hole pressure, added to give them a relatively high recovery in order to compensate them in part for the relatively short producing life of their leases.

Early efforts of the Railroad Commission to distribute the allowable from the East Texas field on the flat per-well basis were stricken down by the federal courts.[23] It was not until the order of April 1933 was written that a method of proration was found which the federal courts would accept. In the meantime, the field had gone through the experiences of unlimited production, ten-cent oil, and martial law. The federal district court in the Amazon case[24] finally withheld its condemnation of a method of proration where a minimum per-well allowable was granted, with the rest of the allowable distributed on the basis of the potential producing capacity of each well.

Between 1933 and 1939 there were no attacks made in the courts on the method of proration in the East Texas field. It was apparent, however, that further attacks would become inevitable. The distribution of the field allowable on the per-well potential basis undoubtedly encouraged the drilling of additional wells, because each well carried with it at least the minimum per-well allowable. Between 1933 and 1939, the number of wells drilled in the East Texas field increased from about 10,000 wells to about 26,000 wells. Each of these wells represented an investment of at least $10,000 in drilling costs alone, and the Railroad Commission could not too drastically reduce the allowable of each of these wells without causing their premature abandonment, resulting in the confiscation of the owner's property and the loss of oil which could be produced only from such wells. At the same time, the Railroad Commission was not free to increase correspondingly the total daily field allowable, because most engineers agree that an average production of about 450,000 barrels per day is approximately the maximum which can be produced without danger of creating physical waste of oil, principally through the rapid drop in the bottom-hole pressure and the consequent loss of reservoir energy. With an increasing number of wells and with a fixed ceiling or total allowable, the Commission was forced to reduce the per-well allowable and the advantages given to the better wells. The per-well allowable was reduced from 40 barrels to 20 barrels per day and the well-potential factor was reduced from 15 per cent to 2.32 per cent of the hourly potential. By 1939, the result was that 19,000 wells in the field received exactly twenty barrels per day, and the best wells received only about twenty-six barrels per day. The average production was further reduced by requiring that all wells in the field be shut down for two days out of each week.

In the fall of 1938, a course of litigation in the federal courts was begun which had as its object to compel the Railroad Commission to change its method of proration. The lineup of the opposing parties was the opposite of what it had been in 1932 and 1933, for the independents were now satisfied with proration while the major oil companies were dissatisfied. While about fifteen applications for changes were presented to the Commission, only three suits, in the nature of test cases, were filed. The plaintiffs in these suits were the Rowan & Nichols Oil Company and the Humble Oil & Refining Company. The former had leases which were slightly more densely drilled than the average of the field, and the latter's leases, on the average, are slightly less densely drilled. Both plaintiffs, however, have their leases located mainly in the "fairway," where the sands are thickest. They therefore took the common position that the proration formula of the Railroad Commission, which was mainly on a flat per-well basis, was so unfair to them as to violate the due process clause of the Fourteenth Amendment, because it ignored the fact that they have much thicker sands beneath their leases than the average of the field, and therefore more recoverable oil. Their contention was that they should be allowed to produce currently an amount of oil substantially in the same ratio to the total field production as the recoverable oil underneath their leases bears to the total estimated recoverable oil in the entire field.

The testimony supporting the contentions of the plaintiffs and the Railroad Commission was both technical and voluminous and will not be stated here. The Railroad Commission's contentions, briefly stated, were that the per-well allowable was necessary to prevent premature abandonment of thousands of wells with consequent destruction of investments and waste of oil, and that the plaintiffs, during the entire life of their leases, would recover a fair amount of oil because their leases would produce much longer than leases in other portions of the field. In connection with the latter contention, it was the position of the Railroad Commission that proration on the basis of current reserves would be unfair, both because reserves are almost impossible to calculate accurately, and also because such method would insure the recovery by leases in the fairway of many times the amount of recoverable oil originally beneath them. As an illustration of the difficulty of calculating recoverable reserves, one of the experts, between the trial which was held in 1939 and the trial of 1940, increased his estimates of the recoverable oil in the field and the remaining reserves about one billion barrels, which represented an increase of thirty-three and one-third per cent in one instance and fifty per cent in the other. He also admitted that he might be as much as thirty per cent inaccurate in estimating the reserves under any lease. Even assuming, however, that reserves can be accurately calculated, it was the position of the Railroad Commission that proration on the basis of current reserves would guarantee to fairway leases much more than the recoverable oil originally beneath them.

In the Rowan and Nichols case, which was the first case to come up for trial in January 1939 after hearing evidence on both sides, and after having the case under advisement for about six months, the Federal District Court held the proration orders of the Railroad Commission to be invalid, and enjoined the Commission from enforcing any method of proration except one which would give to the plaintiff a daily allowable in proportion to its estimated current reserves.[25] This decision was affirmed by the Circuit Court of Appeals[26] but was reversed by the Supreme Court[27] in an opinion written by Mr. Justice Frankfurter, from which the Chief Justice and Mr. Justice Roberts and Mr. Justice McReynolds dissented. This opinion was rendered June 3, 1940, and a petition for rehearing was denied on October 21, 1940. The opinion seems to preclude an independent inquiry by the federal courts into the fairness or reasonableness of the Railroad Commission's orders, even where the issue of confiscation is directly raised.

The court points out that "the record is redolent with familiar dogmatic assertions by experts equally confident of contradictory contentions. These touch matters of geography and geology and physics and engineering."[28]

Its conclusions are stated as follows:

Certainly in a domain of knowledge still shifting and growing, and in a field where judgment is therefore necessarily beset by the necessity of inferences bordering on conjecture even for those learned in the art, it would be presumptuous for courts, on the basis of conflicting expert testimony, to deem the view of the administrative tribunal, acting under legislative authority, offensive to the Fourteenth Amendment.[29]

Plainly these are not issues for our arbitrament. The state was confronted with its general problem of proration and with the special relation to it of the small tracts in the particular configuration of the East Texas field. It has chosen to meet these problems through the day-to-day exertions of a body specially entrusted with the task because presumably competent to deal with it. In striking the balances that have to be struck with the complicated and subtle factors that must enter into such judgments, the Commission has observed established procedure. If the history of proration is any guide, the present order is but one *mote* item in a continuous series of adjustments. It is not for the federal courts to supplant the Commission's judgment even in the face of convincing proof that a different result would have been better.[30]

The true construction to be placed on the decision of the Supreme Court is a matter of dispute among lawyers, and its full legal significance will not be known until the Supreme Court has further filled in the picture by other decisions. From the historical viewpoint, however, it is noteworthy as an endorsement by the court of the State's efforts through the Railroad Commission to regain partial control over great natural resources that it had lightly given away.

Postcard of Santa Rita No. 1 by P. C. McGlasson.
Courtesy of DeGolyer Library, Southern Methodist University, Dallas

JULY 1944

Texas Collection

H. BAILEY CARROLL

MAY 27 WAS THE TWENTY-FIRST birthday of Santa Rita, The University of Texas discovery oil well in the Reagan County area. The anniversary was observed with fitting ceremonies in Austin. About a month before the May 27 date, George C. Gibbons, Executive Vice-President of Texas MidContinent Oil and Gas Association, called from Dallas to say that his Association considered Martin Schwettmann's book *Santa Rita* one of the greatest tributes ever paid to the oil industry, and that his Association was interested in paying tribute upon the anniversary date to the Historical Association, The University of Texas, and the original enterprisers connected with the well.

The story of Santa Rita and the founding of the University was written in a radio script by J. Edward Morrow, Oil Editor of the Dallas *News*. The script was produced by Mrs. Edith Beale Hamilton of Radio House at the University and was broadcast over the Texas Quality Network at 12:30 on Saturday, May 27. Climaxing the day's activities was a dinner in the Maximilian Room of the Driskill Hotel given by the Texas Mid-Continent Oil and Gas Association honoring the Texas State Historical Association and The University of Texas. It was a party that *Life* magazine should have attended. Beauford Jester, chairman of the Texas Railroad Commission and a former member of the Board of Regents of the University, was master of ceremonies. President Homer P. Rainey spoke for the University and called attention to the fact that the permanent fund of the University is now approaching $44,000,000 and that most of these funds have been derived from oil income. George A. Hill Jr., President of the Houston Oil Company and Vice President of the Association, spoke as the representative of the petroleum industry. Among the hundred or more persons present at the dinner were Mrs. Carl Cromwell, wife of the Santa Rita driller, and Mrs. W. E. Peavy Jr., his daughter, Carlene. Frank T. Pickrell, one of the partners in the company which drilled the well, flew in from California to be present on the occasion. His impromptu speech telling of the Santa Rita development was one of the highlights of the program. Dr. Eugene C. Barker spoke as the representative of the Association, making a talk which impressed all present with the necessity for having more history in business. The text of Dr. Barker's and of Mr. Hill's addresses are carried as separate articles in this issue of the *Quarterly*.

SOME THREE YEARS or more ago the Santa Rita derrick was transported from Texon to the campus of the University. It was first expected that the derrick would be re-erected in the mall between two engineering buildings then being constructed. Later, plans appear to have been changed and the regents seem not to have made a designation for a new spot upon which the derrick is to be erected. It is hoped, however, that this can be accomplished quite soon. The University of Texas could not do anything more proper in expressing its appreciation of the contribution Santa Rita has made to the life and material resources of the University.

Texon, Texas, in the 1920s.
Courtesy of Portal to Texas History

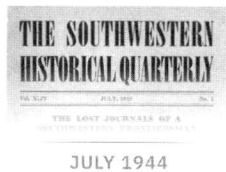

JULY 1944

A Plea for More Business in History

EUGENE C. BARKER*

THE TEXAS STATE HISTORICAL Association comes into this pleasant celebration appropriately by way of a book. The book is Martin Schwettmann's *Santa Rita,* which the Association recently published. It is a history of the completion of the discovery well which opened the University's oil empire in West Texas. Wholly incidentally, it is also a monument to the courage and dogged determination which has characterized individual enterprise in American industry. We need more such books. We need them for an understanding of the complex strands of American civilization. We need them also for a fair appreciation of the services of big and little business.

This brings me to the text of my sermon, which is a plea for more history in business. From the historians' point of view, businessmen—

---

* An address commemorating the twenty-first anniversary of the Santa Rita Discovery Well, delivered at Austin, Texas, May 27, 1944, at a dinner of the Texas Mid-Continent Oil and Gas Association, honoring The University of Texas and the Texas State Historical Association.

and particularly business organizations-are too reticent. We suspect that they are too reticent for their own good. Explanations of their policy leap to mind: partly, no doubt, it is a survival of the buccaneering era of "the public be damned;" partly it is due to the competitive character of business and the natural desire to withhold information from rivals. Whatever the cause may be, the policy creates an atmosphere that is inhospitable to historical investigators, facilitates propaganda that is hostile to business, and stimulates public suspicion.

There is a problem here. The blankest page in Texas history today is that which ought to tell of the growth and contribution of business and industry in the building of the state. The page is blank, not because historians do not appreciate the importance of the subject, but because they can rarely learn enough of the record to enable them to put pen to paper and write. The same is true of industry in the nation. To be sure, there is no lack of reports that corporations and associations are required to file with state and federal governments; but these are the dry skin and bones of history. They become the basis of some textbooks and of speculative discourses on trends, but the average citizen cannot understand them, and they are easily misconstrued. We need a knowledge of the human facts behind the figures. Perhaps we shall never get them, but businessmen and their legal advisers—some of whom are excellent historians—might profitably devise a system for giving us more than we have. For example, what do we know, or what could we learn, about the Texon Company, its successors and assigns after Ricker and Pickrell and Krupp and Cromwell played their respective roles in the history of Santa Rita? There must be other dramatic and heroic chapters in the story. I offer three suggestions for the consideration of business: Follow the example of the Army and Navy and employ a historical staff for each important unit, or open the records to historians with as few reservations as possible, or deposit the records—or selected blocks of records—in public depositories. The University of Texas and the Texas State Historical Association would gladly receive such deposits and would administer them faithfully.

Reunion of University of Texas administrators and
Big Lake Oil Company executives at Santa Rita No. 1 in 1934.
Courtesy of Portal to Texas History

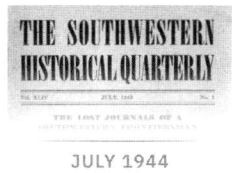

JULY 1944

The Spirit of Santa Rita

GEORGE A. HILL JR.*

UNDER THE AUSPICES of Santa Rita, Saint of the Impossible, on May 27, 1923, the first oil well on University land blew in, out of control, and to the utter amazement of the operators who had toiled for so long and so patiently with unremitting faith, courage, and persistence.

The Santa Rita well in Reagan County was the University discovery well in the great Permian Basin, and its literal eruption was the most fortuitous combination of the forces of nature and the labors of man, heralding a new economic and social era in a vast and largely undeveloped domain, the full significance and beneficence of which is even now hardly comprehensible.

The royalties to The University of Texas ensuing from this and subsequent discoveries, and the wise use to which the same have been and are now being devoted, and the changes wrought in the course of the history of Texas, have made this modest celebration of the Twenty-first Anniversary

---

* *An address commemorating the twenty-first anniversary of the Santa Rita Discovery Well, delivered at Austin, Texas, May 27, 1944, at a dinner of the Texas Mid-Continent Oil and Gas Association, honoring The University of Texas and the Texas State Historical Association.*

of the event an appropriate occasion for the members of the Texas oil industry to appraise the event, and also do honor to two great Texas institutions: The University of Texas and the Texas State Historical Association.

These two institutions are devoted to the exaltation of the spirit, cultivation of the mind, and activation of a virile and dynamic patriotism through the dissemination of knowledge of the experiences of the past, and the advancement of our material well-being under a political system that enlists the fullest expression of the freedom of man and the subserviency of the State to that inviolate freedom. They are each in part custodians of the fruits of this achievement, and worthily have they performed their trust.

But the event which we are gathered to celebrate is not the product of miraculous occurrence, royal beneficence, dictator's edict, or socialized planning. It is the natural consequence of a continuing expression of the fundamental truths that have become manifest through the ageless experience of mankind in its upward surge throughout the centuries for its most cherished aspiration-freedom.

It is a happy concomitance, then, that education, history, and the free enterprise of the individual citizen find mutual satisfaction, justification, and renewed strength in the continuance of achievements alike unto that celebrated upon this day. Santa Rita and all of its beneficent consequences are no more the result of accident than the consequences of the establishment of this great seat of general education at Austin, or the accumulated influence of this great learned society in the field of historical and patriotic endeavor. Each of these crowning accomplishments have come from the natural, yet expected, fruition of a wise, far-seeing, and humanistic policy, rooted deep in the consciousness of the founders of the Republic of Texas, and eloquently expressed in the sapient and profound message of President Mirabeau B. Lamar to the Congress of the Republic of Texas in December 1838,[1] which is, in part, as follows:

> *If we desire to establish a republican government upon a broad and permanent basis, it will be our duty to adopt a comprehensive and well-*

regulated system of mental and moral culture. Education is a subject in which every citizen. and especially every parent, feels a deep and lively concern. It is one in which no jarring interests are involved, and no acrimonious political feelings excited; for its benefits are so universal that all parties can unite in advancing it. *It is admitted by all that the cultivated mind is the guardian genius of democracy and, while guided and controlled by virtue, is the noblest attribute of man. It is the only dictator that freemen acknowledge and the only security that freemen desire. The influence of education in the moral world, as in the physical, renders luminous what was before obscure.* It opens a wide field for the exercise and improvement of all the faculties of man, and imparts vigor and clearness to those important truths in the science of government, as well as of morals, which would otherwise be lost in the darkness of ignorance. Without its aid, how perilous and insufficient would be the deliberations of a government like ours! How ignoble and useless its legislation for all the purposes of happiness! How fragile and insecure its liberties! *War would be conducted without the science necessary to secure success, and its bitterness and calamities would be unrelieved by the ameliorating circumstances which the improved condition of man has imparted to it. Peace would be joyless, because its train would be unattended by that civilization and refinement which alone can give zest to social and domestic enjoyments; and how shall we protect our rights if we do not comprehend them?* And can we comprehend them unless we acquire a knowledge of the past and present condition of things, and practice the habit of enlightened reflection? Cultivation is necessary to the supply of rich intellectual and moral fruits, as are the labors of the husbandman to bring forth the valuable productions of the earth.

But it would be superfluous to offer this honorable congress any extended argument to enforce the practical importance of this subject. I feel fully assured that it will, in that liberal spirit of improvement which pervades the social world, lose not the auspicious opportunity to provide for literary instructions, with an influence commensurate with our future destinies. To patronize the general diffusion of knowledge, industry and charity has been near to the heart of the good and wise of all nations, while the ambitious and the ignorant would fain have threatened a policy so pure and laudable. But the rich domes and spires of edifices consecrated to these objects, which are continually increasing in numbers, throwing their scenic splendor over civilization and attesting the patriotism of their founders, show that this unhallowed purpose has not been accomplished. *Our young republic has been formed by a Spartan spirit. Let it progress and ripen into Roman firmness and Athenian gracefulness and wisdom.* Let those names which have been inscribed on the standard of her national glory be found also on the pages of her history, associated with that profound and enlightened policy which is to make our country a bright link in that chain of free states which will some day encircle and unite in harmony the American continent. Thus, and thus only, will true glory be perfected; and our nation, which has sprung from the harsh trump of war, be matured into the refinements and tranquil happiness of peace.

Let me, therefore, urge upon you, gentlemen, not to postpone the matter too long. *The present is a propitious moment to lay the foundation of a great moral and intellectual edifice, which will in after ages be hailed as the chief ornament and blessing of Texas.* A suitable appropriation of lands to the purpose of general education can be made at this time, without inconvenience to the government or the people; but defer it until the public domain shall have passed from our hands, and the uneducated youths of Texas will constitute the living monuments of our neglect and remissness.

To appraise faithfully the paramount and enduring performances that have eventuated from this chartered course, outlined for the infant Republic, we must briefly examine the stormy past of Texas in contrast with the future evolved in the climate of enlightened freedom so soundly portrayed and so eloquently and wisely adjured.

Frank Pickrell, Haymon Krupp, Rupert Ricker, Hugh Tucker, and Carl Cromwell were not the first pioneers to camp near the waters of the Concho in an enterprise requiring courage, vision, hardihood, intrepidity, and skill, but they were clearly envisioned in the enlightened concept of President Lamar. The Indians that first occupied this region in undisturbed possession were "unattended by that civilization and refinement which alone can give zest to social and domestic enjoyments," and they did not hold to the truth that "the cultivated mind is the guardian genius of democracy, and while guided and controlled by virtue, is the noblest attribute of man."

The advent of civilized people to the region of Santa Rita and the Concho was not on a mission of peace, but upon an enterprise of conquest, and the Conquistadores were not the exponents of a republican form of government for free men, but were the paladins of a royal autocracy.

The primary purpose of Coronado and the early Conquistadores was the conquest of new lands, actually or supposedly rich in hard mineral wealth; the seizure of the gold and silver; the subjugation and pacification of those peopling such lands; and, in many instances, to their enduring credit, the paralleling effort of courageous and zealous priests to accomplish an extension of the Christian faith.

Over four hundred years ago, Hernando Cortés, Captain General of New Spain, was occupying his palace at Cuernavaca. He was the Conqueror of a New World, but he was the subject of the Crown of Spain and the servant of the Council of the Indies. In his intrepid explorations in search of mineral wealth for his Royal Master, he surveyed wide areas, gathered vast riches, and paid to Royalty its bountiful dues.

Notwithstanding the wealth in bullion poured into Royal Spanish coffers by the Conquistadores in Mexico, Peru, and in the Indies, a restless and untiring spirit of daring and adventure kept exploration, conquest, seizure, and pacification the rule of procedure under Royal Commissions for centuries, with the extension of the Faith a subsidiary and largely separate phase, although notable in its accomplishments.

The early Conquistador Cortés conquered the Valley of Mexico and subjugated the Mayas; Coronado sought the fabled Seven Cities of Cibola, intent upon the confiscation of fabulous mineral wealth, leaving a long trail of failure and disappointment; but Pickrell, Krupp, Ricker, Tucker, and Cromwell, and their contemporaries and successors, by the employment of the arts of peace, science and industry, have penetrated the realms of the Permian, the Ordovician, and other geologic regions with an incomparably greater yield in riches, and actually found the veritable Seven Cities of Cibola in Big Lake, in the Pecos, in Hobbs, in Yates, in Winkler, in McCamey, in Texon, and in numerous subterranean provinces of unimagined wealth.

The early Conquistador Juan de Oñate engaged in the search for the mythical Straits of Anian, which were believed to connect the Atlantic and Pacific Oceans and an intermediate "North Sea," the harbors of which were to be carefully mapped, but not used until appropriate regulations could be prescribed therefor, with the usual eventuality of pursuing false rumor; but Pickrell and his pioneering associates reduced to possession the fruits of a successful exploration of the actual "North Sea"—the Permian Basin.

The galleons of old, laden with gold and silver, brought their wealth to Spanish royalty; but the dues paid to the viceroy and the council of the Indies, and the total exactions of Spanish royalty and all of the prizes of the gold hunters' era are dwarfed into insignificance compared to the royalties accruing to the sovereign citizens of our State and their great educational institution, and were a mere triviality compared with the one billion, seven hundred million dollars paid during the past twenty-one years in lease rentals and royalties to the farmers and ranchers and landowners of our State, and the sum of one billion, three hundred and fifty million dollars paid during the same period in various forms of taxes to our State and local governments.

During this period of time, the oil industry of Texas has paid in taxes, for the support of the public schools of this State, a grand total of over two hundred and forty-three million dollars.

In the past twenty-one years oil has accomplished prodigious changes:

(1) Average daily production in May 1923 of approximately three hundred thousand barrels per day is now approximately two million barrels per day
(2) A similar increase in refining capacity has merged into its manifold activities hundreds of millions of dollars invested in aviation gasoline and synthetic rubber plants.
(3) Great trunk line transportation systems now traverse the inland and overland routes to the Great Lakes, the Gulf, and the Atlantic Ocean.
(4) Natural gas has been discovered, developed, and distributed in an expansion paralleling the prodigious performances in oil.
(5) Twenty-three oilfields are now yielding royalty revenues to The University of Texas, from University lands in Andrews, Crane, Crockett, Ector, Pecos, Reagan, and Ward counties.
(6) Increased wealth widely diffused throughout our entire population has made itself manifest in the almost miraculous statistics of population increase, added property values, astounding expansion of life insurance, the migration of related and associated industries and manufacturing enterprises to Texas, the total effect of which is typified by the striking contrast between The University of Texas of today and over twenty-one years ago.

The history of the accomplishment of the oil industry in Texas during the past twenty-one years can only be hinted at in this brief resume. The advancements in technology have even exceeded, in proportion, the comparative production in volume and the comparative proven reserves in quantity. The improvement in quality, and the increased yields in gasoline content due to improved refining methods, are only matched by the reduced retail price of gasoline, exclusive of tax.

All of this has been a necessary progression in every phase of the industry as an indispensable prelude to the maximum effort now being expended by the oil industry in Texas as a contribution to the winning of a war completely mechanized and motorized, whose bomber and fighter planes, whose battleships, cruisers, submarines, transports, and landing ships, and whose tanks, tank destroyers, and artillery are all propelled by the products of oil.

But it is not of material resources alone, and the accomplishments of industry and science, that I would speak. There has been nurtured and preserved in the mind and heart of our people that indomitable attitude toward life that is "Texian," and that has its truest reflection in an unchallenged position of primacy in the number of volunteers in the Army, the Navy, the Marine Corps, and the Air Corps in this War, and the courage and heroism that they have exhibited upon the seven seas and throughout the earth. The spirit of the pioneer is still within them—undiminished, undaunted, and unafraid.

This spirit of the pioneer has a special quality and flavor that animated the pioneers at Santa Rita, the Saint of the Impossible. As I said upon another occasion of Dad Joiner, I may with equal truth say of Frank Pickrell and his comrades: No chart of government pointed the way. No managed economy underwrote the risk. No authoritarian regulation measured the prospect. No bureaucracy supplied the incentive, by mandate or bounty; and not even contemporaneous geologic concept furnished the inspiration. The true spirit of the pioneer, the independent enterprise of a free American citizen who still believed in and cherished the opportunities that America affords; the same courage and self-reliance and indomitable will that conquered the wilderness of earlier years, that peopled the plains and the mountains beyond the far horizons for the beneficent uses of America today, that still guide and animate and propel the sturdy, pioneering Americans of this day, for whom the simple frontiers of our pioneer fathers have been multiplied, many times over, in incalculable number, variety and opportunity, resided in the spirit, and in the heart, and the will of Frank Pickrell. Let us pray that these United States may throughout the future, as in the past, nurture and preserve, and proudly cherish the pioneer and let his courageous, undaunted, and unterrified spirit and faith forever remain the heart and the core of free America.

Electra became known as the "Pump Jack Capital of Texas."
Courtesy of Library of Congress

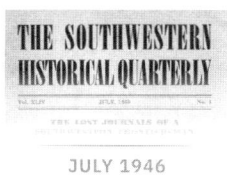

JULY 1946

Electra, A Texas Oil Town

ABBY W. COOPER

ELECTRA IS LOCATED in the western part of Wichita County, two miles east of the Wilbarger County line and about ten miles each from Red River on the north and Beaver Creek on the south. Twice platted and subdivided into town lots and three times sold, the town has had three names: Beaver, Waggoner, and Electra. The first settlement followed the building of the Fort Worth and Denver Railroad through this area in 1885. The first post office was secured in 1889 by C. L. Myers, who was the first postmaster. It was named Beaver, as was the first school. Railway transportation was secured by "flagging the trains." The town consisted of only a few residences, a hotel, wagon yard, school, post office, and a general store. It was a trading post for Chief Quanah Parker and his Comanche Indian comrades from the Comanche Reservation across Red River in the Indian Territory (now Oklahoma).

Daniel Waggoner and son, W. T. Waggoner, cattle barons, had moved their herds westward from Wise County in 1878 and later established headquarters on Red River, north of the present location of Electra. Their holdings almost completely surrounded the town and included a greater part of the original town site. Harrold, Wilbarger County, six miles west of Electra, a thriving metropolis while it was the terminal of the Denver railroad through 1886 and for some years thereafter, had been the shipping place for Waggoner and other cattlemen in this area; but as the fertile land in the vicinity was developed into an agricultural district, frequent clashes occurred between cattlemen and the farmers because the herds, driven in for shipment, tore down fences and trampled the crops. Accordingly, Waggoner secured cooperation with the railroad in building a switch track and loading pens at Beaver in 1900. When the first depot was built, it was designated as Waggoner. Freight and express bills were marked to Waggoner while the mail was still postmarked "Beaver." The citizens in 1902 decided by petition to have the town renamed Electra in honor of Miss Electra Waggoner, daughter of W. T. Waggoner.

In 1905 Waggoner sold the tract of land embracing the Electra town site to Sol Williams, Fort Worth real estate dealer and town site promoter. Involved in the deal were about fifty buildings, including residences, a blacksmith shop, and business houses, ranging in value from $300 to $3,000. Waggoner reserved a large livery stable and the block of land on which it stood. A limited number of other pieces of property owned by individuals, under early deeds, were also reserved. Williams replatted the town, subdividing it into 2,150 lots. Then followed a town-lot sales campaign, which reached nationwide proportions.

The same year that Waggoner sold the Electra town site to the Fort Worth man, he sold 91,000 acres of his ranch land lying between Electra and Red River to Reese S. Allen of Beaumont. This land was subdivided into tracts of 160 acres each for sale to farmers. (Deeds, oil leases, and other legal papers affecting title on permanent records designate this as the Waggoner Colony Survey.) The sales campaign, carried on under the name of the Electra Land and Colonization Company, led to establishment of northern headquarters in Chicago and St. Louis and the bringing of excursion trains regularly from the North and East to accommodate home-seekers, many of whom not only bought raw land in the Waggoner Colony but bought town site lots in Electra. The town site opening set for October 23, 24, and 25, 1907, was nationally advertised. The proposition, a town lot for $50 with the added incentive of the improvements on some of the lots, proved so popular that by opening day the promoters found they had "over sold." The problem was quickly remedied by extending the proposed business district. Residence lots were 50x120 feet, twelve lots to the block. Business lots were 25x120, four lots to the block. Adding several blocks to the business district by splitting the fifty-foot lots into twenty-five-foot lots was a simple matter; and enough lots were found for all of the cash customers as well as to enable Williams to donate a block of land for a future park, a lot each to the Baptist, Methodist, Presbyterian, and Catholic denominations for church purposes, and a lot for the schoolhouse.

A large revival tent was rented for use as headquarters for the town site opening celebration. Services of the Iredell, Texas, Cornet Band were secured for entertainment. A free fair and livestock show with a generous list of prizes offered on farm products, horses, mules, ladies' and gents' saddle horses and "rigs" including horse, buggy, and fancy harness, attracted hundreds of people for miles around; and an excursion train brought other hundreds of visitors. J. E. Powers of Chicago, Illinois, was the auctioneer. Judge M. B. Briggs of Gilmer was named as legal adviser. In order to conform to certain technicalities under which Texas statutes forbade "lotteries" in connection with town-lot auction sales, the title was executed by three trustees, elected for the occasion, namely H. W. Wiseman of Cleburne, Texas; George McDaniel of Abilene, Texas; and Dr. J. P. Brun ton of Frederick, Oklahoma. Thus was created the Special TownLot Deed, City of Electra, Texas, used in the transfer of title for all real estate in the original town site.

M. V. Adams of Blum drew the high prize in the sale, the large general merchandise store at the corner of South Main Street and Front Avenue. He was offered and refused to take $3,000 for the property, bought at $50. Many other pieces of property, however, changed hands several times before the deeds were finally delivered.

The growth of the town was rapid. Supported by the newly developed agricultural lands in the Red River Valley, it became a shipping center for wheat, corn, cotton, and hogs. It retained its pre-eminence also as a cattle-shipping center as the herds on nearby ranches were improved with introduction of purebred breeding stock. Dairying and poultry raising played a prominent part in the rapidly mounting resources.

Traces of oil had been found on the town site when Waggoner had a deep well drilled in 1900, hoping to secure water for his cattle. A second and a third attempt to uncover a supply of artesian water proved equally disappointing, and after the wells were abandoned, the oil which rose to within a few feet of the top of the ground proved useful to farmers and ranchers who used it to dope cattle to rid them of stock flies and ticks. It was also used in combating bluebugs, which infested henhouses. In 1906, representatives of an oil company in Pittsburgh, Pennsylvania, secured a block of leases for a proposed oil test. The project was abandoned because Waggoner, who owned a greater portion of the land wanted, refused to lease. He later leased a large tract to the Producers Oil Company, which started its first oil test on August 8, 1909, the location being adjacent to the town site on the south. Drilled to a depth of 1,965 feet, it was abandoned. Other tests followed in 1910, three being pronounced to be dry holes, but the fifth well was said to have made a strong flow of oil before the owners barricaded the site with a barbed wire fence and placed a guard over it. The townspeople were kept in the dark as to oil's having been discovered there until after the Clayco No. 1, Woodruff-Putnam, a wildcat test one mile northwest from the center of the town, blew itself in on April 1, 1911, setting off an oil boom which not only brought wealth and fame to Electra but has contributed abundantly to the material resources of the southwestern part of the United States.

The sand from which the discovery well made its spectacular performance was found at 1,600 feet, but within a year, five distinct sands had been developed. In 1946, the Electra oilfields, pronounced the most outstanding in Texas because of the longevity of the wells, are producing from twenty or more levels ranging from "grass roots" sands around 350 feet to the famous Ellenberger lime from 4,000 to 5,000 feet.

The town followed the usual pattern of oil booms in phenomenal growth, but because of the fact that with the waning of old pools, new pools have been discovered and developed from time to time, it maintained its place in the ranks of the oil industries as the following statistics will show : the Electra area has four major pipe lines gathering oil from a district in which approximately 8,500 wells have been drilled since 1911, five gasoline plants, a refinery which produced millions of gallons of aviation gasoline for the government during World War II, two cracking plants, twelve oilfield supply houses, a steel tank manufacturing plant, five machine shops capable of making and servicing all sorts of oilfield equipment, six welding shops and all necessary facilities such as pipe line and construction machinery-producing a monthly pay roll of more than $400,000 from oil and its affiliated industries.

Transportation facilities include one railroad, two bus lines, state and federal highways, and more paved and graveled roads within Precinct No. 4, Wichita County (in which Electra is the only town) than in many populous counties.

Four brick school buildings, eleven churches, civic clubs, fraternal organizations, USO, and headquarters for a fully organized and fully staffed company of Texas State Guard serve the town.

Bank deposits at the end of 1945 totaled $2,645,441.11. Postal receipts at the attractive federal government-owned post office were $41,545.89. The community went over the top on its quota in each of the War Bond sales campaigns and provided more than a thousand men for military service during the war, including a fully equipped, completely staffed, and well-trained unit of the Medical Detachment of Texas National Guard, 142nd Infantry, 36th Division. Sixty gold stars on the huge Honor Roll, erected by the American Legion in honor of men and women in service during the war, represent that number of Electra men who gave their lives for freedom.

Other data concerning Electra are: population last federal census, 5,446; commission form of government;- municipal and school tax rate $2.00 per $100; municipally owned light and power plant, also served by Texas Electric Service Company; abundant natural gas for domestic and industrial use; adequate water supply and postwar plans include improving and extending sewer system; tax-supported public library; well-equipped fire department and low insurance rate; fertile soil, growing vegetables, fruit, and flowers; average rainfall twenty-four inches per year; altitude above sea level 1,229 feet.

Beaumont Oil Exchange and Board of Trade in 1901.
Courtesy of Library of Congress

JULY 1946

Spindletop

BOYCE HOUSE

ON JANUARY 10, 1901, an event occurred which was destined to transform the economic life of Texas and, to a lesser degree, affect the history of America and the world, for it was on that day that the Lucas gusher roared in.

But for the beginning of the story, one must go back, far back, of the time that Captain Anthony F. Lucas began drilling his well at Spindletop. For it is a story of Spanish adventurers, of a mysterious pool of oil out in the Gulf of Mexico, of a pioneer geologist with a queer contraption, of "sour wells," of Pattillo Higgins, a home-made scientist. There is even a suggestion of or a touch of the supernatural.

The first known use of petroleum by the white man in North America occurred not far from Spindletop in 1543, when survivors of the DeSoto Expedition, sailing along the coast, were forced ashore by a storm and took advantage of the delay to caulk their boats with tar which they found near the beach. The substance doubtless was the residue of petroleum after the evaporation of volatile elements. The tar could have been the result of seepage from Spindletop.

There was such a seepage, for centuries probably, as evidenced by the "oil pond," or lake of oil, in the Gulf. In 1901, a statement, signed by six shipmasters and the harbor master of Sabine Pass, declared: "From time immemorial, there has existed directly off and along the Gulf beach of this section an immense oil pool, about a mile and a half in width and four miles in length."

The statement declared that, after the storm of 1886, the pool shifted some distance eastward toward Sabine Pass, because of accretions of mud and sand. The document relates: "We the undersigned, have always made this 'oil pool' a place of safety which we sought with our sea-going vessels in times of peril from severe gales or storms, for when we anchored our vessels in this oil sea, we were safe and everything was calm."

After 1902, the "oil pond" vanished. Perhaps the supply of petroleum that had coursed underground to flow out under the coast into the Gulf and rise to the surf ace was intercepted as the result of the drilling of the Lucas and other gushers. At any rate, the miraculous stretch of calm, "oil on the troubled waters," disappeared. Numerous geologists do hold that the disappearance of the oil seepage in the Gulf was purely coincidental with the discovery of Spindletop. Bituminous deposits washed up on the beach near Sabine Pass are still in evidence and can be seen clearly from an airplane.

As far back as the 1860's, there were sour wells on "the Hill," as Spindletop was first known. The water was regarded as possessing medicinal value, and tiny bubbles formed on the suface. A year after the Civil War ended, Dr. B. T. Kavanaugh arrived in Beaumont with an odd-looking contrivance in his hack. The device was the invention of his brother, the Reverend W. B. Kavanaugh, and was designed to discover oil. In a letter written in 1878, B. T. Kavanaugh told of his visit: "Here I found some fine veins, one passing under the sour wells some mile or two southwest of Beaumont… Also I visited Sour Lake, where I found oil upon the surface in greater quantity than at any other point." Near Sour Lake, he drilled to a depth of 142 feet before quitting because of the quicksand and the expense.

Kavanaugh's letter states further, "On the Gulf coast, near Sabine Pass, there is a substance found in lumps like wax, which the people call 'sea wax.' When examined, this wax is found to consist of bitumin and paraffin. The petroleum, being a thin liquid, is washed out from the mixture, leaving the bitumen and paraffin as a wax or gum which is found on the beach." This was the same kind of substance, no doubt, that the Spaniards had used in 1543.

In 1890, Pattillo Higgins began asserting that there was oil under "the Hill." Higgins was born in Beaumont in 1863, worked in a shingle mill and a lumberyard, and then began to run a brickyard. He visited Pennsylvania, Ohio, and Indiana to study brick-making machinery and found that many plants used natural gas or fuel oil. So he began to study the subject of petroleum, reading all the United States government geological reports and other documents that he could lay hands on. He evolved his own system of geology and, from the surface indications, concluded there was oil under the Hill. He went so far as to declare that "gushers" would be drilled, producing thousands of barrels a day. When this prediction was first uttered, the entire output of Texas for the year was forty-eight barrels.

Most of the townspeople considered Higgins obsessed on the subject; but he interested George W. Carroll, wealthy lumberman, and Captain George O'Brien, Confederate veteran and attorney, the result being the Gladys City Oil, Gas, and Manufacturing Company. The "city," which existed only in Higgins' imagination, was named for little Gladys Bingham, member of a Sunday School class which Higgins taught.

A contract was made with M. B. Looney for a 1,500-foot test. The driller was W. B. Sharp, and the equipment was "a rattle trap outfit of the type used in drilling water wells," Higgins related. Gas was struck, but the quicksand halted the drill at four hundred feet. Then Savage and Company of West Virginia drilled, but the second test was foiled by the quicksand.

Undaunted, Higgins advertised in northern newspapers about the possibilities and wrote letters to men he thought might be interested.

One of these letters was to Captain Anthony F. Lucas.

Antonio Francisco Luchich, born in 1855 in Spalato, Dalmatia, Austria, was graduated from the Polytechnic Institute at Gratz as an engineer, entered the Austrian navy, and became a lieutenant. In 1879, he came to the United States and, six years later, became an American citizen, changing his name to Anthony Francis Lucas. Until 1895, he engaged in lumbering, then was a consulting mechanical and mining engineer, his home and offices being in Washington, DC.

Joseph Jefferson, famed for his portrayal of Rip Van Winkle, bought an estate in Louisiana at Bobacres, three miles southeast of Jefferson Island, and decided to drill a mineral water well. He obtained the services of Captain Lucas. Lucas discovered not mineral water but a highly valuable commodity, salt, in the vicinity of Jefferson Island. Then he developed salt and sulphur mines at Belle Isle and became an authority on salt domes along the Gulf Coast.

When Higgins induced Lucas to visit Beaumont, the Captain's chief interest, according to Higgins, was not oil but sulphur. Lucas' first test struck a showing of oil before the quicksands stopped the drill at around six hundred feet. With a sample of the oil in a bottle, he interested Guffey and Galey, prominent oil men of Pennsylvania, who had been active in the development at Corsicana, Texas. Oil had been discovered there in 1895, when a well was being put down for artesian water for the municipal water supply.

Hamill Brothers—J. G. and A.W.—oil well contractors at Corsicana, received a letter from John H. Galey, informing them that "a Mr. Lucas" would see them about drilling a well at Beaumont and that Guffey and Galey would back any agreement Lucas made. The price agreed on was $2.00 per foot for a 1,200-foot test. Hamill Brothers were pioneers with rotary, the new method of drilling, which was a string of pipe with a bit at the end, contrasted with cable, or "standard," tools, with a bit at the end of a cable. Cable tools had failed at Beaumont. It was hoped that perhaps the solid length of pipe would conquer the sliding sands.

Although Lucas' backers had assured the financing of the well, no provision had been made for the captain's living expenses, and, during the winter of 1900, the articles of furniture in his home were sold, one by one. Only the courage of his wife had sustained Lucas when he had wanted to give up, and now she kept a brave smile, though the food was simple and the dining table was only a box with a calico covering. On New Year's Day, 1901, Lucas bowed his head to ask the blessing over the dinner and prayed that the well would strike oil.

Because the bit was not making any headway, Al Hamill telegraphed to his brother at Corsicana for a new fishtail bit, and on January 10, Al met the train to get the bit; then he drove back to the well. And here is the story, in his own words, of the happenings that followed:

> We put the new bit on and had about 700 feet of the drill pipe back in the hole when the rotary mud began flowing up through the rotary table. It came so fast and with such force that Curt, who was up on the doubleboards, was drenched with mud and had a hard time getting out of danger.
>
> Soon, the four-inch drill pipe started up through the derrick, knocking off the crown block. It shot up through the top of the derrick, breaking off in lengths of several joints at a time as it shot skyward.
>
> It all happened in much less time than it can be told.
>
> After the water, mud and pipe were blown out, gas followed, but only for a short time. Then the well became very quiet.
>
> We boys ventured back—after a wild scramble for safety—to find things in a terrible mess. There was at least six inches of mud on the derrick floor and some damage had been done to our equipment. Naturally, we were all disgusted.
>
> We started shoveling the mud away when, without any warning, a lot of heavy mud was shot out of the well with the report of a cannon!

It was followed by gas for a short time, when oil showed up in head flows.

In a very short time, oil was going up through the top of the derrick and rocks were shot hundreds of feet into the air. Within a very few minutes, the oil was holding a steady flow at more than twice the height of the derrick.

As soon as I pulled myself together, Peck Byrd was started on the dead run for Captain Lucas. Peck breathlessly gave the report to Mrs. Lucas and she at once located the Captain, by phone, at Louie Myers' store in Beaumont.

It was not long before we saw Captain Lucas coming over the small hill with his horse in full run. He decided his horse was too slow, so he jumped or rolled out of the buggy and ran to me, shouting: "Al, what is it?" When I answered, "Oil," he exclaimed, "Thank God," and hugged me, good and hard.

From the doorway of their home, Mrs. Lucas could see the great column of oil. Soon the captain saw her hurrying to the scene, and, as he said afterward, "the look of joy which illuminated her countenance was reward sufficient for all the worry and work."

The roar of the untamed geyser of petroleum caused negroes to flee in terror; they thought the end of the world had come. Many persons feared the earth would cave in. A minister delivered an indignant sermon: the Almighty did not intend that His creation should be disturbed in this way.

Tidings of the Lucas gusher, located at tidewater, the mightiest well the world had ever seen, flashed around the globe; and thousands swarmed in to view 100,000 barrels of oil a day soaring into the air.[1] A great lake of oil formed, and suggestions poured in as to methods for taming the monster. One group offered to close it in for a mere $30,000.

For nine days, it raged. When the awaited valve arrived, the drilling crew tackled the danger-laden task. The men worked five minutes or so in the gas-impregnated air, goggles over their eyes, gauze shields over their noses, and cotton plugs in their ears, then dashed back to comparative safety.

The well was capped—and then a spark from a locomotive set the lake of oil on fire, and the hundreds of thousands of barrels went up in huge black clouds.

More gushers were drilled, and railroads ran special trains from Galveston, Houston, and other cities to see "the greatest sight on earth." Wells were permitted to flow into the air to entertain the thousands of Sunday visitors.

Beaumont looked like circus day, every day, with map vendors and peddlers of souvenir bottles filled with oil crying their wares; lease brokers shouted their "bargains" from boxes or wore signs in their hats as they mingled with the crowds that sometimes filled the street from building line to building line. Booths were built in the yard of the Crosby House, customers standing on the sidewalk. One tiny office was headquarters of five promotional companies—for the first nationwide speculation in oil stocks reached a "Mississippi Bubble" magnitude. The *Manufacturers' Record* published an estimate that the actual investment in the field was $11,000,000 but that the total capitalization of Texas oil companies was almost $232,000,000. Incidentally, some metropolitan newspaper writers gave the field a new name, Swindletop.

Lines in front of cafes were a block long; grocery stores never closed; in fact, night and day meant little, for men would set out at midnight with lanterns to search for "gas bumps" and indications of oil. Unable to find a place to sleep, two men bought a mattress and placed it on the sidewalk on the principal street. A man, flipping through a roll of $100 bills, came across a "ten-spot," which he tore up with the remark, "Small change, what are you doing here?" A woman who owned a little truck patch and a few hogs for which she hauled slop from town in two barrels on a dilapidated wagon leased her land for a fortune. A printer, who bought a lease and resold it the same day for a profit of $30,000, put on a celebration in which nearly all the printers in town joined; with a band, they went from bar to bar, drinking wine until the entire $30,000 was gone.

Out on the Hill, hundreds of wells were crowded on 140 acres; the legs of derricks interlapped; and some leases, notably in the Hogg-Swayne tract, which was divided up and sold by former Governor James S. Hogg and associates, were so small that there was only room for the derrick and space for the boiler had to be rented. And, speaking of boilers, it is related that a drilling crew left a well for lunch and, when they returned, the boiler had been stolen, though it had one hundred pounds of steam. There were explosions, raging gas wells, and fires that claimed men's lives.

What was Spindletop? A mound, about three miles southeast of Beaumont, which rose ten or fifteen feet above the flat coastal country. But actually the mound that the world knows as Spindletop was not Spindletop at all; originally, it was called "the Hill" or "the Big Hill." The Beaumont *Enterprise* of October 30, 1901, says:

> The way this name [Spindletop] was switched from its original home to its present one was remarkable and happened in the twinkling of an eye. Indeed so quick did it happen that it must have been through the means of the fertile brain of a newspaper correspondent or reporter that it came about.
>
> Spindletop was, before the great oil discovery, the name of a mound of trees to the east of the oilfield about a mile and a half and almost on the river. The trees arose in the form of a mound and towered above all the other landmarks in the county and could be seen. easily from the prairie where now stands Port Arthur... And why was it called Spindletop? Years ago, a lone tree stood out above all the rest and right in the center of the mound. It ran up in spiral form and the whole picture was like that of a top inverted and with the spindle in the center... The old spindle tree is dead now and no trace of it remains but the large green mound can be seen plainly from any point off to the south.

A suggestion of the supernatural was mentioned. Before the discovery of oil, the Hill was in a pasture; and cowboys, crossing the prairie at night, claimed to have seen a ball of light near the spot where the Lucas gusher later was drilled. As they approached, the light melted away. Sailors have told of seeing a ball of fire high in the spars of ships at sea, and they called such a manifestation "St. Elmo fire," from the patron saint of sailors. Perhaps the light on the Hill was the equivalent of the will-o'-the-wisp of European folk tales.

It was said that Captain Lucas himself had seen the light on the Hill. He may even have been the last to behold the weird glow, for no one since the drilling of the gusher has claimed to have seen it.

Spindletop and its consequences transformed Beaumont from a town of ten thousand persons to a throbbing city, changed Port Arthur from a village in a marsh to the world's greatest refining center, gave much of the impetus that has made Houston the metropolis of the Southwest and one of the greatest ports of earth, was the beginning of such major companies as the Texas, the Gulf, and the Humble, was the training ground for many o. f the leaders of the petroleum industry of the nation for the following forty years, and lifted Texas from a negligible position in oil to foremost rank among the forty-eight states.

A shaft was unveiled on the site of the Lucas gusher in 1941 as the highlight of the convention of the Texas Mid-Continent Oil and Gas Association. It is fitting that, next to the shaft at San Jacinto, this is the highest monument in Texas. Carved in the eternal granite are these lines:

On This Spot
on the Tenth Day of the Twentieth Century
a New Era in Civilization Began
Petroleum has revolutionized industry and transportation; it
has created untold wealth, built cities, furnished employment
for hundreds of thousands, and contributed billions of dollars in
taxes to support institutions of government. In a brief span of
years, it has altered man's way of life throughout the world.

But even this magnificent vista in words could not reveal all, for, a few years later, Texas was producing almost exactly the amount of oil that America needed to win World War II; Texas oil saved civilization and averted world-wide slavery. And Texas oil received its initial impetus when the Lucas gusher roared in.

Such, in outline, is the story of Spindletop.

Wooden Oil Derricks at Sour Lake, Texas.
Courtesy of Wikipedia

JULY 1946

Reminiscences of Sour Lake

CHARLIE JEFFRIES

DURING THE FIRST WEEK of October 1903, I went to Sour Lake. Boll weevils had ruined the cotton in my part of the country, and, like thousands of others, I went to the oilfield to tide over a hard time. By pawning my fiddle and six-shooter and borrowing fifty cents from a friend, I scraped up enough money to buy a ticket; I got there without a cent.

Hardly had I arrived before I was introduced to one of the town's most prominent characteristics—rascality. Two young fellows at the depot came up to me and gave me a drink of beer. Then they began a game of matching nickels on the counter. After playing a short time, they invited me to join in the game. For more reasons than one, I declined. They continued the game between themselves, but every now and then they would invite me to take a hand. After a while one of them got lucky or something and speedily broke the other one. The loser, in a huff, left the room, vowing he was going to get more money and come back and clean up on the winner. As soon as the loser left, the other boy came to me eagerly and proposed that I come in and that he and I work together and fleece the other fellow. I understood something of the game and knew that the trick could be worked readily enough, but I was hardly so gullible as to think it would be worked in my favor; and again, in mild tones, I declined.

At this late date, I do not remember why I remained at the depot since I had come to Sour Lake to work, and especially since I knew that a skin game was being played for the express purpose of catching me; but I did.

Presently the boy who had lost came back and, true to his word, brought a handful of money, not nickels and dimes, but long, green paper money. They started the game again with gusto. From time to time, they would stop and invite me to come in, but I continued to shake my head and tell them I did not want to. They paid little attention to my repeated refusals and soon became highly insistent. Finally, I came out with my more solid reason—told them I was broke. No doubt they were as well acquainted with people without money as they were with those with it. At any rate, they ceased their importunities, and the game stopped. In keeping with the larger life of the place, however, when I asked them the way to the oilfield, they good naturedly showed me the road. As I went down the road, with a sneaking grin I thought of the incident as typical of Sour Lake, for instead of the scamps fleecing me, I had got them for a glass of beer.

I landed at the town in the afternoon. I had had no dinner but was not particularly hungry. I had nowhere to go, no definite plan for the immediate future. I had simply come to the place to get work and was blandly meeting difficulties as they arose. Several young men whom I knew worked around the oilfields, and one of these, Will Collins, I particularly hoped to find with the purpose of getting him to help me until I could get a start. I had not counted on the difficulty of finding a man in a seething mass of humanity, ten thousand souls perhaps, scattered over several miles of territory; but I set out, confidently hunting the needle in the haystack.

By chance, toward night, I did meet Ben Roberts, another boy whom I knew. The ties of acquaintance between Ben and me were strong enough to justify my applying to him for assistance. By way of reply, he said he was broke, too. He said he had been sick, and I could see that he was not in a cheerful mood. We strolled along together on the edge of the oilfield and after a while we met a man whom Ben knew. After a few words with the man, Ben asked him how much money he had. The man told him thirty cents. Ben told him to give it to him. The man did so, and Ben gave the money to me.

By late evening I was beginning to feel a little weak. I had had an attack of malaria a short time before, and the hardship of riding all night without sleep and doing without meals was no doubt telling on me. I went on to the business part of town that night and ate a five-cent supper; then I spent the other twenty-five cents for a bed. Next morning the proprietor of the sleeping place kindly gave me a cup of coffee and some tea cakes for breakfast.

That morning, I began hunting in earnest for someone I knew, particularly Will Collins. What I did throughout the morning I can not now remember in a detailed way, but the events of the evening are more clear. I recall having a fever and lying down on a pine log by the roadside and sweating it off. The fever was not severe, and after it left me, I got up and went on my way, not a great deal the worse. The day was Saturday, and an unusual number of people were on the streets; I continued walking around, looking through them, hunting for someone I knew. I was becoming bothered by this time. Two days without anything like a square meal and with little prospect of a place to stay that night were making an impression on a young fellow not too well acquainted with hoboing.

Tired and feeling bad, I gave up walking after a time. Reasoning that I could look people over as well sitting down as moving around, I took a seat on a syrup barrel out in front of a store. There I watched the people go by. They went by in a stream, hundreds and hundreds of them; I scanned every face that came in view. In my recollection of the many things I experienced at Sour Lake nothing is more strong than the memory of sitting on the barrel that Saturday evening and watching for someone that I knew.

Finally, about sundown, my attention was attracted to a man ambling along down the sidewalk. I had probably become somewhat weary from glancing at so many faces, and the first thing I noticed about this man was that his hand was in a sling. In a subconscious sort of way, at the same time, I noticed that the ambling gait was familiar. These little acts of perception, of course, took the briefest amount of time; and when I took a square look at the man's face, I saw that he was George Wentz, another one of the boys from home. In my whole life, I do not remember having been so glad to see a person as I was that evening to see George Wentz.

George was really glad to see me, too. He and his brother John owned a tent and a complete batching outfit, and they took me in.

For surging energy, unrestrained openness, and diabolical conditions otherwise, Sour Lake was head and shoulders above anything Texas had seen up until that time or perhaps has seen since. The site is on low ground. At that time little effort was made at drainage; and a short while after operations began, a large part of the field was worked up into such a mess of mud as can hardly be imagined.

One thing that made the mud so bad and rendered the place such an inferno in other ways was the crowded condition. There were few, if any, laws governing oilfield operations; no such thing as restrictions on drilling existed. Landowners sold their land to anyone who came to buy it and in as small amounts as the buyer's purse spoke for. Aided by the ignorance of the people and the get-rich craze that swept the country, many men of small means came into the field and bought acreage. In many instances land in as small amounts as one-sixteenth, or even one thirty-second, of an acre was sold. The result was that the greater part of the field was soon a forest of derricks. As quantities of water are required to run a rotary drill, the slush which spread from these hundreds of wells and which was stirred up by the men working in it made the place a sight to behold.

As the oilfield was the important feature of the Sour Lake scene as a whole, so was Shoestring the center of interest of the oilfield. Shoestring was a long narrow strip of land in the middle of the oil-bearing district, where development was most intensified. In many ways it was the pulsing life center of the oilfield. Here the wells were thickest; here the mud was deepest; here the gas was strongest; here the boilers roared the loudest; here the efforts of men had the fullest play. Things of magnitude went on in other parts of the field, in the Cannon tract, and in outlying leases, but they were overshadowed by the activity at Shoestring. This was the place with which men with pride of action liked to identify themselves. As the elect viewed it, no one was deemed worthy of being connected with Sour Lake unless he had undergone his period of seasoning in Shoestring.

Not all the men in the field were in the mud wading around like turtles; not many of them, to be accurate, were reduced to that. Most of them were up out of it, or at least trying to stay out of it. The constant effort to stay clear of the mud added no little to the interest of the scene. The derrick floors were high, if not always dry; and other places absolutely essential to the drilling, like the ground around the boiler and engine, were by a never-ending effort kept comparatively clear. But always nearby, even on the holdings of the larger companies, was the waste from the overflowed slush pits, giving the place the appearance of a freshly drained pond.

The struggle between mud and men was close-locked. There were no roads, that is high, dry roads in Shoestring. The only way of getting around in that part of the field was by whatever means one could devise. A network of large pipes, not unlike a badly constructed spider web, ran about over the field. They had been laid without any regard to system, but they were usually up out of the mud, and these, to some extent, served as causeways. The pipes, together with the derrick floors and the little islands about the boilers, served as foundations for more bridging; the bridges usually consisted of two by twelve planks thrown down wherever the crying need of some little piece of work had demanded. On these frail structures the traffic of the field was conducted.

The statement that there were no roads in Shoestring needs qualification. Along the south border of that seething section there was one good, graded road. This road, however, was owned by one of the large companies of the field whose holdings took in all the land immediately southward. The company maintained this road for its own benefit. The company had it fenced into a strong lane with a locked gate at each end and with armed guards to keep trespassers out. In the unruly condition of the place, however, they could not keep out pedestrians; and because of the convenience of the road, it was a great thoroughfare for those walking any considerable distance in those parts. Whether because they could not prevent it, or because after a time they grew more lenient, the officials came to allow such things as could be packed bodily to be transported along the road. That was the means, when I knew the place, by which all material, be it light or heavy, was moved into and out of Shoestring.

Whenever anything heavy was needed to be brought in, it was hauled by wagon as close to the road as possible; then a gang of men would take it and carry it on to its destination. Packing along the road was fairly easy, but when it became necessary to turn out into the mud, that was another matter. The packers often had to lay down more planks; they had to twist like snakes around obstacles. Sometimes they had to lay the load down on a friendly derrick floor, skid it across to the other side, and then take it up again.

One hard day's work that I remember was helping pack a lot of eight-inch pipe. There was a good-sized crew of us, and we would line up on each side of a joint and lift it up with a handstick; then with measured step we moved along the road to where we had to turn off into the tangle of Shoestring. Then the cautious creeping commenced. Slow and easy was the word as we felt our way along the insecure footage. All day we went thus, back and forth, back and forth, taking plenty of time, but the work was hard, and glad we were when quitting time came.

Sometimes when an object was too heavy to be carried bodily, it was put on rollers and pushed along. I remember one day coming upon an old acquaintance whom I had not seen in many years, who with a gang of five or six men was moving a large pump in this manner. They had it on a wobbly track slowly pinching it along. "Hello there, Ed, what you doing there," I said, by way of salutation, thinking at least he would stop and have a word or two of confab.

"Working like a _____ ," he said, and never raising up and with the sweat dripping from his face, he kept urging the men "scoot," "scoot."

Of course, the really heavy material, boilers, engines, and the like, were not moved in this way. In fact, I do not know how they were brought in. As mentioned, it was October when I reached the place, and the main part of the heavier work had already been done. Doubtless, however, in the earlier days, before the ground became so badly crowded and before it had become worked up into a quagmire, wagons could get about over it freely.

Another highly noticeable feature of the field was the gas. The region is sulphurous, and the gas that comes out of the wells is highly impregnated with the mineral. As the pressure was enormous, forcing out millions of cubic feet of the poisonous fumes daily, it rendered the place highly dangerous. In the early days little effort was made to dispose of the gas; generally, it was allowed to escape at the mouth of the wells, spread, and do such mischief as it would. On damp, still days it could be smelled a mile or more from the field. It had a scent something like rotten eggs and at first was quite offensive; but, strange to say, when a person got used to it, he rather liked it. This particular kind of gas was what the people about the oilfield called "rotten" gas. While it was disagreeable to be in, it was not the kind that was dangerous.

It was the gas fresh from the wells, less diffused and more highly impregnated with sulphur, that the workers dreaded. This kind had hardly any scent, but it was as deadly as a murderer. Its effect when breathed was much like that of chloroform. If a person, or any other living animal, inhaled a few strong breaths of it, he would fall over unconscious; and if he lay in it and continued to breathe it, he would die as surely as if chloroformed.

As results actually went, however, the gas did not cause a great number of fatalities. A person had to get an extremely strong dose and keep breathing it for some time for it actually to kill him; experienced workers in the field understood its ways and were constantly on guard against it. They knew when they were breathing gas, and they knew about how much they could stand. When one felt that he was getting too much, he would go away a short distance and breathe fresh air till refreshed. Still sometimes, in spite of every precaution, one would be overcome, and if help were not at hand, his life would be the forfeit.

One evening we were working at a bad well. We were, I think, pulling pipe, and the gas was coming out of the hole, not in the strong pressure of a newly-made well, but plainly visible, looking like hot air rising from a boiler. We would work awhile, bucking the chain tongs till we got as much of the poison as we could stand, then go away a few yards and breathe good air awhile, and then come back and go to work again. I had done this many times during the evening, and after a while, on getting an extra strong dose, I started for air again. It happened that as I walked away, a little breeze blew the gas straight after me, and I drew in another breath or two. That proved too much. I got to the edge of the derrick floor, and I remember putting out my hand, trying to reach a post for support, but I could not reach it. Consciousness left me, and over into the mud I went. When I came to, the well crew was carrying me out to safety.

Another bad effect of the gas, while not so dangerous but much more painful, occurred when a person got it in his eyes. This affliction did not give much warning of approach. A man might be working along in a gassy place, thinking he was doing well; then perhaps late in the evening, his eyes would begin to itch a little and feel as if they had dust in them. That would be a signal that he had better quit and get away from that place. If he did not quit immediately, the chances were that he was in for some days of near blindness and about as keen pain as he ever felt.

We had been working on a well two or three days. The gas had been rather bad, but we had managed to keep clear of it. Then on the third day, awhile before quitting time, my eyes began to bother me a little. I did not know much about gas at the time and paid little attention to this warning. The work was dirty; my hands were covered with black oil, and fortunately I could not rub my eyes, but kept working, like one in a smoky room, till the end of the day. When I reached the boarding tent, I washed my face and hands and gave my eyes a good rubbing. They had given me hardly any pain until then, but that rubbing seemed to set them on fire. It must have irritated them slightly so that the sulphur could get at them better. At any rate, they grew rapidly worse. Supper was presently announced, and I went to the table. I should have been ravenously hungry, but the pain in my eyes drove away all desire for food. I ate a few bites in a perfunctory sort of way, then got up from the table, and went to bed. That was as miserable a night as I ever spent. I remembered back in mythology that some god or demigod dug out with a stake the eyes of Polyphemus, and in my heightened imagination, I reckoned that he suffered no worse than I was suffering right then.

When morning came, the men of the place looked at me, and they said that I had as bad a case of gassed eyes as they had ever seen. Indeed, they must have been a sight, swollen and red and strutted like those of a crawfish, and with tears running out of them like rain.

I lay in bed all day. If from necessity I had to open my eyes for something, it would be only for the fraction of a second, so painful was the light. I continued to lie there another day, practically as blind as a bat. Then, toward morning of the third day, the affliction left me. Not a great deal the worse from the experience, I was able to get up and go about my business.

That much for the struggle of men against natural forces. Other things went on there of a more personal kind and of fully as much interest. One of the most prominent of these was work: the strenuous work, the work in the gas, the work in the heat, the work in the danger, this last especially. How many men in the hurry, scurry, and irresponsible management in the field were taken out maimed, mashed, struck dead, will never be known. To get the oil out of the earth and get it converted into money was the sole thought of acreage owners; and those engaged in other forms of business were moved by like motives. They halted at no obstacles. Employers paid good wages for what they had done, and slam, bang, clang, they had to have results. Hence firemen with eyes so badly gassed they could hardly see the steam gauges worked around boilers; hence well crews worked with old rattletrap outfits that were liable any minute to fly to pieces and knock them to kingdom come; hence men worked in the top of derricks, hanging on with one hand, straining with the other to the limit of their muscles to adjust something that had gone wrong. After forty years of sobering absence, it still seems to me that there was more high-pressure work going on in Sour Lake than in any other place I have ever seen.

Amid this orgy of work, there was plenty of idleness, be not mistaken in that. Probably in the previous months, during the high tide of development, there had been work for all applicants, but when I got there, there were not a few men hunting jobs. I was not acquainted with anyone of importance in the place, belonged to no fraternal order, and perhaps had little aptitude for approaching employers. Those who did hire me, I imagine, had happened to be needing hands badly at the time, as during the first few months the jobs I did get lasted only a few days. Consequently, much of the time I was without work. Being without work meant being without money, and being without money, in that place, meant being without food.

Some of the other boys of my acquaintance were in my situation. We lived in various ways. Sometimes we boarded at regular boarding places; sometimes we slept in sleeping tents and took our meals at restaurants; more often we batched straight. But anyway, we lived; we were on our own resources; and our experience in keeping the wolf from the door would fill a thin volume.

One morning, Will Collins and I awoke to the fact that we were dead broke and without a bite to eat. We separated and went different paths to try to make a raise. I had no success whatever, but when I came back that night, Will displayed a bright silver dollar. He had hit some doctor, or somebody that he knew, and struck it lucky. Hungry as he must have been around dinner time, he had not broken the dollar, but had faith fully waited to share it with me.

Another night I was hungry with long developed hunger. I was working hard at the time, and had money coming but had none in my pocket. For several days my provisions had been running low. The day before, I had not had half enough to eat, not a third enough. That morning for breakfast, I had a few fried Irish potatoes; for dinner, potatoes again, but in a still smaller quantity. I remember well that when we went to eat, I slipped off to one side so the others of the crew could not see how scant my dinner was and how I gobbled it down. That night, my cupboard was completely bare.

Standing around a little fire in front of my tent, I wondered what to do. I had a pair of old overalls that I had not worn in some time hanging out in front of the tent on a pine tree. My mind groping, I thought I would feel in the pockets to see what I could find. I found a nickel. There was a baker shop a half mile or so away, and for this I headed. When I came in smelling distance of the shop, the odor of bread baking drove me a bit wild. I walked in and called for a loaf. The man wrapped it up and gave it to me; and I could hardly wait till I got out of the door before I bit into it. All the way back to the tent, without water, I continued to tear off the bread and swallow it, a highly relished meal.

One more string of these pronouns, first person, singular number. The boarding tent that I went to the time my eyes were gassed was a new place to me. I had never seen the proprietor before and had gone there at the suggestion of some of the well crew and on the strength of paying my board when I collected my wages. When I went in that night, I knew that my top shirt was badly soiled with oil but did not know that the oil had gone through all my clothes. When I stripped to go to bed, I could not see and still did not know that my underclothes were greasy, too. Nor did

I know it till the morning I got up, and then I saw I had ruined the bed.

After breakfast, I told the proprietor that I had no money and asked him if he would mind waiting for a settlement until I could go to collect my wages. He agreed readily. I then went further with my assurance. The man had happened to mention that he was going to town on some errand, and I asked him if he would buy and bring me back a clean undershirt. He said he would do this too. True to his promise, when he returned, in an hour or two, he brought a new shirt, for which he had paid fifty cents out of his own pocket. I washed and put on the shirt and left. As I went away, I wondered if he thought he would ever see me again. He saw me. It would have taken chains around my neck to prevent his seeing me again.

It turned out that he was to see me yet again. Several months later, when we had left Sour Lake and were living at Saratoga, another small oil town nearby, this same man came along late one evening. He had lost all the money he had, he told us, and was now out and down. As fortune would have it, I was now up on my feet. Three others of us were batching; we owned three tents, had good jobs, and were in money. I was glad to take this wholehearted man in and furnish him a bed and two good meals.

In saloons, Sour Lake ranked high. These were of all sizes and quality; they had appropriate names. There was the House of Lords, a place where the big boys gathered and played pool and rowdied around. There was the Derrick Saloon, and there was the Big Thicket Saloon, and there was Dad's Saloon; this last was a noted hangout for blacklegs and cutthroats. Considering the character of the town, it is almost a waste of words to say that the saloons were well patronized; but the extent to which the patronage sometimes went was an eye-opener to even an old denizen. After payday, when a gang of pipe-liners came to town, especially if it happened to be a chilly, drizzly evening, the sidewalk for a block or more would be filled with jabbering, reeling men.

As for other evidences of heavy drinking, there were plenty of these too, such as empty flasks by the wayside. It was a sight I never did quite become indifferent to, the number and variety of whiskey bottles lying in the weeds along the paths through the oilfield.

The saloons served other purposes than mere drinking places. They were recreation centers of a sort. Here often men met and talked and played dominoes and transacted business without drinking much, if any. Also, when a man was cold, he could go in one and warm. They were convenient places, too, in which to get checks cashed. Dad's Saloon had the reputation of cashing a check when no other place in town would.

In the back end of nearly every saloon was a gambling house. They were all wide open and, like the saloons, did a land-office business. My experience with these was limited, but what experience I did have was to the effect of putting my money back into circulation.

Of skin game places and other tough joints, they were likewise there in plenty. Judging from general appearances, they, too, were there for something besides their health.

Apology may be due for so little being said of the gentler side of the picture; for a gentler side there indubitably was. Friendships were strong; generosity flourished; and deeds of noble conduct in many ways were to be seen constantly. But it is not these softer things that the old-timer usually recalls when his mind runs back on the past in this place. The riproaring side of life was typical of Sour Lake in the boom days.

Gulley #2 Largest Gasser in the World 8 Miles South Sinton Texas. Daily production 100,000,000 Cubic Feet

Copyright, 1916 by Fred H. Kurtz

This gas well erupted on New Year's Eve 1915 and was not brought under control for almost two months. *Courtesy of Library of Congress*

JULY 1946

Texas and the Oil Industry

CHARLES A. WARNER

THE OIL INDUSTRY is as much a part of Texas as its cattle ranches, its missions, its plantations or its Llano Estacado, and knowledge that Texas ranks first in the oil industry is worldwide. Extending approximately 800 miles from Brownsville to Tex line and about 760 miles from El Paso to Orange, Texas has a coastline of about 400 miles and a total area of nearly 264,000 square miles. Its surface topography varies from the flat coastal plains to the rugged mountainous areas of the Big Bend region and the extreme western part of the state. It has land suitable for practically every purpose; its agricultural products are as varied as its climate and its topography; cattle-raising is one of its oldest industries; and metallic and nonmetallic minerals are mined or quarried in several areas. Of all its products, however, those taken from the earth by the oil industry are by far the most important economically, and they are indigenous to all portions of the state.

Texas contains 254 counties, 175 of which produce oil or gas or both in commercial quantities. It contains the largest oil and gas fields in the world, and its reserves of crude oil represent approximately 55 per cent of the estimated reserves of the nation. It has more than 37,000 miles of oil pipelines, more than 13,250 miles of gas pipelines, 95 refineries, 199 natural gasoline plants (including 33 cycling plants), and 45 carbon-black plants. Its reported production has increased from forty-eight barrels of oil and a small quantity of gas in 1889 to more than seven hundred million barrels of oil and more than two trillion cubic feet of gas per year.

The oil and gas produced in Texas are secured from strata of many geologic ages at depths ranging from a few feet to below 11,800 feet. It is the only region in the world from which oil and gas are produced from altered igneous rocks, salt dome cap rock, sandstones, sandy shales, limestones, chalk, and dolomite of various geologic ages. It is the only area in the world in which oil and gas fields are associated with salt domes, igneous intrusives, major and minor folding and faulting, sand lensing, erosional unconformities, and depositional unconformities.

HISTORY *of* DEVELOPMENT

THE USE OF PETROLEUM is no new thing to the natives of Texas. The Indians who dwelt within the borders of what is now the Lone Star State were familiar with oil seepages and with sour waters. They journeyed from far and wide to heal battle wounds and skin diseases at Sour Lake, Oil Spring, Tar Spring, Damon Mound, and other places well known to them. It is also quite probable that in religious ceremonies gas seepages were burned.

A scant fifty years had passed after the discovery of the western hemisphere by Columbus before the survivors of the De Soto Expedition used asphalt from near Sabine Pass to repair their crude boats. This account is the first record of white men's knowledge of the existence of petroleum in America. The earliest settlers, like the Indians, appreciated the many uses of the crude oil. They employed it to soften and preserve leather, to lubricate cart axles and such machinery as they possessed, and they used it as an insecticide and as an external ointment. Legends handed down from pioneer families tell how the oil was collected by skimming it from the surface of the water, if present in sufficient quantities, or by dipping bunches of pine straw in the thin scum on the water and then stripping it off into jars or other containers.

Authentic information as to the location and the number of seepages of oil and gas known to the hardy pioneers of Texas is difficult to secure, but it is known that seepages along the Old Spanish Trail were familiar places to explorers and settlers, that a health resort was in operation at Sour Lake for some time prior to 1850, that there was a seepage near Toyah in western Texas, and that oil from wells in various parts of northern, eastern, and southern Texas made the water unfit for human use. It is also known that two tar barrels of oil were collected at Nacogdoches about 1832 and shipped to Europe. One barrel was consigned to Liverpool, England, and the other to Germany. The barrel shipped to Liverpool never reached its destination because no provision was made in British customs regulations for the admission of anything of that nature. The other barrel, however, reached its destination; its contents were analyzed; and the analysis was returned to this country. It is also well authenticated that prior to 1900 the existence of oil, gas, and allied hydrocarbons had been recorded in nearly fifty counties scattered over all of the present major producing districts within the state except the Panhandle.

Although there have been numerous claims advanced as to the location in Texas at which the present oil industry had its inception, there is now no doubt that it was relatively near the world's premier producing area, the East Texas Field. Reliable data indicate that the first efforts by white men to secure larger quantities of oil from beneath the surface of the ground than were available at a seepage were made near Tar Spring in Angelina County and near Oil Spring in Nacogdoches County. Shortly before 1859 Jack Graham dug a pit near the spring in Angelina County and collected the oil which seeped into it. In 1859, the year of the Drake Well in Pennsylvania, Graham was instrumental in having a well sunk near this pit by use of a spring pole, but he failed to secure any considerable quantities of oil.

At about this same time, Lynis T. Barrett conceived the idea that it would be possible to secure greater quantities of oil from a well than from the surface seepage at Oil Spring. He accordingly acquired a lease in 1859 covering the Skillern tract with the intention of boring a well there with an auger. (This was the first oil lease ever taken in Texas.) The growing seriousness of the slavery question and the outbreak, shortly afterward, of the Civil War resulted in the temporary postponement of his efforts.

Immediately after the war, Barrett and his associates secured a new lease on the Skillern tract, and on December 20, 1865, they commenced boring for oil. The boring was done by an auger eight feet long and eight inches in diameter. The auger was purchased in New Orleans and transported by boat and wagon to the location. Resembling a gin screw, this auger was securely fastened by clamps to a joint of pipe and turned by means of a large wheel actuated by cogs from a drive shaft driven by a steam engine. It was mounted under a tripod, and additional joints of pipe were added as it bored deeper and deeper into the earth.

The well was bored through several "veins of oil" before reaching a depth of 106 feet where the auger, according to Barrett, "dropped through a vein six inches deep, when oil, water, and gas gushed to the top of the well." Although the initial production of this, the first oil well to be completed in Texas, was only about ten barrels per day, Barrett was convinced of the future potentialities of the area. He cased the well with iron pipe, capped it, and went to Pennsylvania in October 1866 to secure assistance in developing the new field. There, he interested John F. Carll in the project, and they began operations with approximately $5,000 worth of equipment shipped from Pennsylvania. Their explorations were unsuccessful, and Carll returned to Pennsylvania, while Barrett, unable to secure financial assistance, was forced to abandon his efforts to develop the area.

Nacogdoches was not the only locality in Texas where there was interest in the acquisition of leases and in the exploration for oil in the years immediately after the War between the States. On August 2, 1865, Edward von Hartin, of Galveston, and John F. Cotton entered into a co-partnership "for the purpose of obtaining Petroleum by boring wells or otherwise" on lands owned by Cotton, and a test well was sunk to a depth of about one hundred feet in what is now the Saratoga Field. Showings of gas and heavy oil were encountered, but the well was abandoned because of inadequate machinery.

Richard W. Dowling, the hero of Sabine Pass, had also been acquiring oil and gas leases, including one in what is now the city of Houston, and in 1866 he and his associates acquired leases covering lands in various counties from Jefferson to Clay and from Tyler to Bexar.

Although numerous attempts were made to secure oil by drilling, boring, and digging over widely scattered areas prior to 1866, they were not attended with any degree of success, other than at the one well at Nacogdoches. Gas was found near Graham in Young County in a well being drilled for salt water in 1871 or 1872, and in 1879 appreciable quantities were located in southwestern Washington County, where it was piped to a nearby house and burned as fuel.

It was not until the period from 1886 to 1890 that the producing and marketing of oil and the production and reported utilization of gas actually began in Texas. There was a revival of interest in the Nacogdoches area in 1886, when B. F. Hitchcock, who had been studying the area, was instrumental in the organization of the Petroleum Prospecting Company and in the resumption of drilling at Oil Spring. The first well drilled encountered flowing production rather unexpectedly, and the first day's production, estimated to have been 250 or 300 barrels, was lost. The well did not flow after the first day but was later completed as a pumper. This well opened the first of the many Texas oil booms. Several companies were formed; extensive operations soon commenced; and plans were made for development of a field comparable to those of the Pennsylvania area. The Petroleum Prospecting Company, operating near the spring, completed thirty producing wells prior to 1890, erected the first steel storage tanks for oil in Texas, and built the first oil pipeline in the state, a three-inch line extending from the field to Aaron Hill at Nacogdoches. The Lubricating Oil Company, operating about three miles northeast of the spring, had an extensive plant, including a crude method for refining the oil of impurities by heating it in an iron evaporating pan and then filtering it before running it into iron shipping drums. The small production of the wells and other economic factors contributed to a rapid decline of the field and its practical abandonment about 1890. Many of the early wells even now yield a few gallons of oil, although practically forgotten among the pine trees which have grown up around them.

Concurrent with the activity in the Nacogdoches Field, development was being carried on several hundred miles to the southwest where George Dullnig had encountered oil at 235 feet while drilling for water in 1886 on his ranch just southeast of San Antonio. A second test nearby also secured minor production, and a well to the northwest was completed as a gas well. This gas was used as a fuel supply in the oil operations and on the ranch. The production from the Dullnig wells was the first to be reported in governmental statistical summaries in 1889, when Texas was credited with a production of fortyeight barrels of oil and with natural gas valued at $1,728. The value of the gas produced was computed by assigning to it the value of the amount of wood or coal necessary to fire the boiler at the rig for the same length of time that the gas was used. The oil was sold in barrels at twenty cents per gallon, in five-gallon containers at thirty cents per gallon, and in smaller quantities at thirty-five cents per gallon.

The next discovery was in the fall of 1890 on the ranch of Colonel William L. Prather near Waco, in McLennan County, where a well being drilled for water encountered a substantial amount of oil at a depth of 265 feet. This oil, unlike that from Nacogdoches and the Dullnig ranch, proved excellent for purposes of illumination, but no particular or immediate attention was paid to the discovery.

Some interest was manifested in the Gulf Coast area shortly after

1890, when gas was reported from several wells and a little oil production was secured at Sour Lake. Savage Brothers, of West Virginia, completed several small wells there in 1895, after they had been unsuccessful in an attempt to secure pro duction at what was later the Spindletop Field; and in 1896 W. B. Sharp drilled a well at Sour Lake for the Trinity Lubricating Oil Company, which had a small test refinery near the lake. The operations of this refinery and those of the Gulf Coast Refining Company plant, which was constructed there in 1898, marked the beginning of actual refining operations in Texas other than the crude method previously employed at Oil Spring.

With all of this activity, however, Texas continued to be unimportant from the standpoint of oil production until after the discovery of oil at Corsicana. Here, again, discovery of the presence of oil was accidental. A well being bored for water in Corsicana in 1894 encountered oil at a depth of 1,027 feet; and considerable difficulty was experienced, including the loss of the rig by fire, before the oil was successfully cased off and the test completed at a depth of 2,470 feet as an artesian water well. The oil continued to come up on the outside of the casing, and the second Texas oil boom was soon under way. The Corsicana Oil Development Company was organized by Ralph Beaton and H. G. Damon, of Corsicana, and John Davidson of Pennsylvania. Several leases were acquired and a contract made with John H. Galey of Pittsburgh, Pennsylvania, for the drilling and equipping of five wells. The first well was bored two hundred feet south of the artesian well and completed on October 15, 1895, for a production of two and a half barrels of oil per day from a depth of 1,040 feet. A second well was of no importance, but the third well, located at Fourth and Collins Streets, was completed in May 1896 as a flowing well with an initial production of twenty-two barrels per day. A total of five wells was completed before the end of 1896, and the production for that year amounted to 1,450 barrels.

Oil production at Corsicana began in 1895, and it has been continuous there for the past fifty-one years. Several of the earliest leases are still perpetuated by production. The first great steps in the advancement of the industry in Texas were taken in 1897, when J. S. Cullinan agreed to install a pipeline system, erect storage tanks and a refinery, and develop a market for the oil. The stills of the refinery, built and operated under the supervision of E. R. Brown, were fired on Christmas Day, 1898, a true Christmas present for that community and for the state of Texas. The first shipment of refined oil left Corsicana on February 24, 1899. Production from the field increased steadily to 544,620 barrels in 1898, and to 668,483 barrels in 1899. Corsicana gave Texas its first sustained commercial production, its first efficient and complete refinery, the rotary rig, the gas industry, and a firm foundation for the future growth of the entire industry. The Corsicana Field also resulted in the first legislation relating to field development by the enactment of House Bill No. 542, which was approved and became effective in March 1899. It prescribed practices for casing wells, for plugging and abandoning wells, and for preventing gas wastage and stipulated that gas was not to be burned for illumination between 8 A.M. and 5 P.M.

In connection with the rotary rig, it is interesting to note that it originated about 1882 in the territory of Dakota, where the Baker brothers used it for drilling water wells. In its first operation, water was poured down outside of the drill pipe and cuttings washed back up through the pipe. Later, water was poured down inside the drill pipe from an elevated platform, but these rather tedious and difficult methods of securing circulation of the water were superseded when a windmill was used to pump water into the drill stem. It was then a natural step for power-driven pumps to be used, but this simple outfit, originated in Dakota and first powered by one horse, revolutionized deep drilling and made it possible in areas of soft unconsolidated sediments.

While the field at Corsicana was forging rapidly ahead, Pattillo Higgins was continuing his efforts to secure production at the Big Hill south of Beaumont. Convinced of the possibilities for production in the immediate vicinity of the mound, he had been instrumental in the drilling of test wells there as early as 1893. In 1899, he and Captain A. F. Lucas entered into an agreement, and a well was drilled to a depth of 575 feet. This well encountered showings of oil and gas before it was abandoned. The two determined prospectors were now more firmly convinced than ever that the area would prove productive, but they were confronted with a lack of financial resources. They succeeded, however, in securing the backing of Guffy and Galey of Pittsburgh, Pennsylvania, and commenced a second well on October 27, 1900.

On January 10, 1901, this well blew in at 10:30 A.M. from a depth of 1,160 feet. Spindletop had been discovered. It is doubtful whether any discovery in the history of the industry has had a comparable significance. The capacity of the well, estimated at from 35,000 to 100,000 barrels per day, staggered the imagination; and the force of the flow demonstrated conclusively that the industry must devise heavier equipment and new methods for controlling wells of such tremendous proportions.

A new era had dawned in the oil industry. Spindletop became the Mecca for executives of eastern oil companies, independent operators, investors, promoters, and speculators. Prospectors began searching both day and night for similar mounds in the vicinity of the coast, expecting each such surface elevation to prove another Spindletop. Prices for land jumped from a few dollars to several thousand dollars per acre, and in some instances as much as $30,000 was paid for a single location on the mound at Spindletop. Gusher after gusher was completed in the new field, and train loads of prospective investors were treated to the spectacle of seeing wells opened up and flowing a solid stream of oil high into the air. That practice undoubtedly heightened the desire of the investor to own some of the gaudily colored stock offered him, but it was also fraught with possible disaster through the ever-present hazard of fire.

It was apparent that some action must be taken to safeguard life and property, and the result was the first organized effort in Texas, if not in the world, to prevent unnecessary wastage of oil as well as to protect the lives of the workmen and property of the operators. A meeting of operators and representatives of oil and supply companies was held on August 30, 1901, and a committee was appointed to formulate proper measures of safety. This committee, under the chairmanship of George A. Hill Sr., adopted, published, and, through its watchmen and inspectors, enforced such rules. Texas, even then, was taking the lead in oil and gas conservation.

Following the discovery and early development at Spindletop came additional salt dome fields in Southeast Texas and the construction of pipelines and refineries in that area. Saratoga was proved productive in the fall of 1901, Sour Lake in 1902, Batson in 1903, and gusher production was secured at Humble in 1905. By the end of 1903, the total storage facilities in the Beaumont district were reported to be 19,226,000 barrels. It was estimated that the total capital invested in the district at the end of 1901 was $3,951,085, while at the end of 1904 it was estimated to be $34,036,500.

Exploratory efforts were by no means confined to the southeastern part of the state during the five years following the discovery of Spindletop. In most instances, however, they were unsuccessful in the other areas of Texas and merited little attention until 1904. In that year, the industry began to notice North Texas as a result of the production of 65,455 barrels of oil from a depth of about three hundred feet in the Petrolia Field of Clay County. Although a few small wells had previously been completed there following the encountering of oil at about 150 feet in a well being bored for water on the Lochridge farm, the actual discovery of the field is generally credited to the year 1904.

The development of the new producing area, the greatly increased production in the coastal region, and the widened interest in the oil industry were followed by additional legislation in 1905. The new legislation provided, among other things, that when an operator could not case off water encountered in a well being drilled for oil or gas, he must immediately plug and abandon it.

South Texas became the fourth producing area of the state in 1907 with the discovery and early development of the Mission Field in Bexar

County and the discovery of oil at Piedras Pintas in Duval County. Neither area was to prove of especial significance for many years.

During the period 1905-1910, the oil-producing capacity of the state was further enlarged by the discovery of production at North Dayton, Goose Creek, Markham, Potters Point, and in Brown, Coleman, Shackelford, and Wichita counties. The transportation facilities of the state were expanded and extended by the construction of several minor pipelines and by the construction of eight-inch oil lines from Oklahoma to the coast of Texas by the Texas and Gulf Pipe Line Companies.

In the meantime, the development and utilization of natural gas had been progressing rather rapidly. During the first few years of the century, small amounts of gas were consumed for lease and domestic purposes at Corsicana, the total value of the gas thus utilized in 1903 by seventy-eight domestic and eight industrial consumers having been placed at $21,351. The gas was transported and distributed through a total of twenty-eight miles of pipeline in or adjacent to the field, and the sales were made at a fixed price per month for a house and on a yearly basis to an industrial consumer, the price depending upon the amount of manufacturing done. Such practices were largely discontinued about 1905, when the use of meters was inaugurated.

Indications of the future importance of the gas branch of the industry were evident soon after the completion of four good gas wells in the Petrolia Field and the transportation of this gas to Henrietta and Wichita Falls for distribution and consumption. The success of this undertaking, under the able leadership of E. R. Brown, was responsible for the organization of the Lone Star Gas Company in 1909 and the beginning of the major gas transportation lines throughout and from Texas. The extensive gas industry as it is known today may well trace its origin to the Petrolia Field of Clay County, Texas. The utilization of gas as a fuel for railroad locomotives did not prove as efficient as hoped for when tried out in 1910 between Atlanta and Bloomburg, and this practice was discontinued.

The search for new fields was steadily advancing, and tremendous strides were made by the industry in the decade 1911-1920. The first discovery of importance in this period was at Electra in January 1911, and the active development of the new field was followed by extensive wildcatting and by new pipeline construction. The Mexia gas area was opened in 1912 and rapidly developed. Additional legislation, which became effective April 2, 1913, related to the plugging of wells and to the waste of natural gas. The discovery of the Thrall Field in February 1915 directed attention to Southwest Texas and a new type of production, that obtained from serpentine rock. Wildcatters immediately began searching for other altered igneous intrusives with a zeal equal to that displayed in the search for salt domes following the discovery of Spindletop. The discovery of the Brenham Field in Washington County in October 1915 proved that production could be secured from salt domes located some distance inland from the coast. Also in 1915, the natural gasoline industry made its first appearance in the state with the construction of a plant by the Clayco at Electra.

The Ranger Field, discovered in October 1917 by Texas and Pacific Coal Company's No. 1, the J. H. McClesky well, started off slowly because of the disfavor with which many operators had looked upon that general area. This apathetic attitude changed rapidly after the completion of a few good wells, and within less than two years the field was producing between four and five million dollars worth of oil per month.

The years 1917 to 1920 inclusive were of outstanding importance to the oil industry of Texas. Exploratory drilling resulted in the discovery of such areas as West Columbia, Barbers Hill, Burkburnett town site and its northwest extension, South Bend, Hull, and Desdemona. It also resulted in the discovery of gas in the Panhandle. Of particular significance during these four years, however, was the enactment of legislation vesting broad powers in the Railroad Commission of Texas. Senate Bill No. 68, approved February 20, 1917, declared pipelines to be common carriers and placed them under the supervision of the commission; Senate Bill No. 350, which became effective June 18, 1919, is the fundamental conservation law of the state; and House Bill No. 11, approved June 18, 1920, gave the commission jurisdiction over all natural gas utilities and appellate jurisdiction in the matter of fixing rates at which natural gas is sold in the various municipalities of the state.

The organization of the Oil and Gas Division of the Railroad Commission was begun on June 18, 1919, and proceeded rapidly. The first shut-down order, suspending production and the completion of wells in the Burkburnett area, was issued on July 11, 1919; the first proration order affected the northwest extension to Burkburnett and was issued July 18, 1919; the first rules regulating the methods of oil and natural gas conservation were adopted July 26, 1919 ; and Rule 37, which is so well known to all operators, was adopted November 26, 1919. One of the rules laid down by the commission, early in 1920, classed a well as a gas well if the gas production, computed at fifteen cents per thousand cubic feet, was more valuable than the oil production, computed at $3.00 per barrel.

The operators of the state had had their difficulties with labor in the Gulf Coast area and with excessive production and lack of transportation facilities in North Texas, and the Railroad Commission was struggling with its many problems of administration and conservation when a new boom appeared on the scene. This was the opening of the Fault Line play by the discovery of gusher production from the Woodbine at Mexia in the summer of 1921. Development was rapid, production pyramided to over 100,000 barrels per day within a few months, and exploration seeking similar faulted structure fields was under way. The discovery of Currie followed in November 1921, Powell in January 1923, Richland in February 1924, and Wortham in November 1924.

While hundreds of thousands of barrels of oil were being produced daily in the Mexia district, development operations were being expanded following important discoveries in three other areas of Texas. The discovery of the Westbrook Field in January 1921 added West Texas to the list of oil-producing districts, the Panhandle was included in May 1921, and the Mirando area secured its first commercial production in April 1921. The

Luling Field was discovered in August 1922 and was followed by exploratory drilling for faulted structures in the Bastrop-San Antonio area.

Other events of interest and importance during these years were the purchase of oil on a gravity basis in North Texas; the development of an important natural gasoline business in Eastland and Stephens counties; the introduction of the seismograph and torsion balance into the Gulf Coast area; a renewed activity in the old Nacogdoches Field; the declaration of martial law at Mexia in January 1922; the discovery of production in the Big Lake Field, two hundred miles southwest of Ranger; the discovery of a noninflammable gas in a well in Mitchell County; the granting by the Railroad Commission of permission to operate the first carbon black plant in the state in Stephens County; the construction of an oil pipeline from Luling to Houston (prior to this time the trunk oil pipelines were east of a line drawn from Wichita Falls through Ranger to Houston); and the construction of a gas pipeline from Cotton Valley, Louisiana, to Beaumont, Texas.

Spindletop, the first major discovery in Texas, had continued to produce oil during this entire quarter of a century, but its production had declined from over 17,000,000 barrels in 1902 to 359,000 barrels in 1924. In January 1926, however, it was rediscovered by the completion of a well from a new deep sand on the southeast flank of the field, and a new orgy of drilling followed. Production from the field increased rapidly to a new all-time high of over 21,250,000 barrels in 1927.

The Spindletop of 1901 had been followed by Sour Lake, Saratoga, Batson, Humble, North Dayton, and other fields. The one of 1926 was followed by Hendricks, Yates, Salt Flat, Van, Darst Creek, and other fields; and oil production in the Panhandle increased from some 1,287,000 barrels in 1925 to over 40,000,000 barrels in 1940. In both instances, the operators were confronted with serious overproduction, the net result of which was decreased prices for crude oil. In the Panhandle, however, the additional results of a major expansion of pipeline facilities and regulatory activities of the Railroad Commission were operative. During the year

1928, the commission undertook the proration of oil from the Hendricks, Howard-Glasscock, and Yates pools. It has been estimated that had Winkler and Pecos counties been allowed to flow their maximum potential production, Texas would have been producing more than 2,000,000 barrels per day the week of December 29, 1928, instead of slightly more than 700,000 barrels per day. Proration was extended to include the Darst Creek Field in 1929 and the Panhandle in 1930.

This tremendous increase in oil production was accompanied by an unparalleled expansion in the natural gas industry, particularly in Southwest Texas and the Panhandle, where the completion of many wells had demonstrated the existence of tremendous gas reserves. The first major gas pipeline in either of these areas was that constructed by the Houston Pipe Line Company in 1925 from Live Oak County to Houston and extended to the Mirando area in 1926. At about the same time, the Houston Gulf Gas Company also constructed its line from Southwest Texas to Houston. At the end of 1926, gas from thirty-seven counties in Texas was being delivered to 113 towns and cities and the combined daily open-flow capacity of all gas wells was over three billion cubic feet. Increased facilities for handling, active development of gas areas, and a greater demand for this fuel resulted in the serving of 442 towns and cities in 1928 with gas from forty-nine counties. The total daily potential of the wells at the end of that year was nearly fifteen and one-half billion cubic feet.

The demand for gas in states other than Texas and the success of transportation caused more extensive pipeline construction than ever before. Transmission lines of large diameter were constructed from the Panhandle to such distant cities as Chicago and Indianapolis, and such facilities have since been extended and expanded.

The oil industry in Texas had assumed proportions of great importance in the twenty-nine years following the first discovery of Spindletop. It was represented in 1930 by thousands of producing wells, a network of pipelines, and adequate processing and distributing facilities over the length and breadth of the state. It had advanced in the face of such obstacles as depressed prices during and following the period of overproduction, and it was continuing to advance in competition with other floods of oil from great discoveries in California and Oklahoma when the discovery of the East Texas Field occurred.

The discovery of the Van Field in 1929 had indicated that the possibilities for additional Woodbine sand production from the eastern portion of Texas should not be disregarded. That this was true was demonstrated most spectacularly by the completion of the Joiner well on the Bradford farm in October 1930, the Bateman well on the Crimm farm in December 1930, and the Farrell well on the Lathrop farm in January 1931. Three wildcat wells had opened an area more than twenty miles long within a period of slightly more than three months, and exploration soon spread out rapidly. Consternation previously felt about overproduction from other areas was now crystallized on steadily increasing production from one field. The average production from the field amounted to only about 25,000 barrels per day in February 1931, but by the middle of August 1931, it was over one million barrels per day. Posted prices dropped to below ten cents per barrel for oil. Immediate action was necessary, and the field was shut down under martial law on August 17, 1931. When it was opened up again on September 6, 1931, production was curtailed to 225 barrels per well daily. This production has been steadily reduced by subsequent orders. The history of the East Texas Field is one of superlatives, and its questions of proration, hot oil, bypasses, and tender boards are all familiar enough to need no amplification. It should be noted, however, that as a result of the application of sound engineering principles in the proration of this field, it is still flowing after producing more than 2,170,750,550 barrels of oil during the past fifteen years; and it should continue to flow a considerable portion of its production for many more years.

Activity within the state since the development of the East Texas Field has added many new producing areas and many new horizons in older producing areas. Included in such discoveries are the fields of Conroe, Anahuac, Tom O'Connor, and West Ranch, and such new producing horizons as the Viola lime in northern Texas, Devonian and Silurian strata as well as new horizons in the Permian and Ordovician formations in western Texas, deep Frio horizons along the Gulf Coast, the Edwards lime in the upper inland coastal area, the Smackover lime in Northeast Texas, and new Cretaceous horizons on and adjacent to the Sabine Uplift.

The discovery of large reserves of gas containing substantial quantities of liquid hydrocarbons has resulted in an operating procedure far removed from those of the earlier days of the industry. It was essential that such reserves be developed in a manner capable of maximum production with minimum waste, and the process of cycling was therefore adopted as an integral part of the oil industry. This practice was first employed in Texas in 1937, and since that time it has expanded until there are now thirty-three cycling plants in Texas processing a total of approximately two billion cubic feet of gas daily. The importance of such operations is readily apparent when it is realized that at V-E Day the plant at Katy, Texas, was producing approximately six thousand barrels of aviation gasoline daily.

Operations during the past four years have necessarily been carried on under rather stringent regulations by both state and federal governments. That was necessarily true since it was essential that the maximum production of oil and gas be secured for the minimum expenditure of critical steel. Such operations have not at all times been in strictest accordance with proper engineering practices, but they were carried on in the full knowledge that oil was essential to the successful prosecution of the war and with the firm conviction that no sacrifice by the oil industry was comparable to that being made by its men and their sons and brothers on foreign battlefields. The efforts of the industry, hampered as it was by shortages of material and manpower, have been crowned with success. It now hopes to resume its normal method of operation as an individual, not a governmental, industry in which initiative and private enterprise will continue to make available to all the oil, gas, and allied products upon which the progress of the world so largely depends.

STRUCTURE and STRATIGRAPHY

THE STRUCTURE AND stratigraphy of Texas are of direct interest to the oil industry, for it is the attitude and physical characteristics of the strata that play so important a part in the discovery and production of oil and gas.

There is no single broad classification for the structure of Texas. It varies greatly from one region to another, and there is, in many parts of the state, a considerable variation between the surface and the subsurface structures. Such variations include not only changes in the rate and direction of dip between the surface and subsurface formations but also such structural anomalies as buried hills and intrusives below the surface. Excellent illustrations of such variations are to be found in the variations in dip between the surface and subsurface formations on the flanks of the Bend Arch, in the buried granite ridge of the Red River Uplift, in the serpentine plugs of the Balcones Fault zone, and in the salt domes of coastal and eastern Texas.

A classification of the regional structural provinces includes: (a) the general gulfward dipping monocline with its inward limit bounded roughly by a line from northeastern Montague County to Burnet County and thence westward to Brewster County; (b) the Llano Uplift in the central portion of the state where early igneous, pre-Cambrian, and Ordovician rocks are exposed at the surface; (c) the Van Horn, Marathon, and Solitario Uplift areas of extreme western Texas where formations are exposed varying in age from Paleozoic, or earlier, to the present; (d) the Bend Arch extending northward from the Llano Uplift to southern Archer County, with surface exposures of Pennsylvanian and some Cretaceous formations; (e) the Red River Uplift where earlier formations are covered by strata of Permian, Pennsylvanian, and Cretaceous ages; (f) the Amarillo Uplift with its granite ridge buried beneath Permian, Triassic, and recent formations; and (g) the West Texas Basin where surface strata varying in age from recent to Triassic overlay successively older formations.

All of these general structural provinces may, by closer study, be subdivided into several more minor features. This is well exemplified in the gulfward dipping monocline with its salt dome belt along the coast, its series of interior salt domes in the Tyler Basin, the Balcones and Mexia fault zones, and the Sabine Uplift.

These general structural provinces and their individual minor features are the result of a series of general adjustments be tween the seas and the land masses from the time of earliest sedimentation. They are of particular importance to those interested in the production of oil and gas because of their relationship to the accumulation of such minerals. An analysis of regional structure and conditions of deposition will disclose general areas in which prospecting may be carried on with a greater degree of confidence than in others. A more detailed study of the general area will then disclose whether or not deposition or structural movement has been such as to result in the formation of a suitable trap for the accumulation of oil and gas.

The earliest sedimentation in Texas apparently took place in seas that covered a considerable portion of the central part of the state, with the material deposited derived from the weathering down of a land mass then existing along the present coastal plain. A pronounced early deposition occurred along a belt extending from Fannin County southward through San Antonio and thence westward to Brewster County. Deposition in this area has unquestionably been an important factor in structural movements resulting in the Mexia-Luling fault trend, along which profitable oil and gas production has been secured. This area of deposition is also the locale of serpentine plugs, several of which are productive.

The deposition of these early sediments was followed by that of Cambrian and Ordovician times, during which the Ellenberger lime was laid down over much of northern and western Texas. Subsequent folding has resulted in the formation of structures favorable for production from the Ellenberger, as shown by that secured in Andrews, Cooke, Crane, Reagan, Stephens, Winkler, and other counties of northern and western Texas.

Following the deposition of the Cambrian and Ordovician sediments, some sedimentation of Silurian, Devonian, and Mississippian ages took place over a part at least of central and western Texas. The exact extent of such deposition is not known; but production is now being secured along the Bend Arch from strata of Mississippian age, in Andrews, Crane, Ector, Gaines, Upton, and Winkler counties from strata of Devonian age, and in Ward and Winkler counties from Silurian horizons.

Deposits of Pennsylvanian age spread out over a broad area to the north, west, and southwest from the Llano Uplift. Lower Pennsylvanian strata have been prolifically productive horizons at Ranger and in other fields on the Bend Arch. Horizons of Middle and Upper Pennsylvanian age are major sources of production in North and North Central Texas.

A shifting of seas at the close of the Pennsylvanian age resulted in the formation of the West Texas basin in which were deposited the thick Permian sediments which contain important productive horizons in West Texas and the Panhandle and have yielded considerable oil in North Texas.

The deposition of Triassic formations followed those of Permian age over large areas of western Texas and was succeeded by minor deposits of Jurassic age. Neither is now of any great economic importance as an oil-producing horizon in Texas.

With the close of the Jurassic age came the beginning of another major sea invasion of Texas and the deposition of Cretaceous strata over practically the entire state. Advances and recessions of the seas, accompanied by changes in depth, resulted in the deposition of such important strata as the Trinity series, the Edwards lime, the Woodbine sand, and the Taylor, Navarro, and other formations. The present importance to the oil industry of the conditions under which these strata were deposited is exemplified by the formation of the trap constituting the East Texas oilfield. This formation resulted from the deposition of the Woodbine sand against the Sabine Uplift, followed by erosion and the unconformable deposition of the impervious Eagle Ford shale and Austin chalk which caused a sealing off against the further migration updip of oil and gas in the porous sand members. Cretaceous horizons have proved of major economic importance for oil and gas production. They are the source of the first recorded production from the Dullnig wells, and they have yielded the East Texas and other fields in the vicinity of the Sabine Uplift, as well as the fields of the Corsicana, Mexia, Powell, and Luling areas and other sand and lime pools extending from Rodessa to Maverick County.

The Cretaceous age ended with a readjustment between the land and seas, followed in Tertiary times by another incursion of the sea and the deposition of strata to the east and southeast of the general Balcones Fault zone. Eocene and more recent formations therefore cover the areas known as South and East Texas. The strata of Eocene age are productive along the general Wilcox-Cockfield trend, while strata of Oligocene, Miocene, and Pliocene ages are productive along the coastal trend.

The many adjustments between sea and land have resulted in the formation of faults and of structure and deposition features often buried but contributing largely to present-day fields in the area. The Conroe Field is an excellent example of a pronounced subsurface fold. Faults, traceable at the surface or determined by subsurface methods or geophysical explorations, have accounted for production at Silsbee, Segno, Pettus, and other fields along the Cockfield trend. Changing conditions of sedimentation resulting in a pinching out updip of sand strata have been responsible for productive areas in the Mirando trend and at Nacogdoches. The intrusion of salt masses and the formation of such prolific reservoirs as Spindletop and West Columbia may well be attributed to early lines of weakness developed during such periods of adjustment.

General structure and deposition features controlling the accumulation of oil and gas in the various producing regions of Texas may be classed as follows: *East Texas*—faults, unconformities, and buried folds; *Gulf Coast*—salt intrusives, faults, and folds possibly resulting from deeply buried intrusives; *North* and *North Central Texas*—folds, unconformities, and faults; *Panhandle*—folds and unconformities; *Southwest Texas*—faults, folds, irregular deposition, and salt intrusives; and *West Texas*—folds and unconformities.

A general summary of the major producing formations and the counties in which they are productive is given in the accompanying chart:

GEOLOGIC FORMATIONS AND COUNTIES IN WHICH THEY ARE NOW PRODUCING

Pliocene		undifferentiated	Brazoria, Chambers, Fort Bend, Galveston, Hardin, Harris, Jefferson, Liberty, Matagorda.
Miocene		undifferentiated	Austin, Brazoria, Brooks, Cameron, Chambers, Fort Bend, Galveston, Hardin, Harris, Jefferson, Kleberg, Liberty, Live Oak, Matagorda, Nueces, Orange, Refugio, San Patricio, Victoria, Washington, Wharton.
Oligocene		undifferentiated	Aransas, Brazoria, Calhoun, Chambers, Fort Bend, Galveston, Hardin, Harris, Jackson, Jefferson, Jim Wells, Liberty, Matagorda, Nueces, Orange, R e f u g i o , San Patricio, Victoria, Wharton.
		Frio and Vicksburg	Aransas, Bee, Brazoria, Brooks, Calhoun, Chambers, Colorado, Duval, Fort Bend, Galveston, Goliad, Hardin, Harris, Hidalgo, Jackson, Jefferson, Jim Wells, Kleberg, Liberty, Live Oak, Matagorda, Nueces, Orange, Refugio, San Patricio, Starr, Victoria, Waller, Wharton, Willacy, Zapata.
Eocene	Jackson	Whitsett	Austin, Bee, Duval, Harris, Jim Hogg, Liberty, McMullen, Webb.
		McElroy	Austin, Bee, Duval, Jim Hogg, Live Oak, McMullen, Polk, Starr, Webb, Zapata.
	Claiborne	Cockfield and Yegua	Austin, Bee, Colorado, Duval, Fort Bend, Goliad, Hardin, Harris, Jasper, Jim Hogg, Jim Wells, Karnes, Liberty, Live Oak, McMullen, Montgomery, Newton, Polk, Tyler, Waller, Webb, Wharton, Zapata.
		Cook Mountain	Angelina, Goliad, Harris, Houston, Polk, Washington, Wharton.
		Mount Selman	Angelina, Fayette, Harris, Houston, Karnes, McMullen, Nacogdoches, Starr, Tyler, Washington, Webb, Zapata.
	Sabine	Wilcox	Angelina, Austin, Bee, Brazos, Colorado, De Witt, Fayette, Goliad, Hardin, Houston, Karnes, Lavaca, La Salle, Liberty, Live Oak, McMullen, Montgomery, Polk, San Jacinto, Tyler, Victoria, Walker, Webb, Wilson.
		Midway	Bexar, Milam.
Cretaceous	Upper	Navarro-Escondido	Atascosa, Bexar, Caldwell, Cherokee, Dimmit, Frio, Guadalupe, Limestone, Medina, Milam, Navarro, Panola, Robertson, Zavala.
		Taylor-Anacacho	Atascosa, Bexar, Caldwell, Gonzales, Guadalupe, Limestone, Medina, Navarro.
		Austin	Bastrop, Bexar, Caldwell, Frio, Guadalupe, Hill, Marion.
		Eagle Ford	Maverick, Panola, Shelby, Wood.
		Woodbine	Anderson, Cherokee, Freestone, Gregg, Henderson, Houston, Hunt, Leon, Limestone, Navarro, Rusk, Smith, Upshur, Van Zandt.

Cretaceous	Lower	Washita	Buda	Caldwell, Falls, Frio, Guadalupe.
			Georgetown	Falls, Frio, Panola.
		Fredericksburg Edwards		Atascosa, Caldwell, Frio, Guadalupe, McLennan.
		Trinity	Paluxy	Franklin, Grayson, Hopkins, Hunt, Smith, Wood.
			Glen Rose	Anderson, Cass, Cherokee, Franklin, Freestone, Gregg, Harrison, Henderson, Hopkins, Limestone, Marion, Maverick, Panola, Rusk, Shelby, Smith, Van Zandt, Wood.
			Travis Peak	Camp, Freestone, Harrison, Henderson, Marion, Nacogdoches, Panola, Rusk, Van Zandt.
Jurassic				Bowie, Pecos.
Permian			undifferentiated	Andrews, Callahan, Carson, Clay, Cochran, Crane, Crockett, Dawson, Ector, Gaines, Garza, Glasscock, Gray, Hansford, Hartley, Hockley, Howard, Hutchinson, Irion, Jones, Loving, Lubbock, Mitchell, Moore, Pecos, Potter, Reagan, Scurry, Shackelford, Sherman, Taylor, Terry, Tom Green, Upton, Ward, Wheeler, Wichita, Wilbarger, Winkler, Yoakum.
Pennsylvanian			undifferentiated	Carson, Collingsworth, Gray, Hansford, Hartley, Hutchinson, Kendall, Moore, Potter, Sherman, Wheeler.
			Cisco Canyon Strawn	Archer, Baylor, Brown, Callahan, Clay, Coleman, Comanche, Coke, Cooke, Crockett, Denton, Eastland, Erath, Fisher, Foard, Grayson, Hardeman, Haskell, Jack, Jones, Kimble, King, McCulloch, Midland, Montague, Nolan, Palo Pinto, Runnels, Schleicher, Shackelford, Stephens, Stonewall, Taylor, Throckmorton, Wichita, Wilbarger, Young.
			Bend	Archer, Brown, Clay, Coleman, Comanche, Concho, Eastland, Hamilton, Jack, Montague, Palo Pinto, Shackelford, Stephens, Wise, Young.
Mississippian				Archer, Clay, Stephens, Stonewall, Throckmorton, Wilbarger, Young.
Devonian				Andrews, Crane, Ector, Gaines, Upton, Winkler.
Silurian				Ward, Winkler.
Ordovician			Ellenberger	Andrews, Archer, Clay, Coleman, Comanche, Cooke, Crane, Crockett, Ector, Jack, Montague, Pecos, Reagan, Shackelford, Stephens, Ward, Wichita, Wilbarger, Winkler, Young.
Miscellaneous			Cap Rock on Salt Domes	Brooks, Chambers, Duval, Fort Bend, Galveston, Hardin, Harris, Jefferson, Liberty, Matagorda, Wharton.
			Serpentine	Bastrop, Caldwell, Medina, Travis, Williamson.

PRODUCTION

THE PRODUCING AREAS of Texas are commonly divided into the major producing districts of (a) East and East Central, (b) Gulf Coast, (c) North and North Central, (d) Panhandle, (e) Southwest, and (f) West Texas.

Statistical records indicate that Texas has produced approximately 9,634,006,000 barrels of oil since 1889 and that its marketed value at the well is estimated to have been in excess of $10,500,000,000.

The first production in the state was secured in the East and East Central district in 1866, although accurate records of production from these areas are incomplete until about 1896. Subsequent development in this district has resulted in the discovery of prolific Woodbine sand pools as well as pools from other horizons. The total production from this district has been 2,887,920,424 barrels, of which approximately 91 per cent is from the Woodbine sand. The reported production from the East Texas Field, producing from the Woodbine sand, up to January 1, 1946, is 2,170,750,550 barrels. This total exceeds that of any other field in the world.

The Gulf Coast was the first major producing district, and, starting with the flush production from Spindletop in 1901, it has produced a total of 1,979,169,066 barrels.

North and North Central Texas have produced a total of 1,324,641,461 barrels since 1904. The production in this area is from strata of Permian, Pennsylvanian, Silurian, and Ordovician age.

The Panhandle district, producing from Permian and Pennsylvanian strata, has yielded 537,471,835 barrels of oil since 1921. It has also produced and marketed tremendous quantities of natural gas and is a most important source of carbon black.

Southwest Texas was the first area of the state to be reported in statistical summaries in 1889. Since that time it has produced a total of 1,192,589,442 barrels of oil, of which approximately 20 per cent has been from altered igneous and rock of Cretaceous age along the Fault Line, approximately 28 per cent has been from rocks of Eocene age along the Laredo-Pettus trend, and approximately 52 per cent from rocks of Oligocene, Miocene, and Pliocene age along the coastal area. This district has been the source of gas for much of the industrial development along the coast of Texas, and more recently gas from fields within the area has been piped to West Virginia.

West Texas, while relatively young as a producing district, has produced 1,712,214,305 barrels of oil, chiefly from strata of Permian age, although steadily increasing production is being secured from Ordovician, Devonian, and Pennsylvanian horizons.

SUMMARY

ALL TEXANS ARE proud of the position of Texas in the oil industry, and they are deeply grateful that they were able to produce and deliver ample quantities of essential gasoline and other petroleum products to their kinsmen in the armed forces. Texas has unequaled proved reserves of oil and gas for providing cheap and convenient fuel for millions of people and for facilitating speedy transportation. The revenue from this industry provides food and shelter for thousands and thousands, pays for a substantial part of local and state government, is a major factor in providing education for the youth of the state, and contributes largely to maintaining and expanding the highway system of the state. Every citizen of Texas is engaged either directly or indirectly in the oil industry or is affected by it. The words oil, gas, and Texas are truly synonymous.

TOTAL PRODUCTION OF OIL IN TEXAS*

(In thousands of barrels)

Year	East and E. Central	Gulf Coast	North	Panhandle	South-west	West	Texas Total	Cumulative
1896	1						1	1
1897	66						66	67
1898	546						546	613
1899	669						669	1,282
1900	836						836	2,118
1901	801	3,593					4,394	6,512
1902	618	17,466					18,084	24,596
1903	502	17,454					17,956	42,552
1904	504	21,674	65				22,243	64,795
1905	445	27,616	101				28,162	92,957
1906	1,007	11,450	111				12,568	105,525
1907	827	11,400	83		10		12,320	117,845
1908	636	10,478	86		5		11,205	129,050
1909	569	8,770	113		2		9,454	138,504
1910	843	7,800	127				8,770	147,274

Early oilfield workers in Texas.
Courtesy of Portal to Texas History

TOTAL PRODUCTION OF OIL IN TEXAS—Continued

(In thousands of barrels)

Year	East and E. Central	Gulf Coast	North	Panhandle	Southwest	West	Texas Total	Cumulative
1911	1,183	7,272	1,069		1		9,525	156,799
1912	851	6,458	4,451				11,760	168,559
1913	707	5,824	8,638		1		15,170	183,729
1914	601	10,615	9,039				20,255	203,984
1915	509	17,422	6,557		613		25,100	229,084
1916	420	18,298	9,016		433		28,167	257,251
1917	392	21,479	10,521		190		32,582	289,833
1918	365	21,546	16,303		200		38,414	328,247
1919	404	21,815	71,183		187		93,589	421,836
1920	408	29,856	73,067		306		103,637	525,473
1921	6,237	37,655	67,453		652		111,997	637,470
1922	36,281	37,812	48,091		1,994	34	124,212	761,682
1923	51,032	33,576	44,856		5,561	177	135,202	896,884
1924	49,350	27,543	43,081	284	14,732	1,507	136,497	1,033,381
1925	42,474	31,099	45,115	1,288	16,427	9,566	145,969	1,179,350
1926	20,945	44,114	50,117	26,379	15,239	15,613	172,407	1,351,757
1927	12,904	48,534	55,041	40,090	11,469	51,372	219,410	1,571,167
1928	8,563	40,367	50,599	24,736	10,909	120,148	255,322	1,826,489
1929	7,121	48,360	52,506	31,743	26,344	132,599	298,673	2,125,162
1930	13,116	50,665	46,221	32,492	43,408	107,101	293,003	2,418,165
1931	126,834	39,083	30,168	20,860	34,718	77,397	329,060	2,747,225
1932	142,054	38,272	27,460	18,154	26,067	63,788	315,795	3,063,020
1933	222,603	57,253	27,641	16,604	23,680	54,389	402,170	3,465,190
1934	196,039	53,364	32,812	20,353	26,543	49,748	378,859	3,844,049
1935	176,817	55,519	33,231	21,668	34,639	53,898	375,772	4,219,821
1936	182,024	62,603	34,924	23,631	56,228	60,504	419,914	4,639,735
1937	208,563	72,713	37,986	28,105	84,058	74,446	505,871	5,145,606
1938	182,311	72,746	38,216	23,503	80,805	71,200	468,781	5,614,387
1939	173,891	77,612	41,449	24,097	81,318	78,182	476,549	6,090,936
1940	167,373	78,832	49,059	26,571	81,143	83,683	486,661	6,577,597
1941	158,835	89,789	49,100	27,826	81,043	92,383	498,976	7,076,573
1942	152,111	91,190	50,377	30,747	72,270	81,134	477,829	7,554,402
1943	171,682	139,145	50,379	33,319	94,785	98,126	587,436	8,141,838
1944	184,515	178,653	53,471	33,371	131,200	159,916	741,126	8,882,964
1945	179,536	174,384	54,758	31,651	135,410	175,303	751,042	9,634,006
Total	2,887,921	1,979,169	1,324,641	537,472	1,192,589	1,712,214	....	9,634,006

*Data are compiled from published reports of U. S. Bureau of Mines and Railroad Commission of Texas and from unpublished private files and reports.

The Office of Production Management wanted everyone to understand
the importance of oil and gas to the military during World War II.
Courtesy of National Archives and Records Administration

JANUARY 1958

The Oil Industry in Texas Since Pearl Harbor

CHARLES A. WARNER

THE IMPACT OF PEARL HARBOR on the oil industry of Texas was as pronounced and as far reaching as the outbreak of hostilities was on the youth of the state. The change from a nation at peace to one at war was instantaneous, and it brought with it a necessity for the immediate revamping of all branches of the oil industry. Maximum production had to be established and maintained with the minimum expenditure of steel and highly skilled manpower. Such production had to be moved efficiently and with the least possibility of loss to refining centers. Refinery output had to be adjusted radically, and the production of aviation gasoline, of aviation lubricants capable of successful use in any climate, and of tolulene, butadiene, and other highly specialized products took priority over the then less essential products normally required more in peacetime.

On December 23, 1941, the Office of Production Management, on the specific recommendation of the Office of the Petroleum Coordinator, issued General Preference Order M-68. This order was the first of many which affected directly the entire oil industry, but all were calculated to assure an ample supply of petroleum products to the armed forces of the government and to industry behind those forces.

Immediate plans were developed for the rapid and safe transportation of more oil and products by pipeline to mid-continent and eastern refining centers, and construction work was started under the supervision of the most skilled pipeline men. The first project completed permitted the movement in December 1942 of approximately twenty-five thousand barrels of gasoline per day from the Port Arthur area to Mississippi River terminal facilities at Helena, Arkansas. This project involved the construction of a ten-inch line from El Dorado, Arkansas, to Helena, and the reversal of existing lines from the El Dorado-Shreveport area to the Port Arthur area. Construction proceeded rapidly on the "Big Inch," the "Little Big Inch," and other projects, and within seventeen months from Pearl Harbor Day facilities had been completed for the movement north and east from Texas of approximately 150,000 barrels of products and approximately 350,000 barrels of crude oil daily. Before the end of the war these facilities had been expanded until approximately 800,000 barrels of oil and products were being moved inland or to the Atlantic Coast from Texas daily. Interconnecting or enlarged facilities in Texas, such as those from the Corpus Christi area to the Houston area and from West Texas fields to the Corsicana and East Texas area, permitted the movement of approximately 200,000 barrels more than at the beginning of 1942.

The increasing need for a convenient and efficient fuel in more ample quantities along the Eastern Seaboard was reflected in the granting of a permit to the Tennessee Gas Transmission Company for the construction of a gas transmission line from Texas to West Virginia in September 1943. Construction commenced in December, and the first gas was delivered through the line eleven months later.

Exploratory activity in Texas during 1941 had resulted in significant discoveries along the newly established Wilcox trend of the Gulf Coast region, in deeper production on the flanks of salt domes, in excellent production from Mississippian horizons in North Texas, and in the discovery of deep pay horizons in the Ellenberger and Simpson horizons of West Texas. These proved a sound foundation from which to carry on development and further exploration during the years of war need. The problem of establishing and maintaining an efficient high rate of daily production was increased during 1942 and the years immediately following by difficulty in securing pumping equipment and replacement material for stripper wells, which resulted in a consequently increased rate of abandonment of such wells. The problem was further complicated by the large decline in drilling activity caused by the shortage of steel and the fact that many highly skilled technical men and lease employees left the industry to serve in the armed forces, agencies of the government, and defense plants.

That the industry was able to cope with the situation, however, is demonstrated by the fact that productive capacity was not only maintained but was increased, and by the further fact that while the total number of wells completed in the state dropped 50 per cent from 1941 to 1942, the number of new fields discovered in 1942 was 12 per cent greater than in 1941. Significant discoveries during the first year of all-out effort included first commercial production of oil in Coke, Hunt, San Jacinto, Wilson, and Wise counties, first production in North Texas from the Simpson formation, and the first production in the state from the Viola lime. In the years immediately following were such discoveries as the TXL and Block 31 fields and commercial production from the Devonian in West Texas. At the same time the recovery of liquid hydrocarbons by cycling moved ahead rapidly with the completion of such plants as La Gloria, Katy, and Sheridan, all in the coastal area.

As a result of restricted but most effective exploration and development during the war years, Texas was able to supply necessary production, not only without waste, but also while maintaining excess productive capacity as shown by the fact that shutdown days were continued throughout the period. Development in the Panhandle was greatly restricted in 1942 following a ruling by the Petroleum Administration for War that exploration for gas in that area should be discontinued.

The need for rubber and other highly specialized products caused a tremendous expansion in the petrochemical industry, the foundations for which had been laid along the Gulf Coast in 1941. By the end of 1943 there were eight completed plants for producing butadiene, eight completed plants for producing 100-octane gasoline, and plants for producing tolulene and other products, with additional plants under construction.

With the close of the war in 1945, there came another period of radical adjustment. The end of hostilities in August was almost immediately reflected in a reduction by the Railroad Commission of some 370,000 barrels daily in the state's allowable production for the month of September. Prior to V-J Day the industry had been straining to attain higher peaks of activity, but after that there was an easing of pressure and a letdown in activity.

In the five-year period 1946-1950 inclusive, immediately following the close of the war, exploration and development increased greatly, the construction of big-inch gas lines exceeded anything in the past, oil and products line facilities were expanded, and gas processing and secondary recovery operations moved forward, augmented by new advances in gas conservation and by the initial storing (in 1950) of liquefied petroleum gases in salt reservoirs.

During this period the total number of wells, both wildcat and development, completed in Texas more than doubled. This increase in wildcat activity reflected the return to normalcy of the search for new reserves with adequate supplies of steel and necessary equipment and men to operate it. The results of exploration were evident in such discoveries as the reef areas of Scurry County, the Spraberry trend, and the first Texas offshore production, which was secured in 1949 in the Capano Bay and Corpus Christi areas of southern Texas by the Phillips Petroleum Company and The Texas Company. These developments, plus the discovery of new producing horizons in many districts, added seventeen new counties to the list of those producing oil in Texas. Also during this period, a new producing depth of 13,300 feet was established in March 1950 by General American Oil Company of Texas in Midland County.

That the demand for oil did not necessarily keep pace with the accelerated program of exploration and development during this period is shown by the fact that while statewide allowable producing days gradually increased to 366 in 1948, they then dropped to 230 for the year 1950.

The years of all-out war effort had demonstrated the need for the fullest utilization of material and men and for the greatest degree of conservation of natural resources. The lesson was well learned. Industry and regulatory bodies were becoming more conscious of natural gas. Chemical processing of the constituents of natural gas emerged during the war from a business of comparative obscurity to a prominent role, and the new methods and processes provided the motive for more effective conservation of this great resource.

In the years immediately following the war, advances in gas conservation in Texas paralleled, if indeed they did not exceed, the advances made in oil conservation during the early 1930's. Alarmed by the evident wastage of untold power through the flaring of tremendous quantities of gas, particularly casinghead gas, Governor Beauford H. Jester appointed a committee to investigate the matter and report on it. That committee, under the leadership of William J. Murray Jr., was composed entirely of engineers from the oil industry. Following the committee's report, and as a result of the conditions set forth, the Railroad Commission issued a call for oil and gas operators in the eleven districts of the Commission to meet and consider with the Commission the problem of gas flaring as it was then being practiced. This step marked the transition from the old era, when a well was not considered to be a high ratio one unless a four-inch gas riser could be heard screaming for three-quarters of a mile, to the new in which maximum utilization is made of all gas.

The first of the hearings was held in Corpus Christi on February 6, 1946, and following further investigation the landmark order of the

Commission in the field of conservation of casinghead gas was issued on March 17, 1947. This order applied to the Seeligson Oil Field of Jim Wells and Kleberg counties, where some thirty-five to forty million cubic feet of gas were being burned daily in flares. The order set forth certain beneficial uses for gas and stipulated that unless the gas produced in the field should be so utilized it was not to be produced. Paralleling the course of early oil conservation orders, legal proceedings against the Commission and its order followed immediately. The order was stricken down in the trial court but was supported by the Supreme Court of the state which held, in effect, that the Commission had the statutory authority to enter and enforce such an order, and that it would stand if the fact situation on which it was premised showed that the waste it sought to prevent was preventable. Following these initial steps, and after additional hearings on specific fields where large quantities of casinghead gas were still being flared, the Commission entered orders similar to its Seeligson order on sixteen such fields in November of 1948. Again, court action followed but the net results are considered to be a general achievement of the conservation sought since the volume of gas reportedly flared dropped about 60 per cent from 1948 to 1949. It is unquestionably true that such conservation action, initiated by the Railroad Commission of Texas, has promoted a usage for previously flared casinghead gas in the conservation of reservoir pressure in oilfields, which will result in an increased recovery of oil and in the subsequent sale of the gas. Additional revenue thereby accrues to the operators, to the royalty owners, and to the state.

It was during this five-year period, 1946-1950, that tremendous increases in gas processing capacity were made, especially through such large plants as those at Carthage and Slaughter in 1949, at North Cowden in 1950, and at Old Ocean which was unitized on August 1, 1948, and was then the largest voluntary domestic unit operation. It was also during this period that Governor Allan Shivers early in 1950, after consultation with members of the Railroad Commission, designated the recently formed Texas Petroleum Research Committee as the appropriate agency in Texas to aid in making a survey and in developing a program of research in petroleum engineering with particular emphasis to be given to secondary recovery and the improving of primary recovery. The work of this committee has been outstanding.

In connection with its natural gas investigations, the Federal Power Commission held hearings in Houston late in January 1946. At these hearings, the governor, the members of the Railroad Commission, leaders in the oil and gas industry, royalty owners, consumers, research men, and representatives of the Petroleum Administration for War, and the attorney general, appeared and pointed out the necessity for the oil and gas business to remain in the hands of private industry and for problems of conservation and waste to be handled by proper state agencies if the industry was to continue to grow and to be a bulwark for democracy.

In the six years immediately past, the oil industry of Texas has continued its steady growth, reaching new peaks in the production of oil and gas, attaining greater success in the field of conservation, and developing new techniques for more complete recovery of oil by both primary and secondary methods, as well as for a higher recovery of the end products of the oil and gas produced.

Exploration and development during these years, 1951-1956, have not been restricted to any particular district or districts, but have been widespread throughout the length and breadth of the state. These activities have resulted in important discoveries in West Texas in horizons ranging in age from Permian to Cambrian, in the discovery in McMullen County in 1953 and the subsequent development of deep Edwards lime horizons in southwestern Texas, in the discovery of Ellenberger production in Gray County in the Panhandle in 1955, in the discovery and development of production from horizons of Jurassic age in northeastern Texas, and in the development of deeper and new horizons on the flanks of old producing salt domes, which is evidenced by the wells along South Main Street in Houston on the flanks of Pierce Junction. This exploration and development also resulted in the first commercial production of oil from the Texas tidelands off the coast of Kleberg County by the Standard of Texas in July 1954. It will be recalled that the Supreme Court of the United States had ruled in June 1950 that the federal government had paramount rights off both Texas and Louisiana coasts, that following Congressional action President Eisenhower signed the "Tidelands Bill" in May 1953, and that the first sale of Texas' tidelands oil leases after such action was on December 1, 1953.

A continuation of the increased interest in the prevention of waste and the conservation of oil and gas which had been evident in the preceding five years was particularly noticeable during the past six years. This is well exemplified in connection with the development of the Spraberry trend centering in the counties of Glasscock, Martin, Midland, Reagan, and Upton. Following discovery of production in the Spraberry horizon of Permian age in Dawson County on January 22, 1949, in Reagan County on January 29, 1949, in Midland County on February 24, 1949, and in adjacent counties shortly afterward, development expanded rapidly to 80 wells with an average daily production of 8,576 barrels on January 1, 1951, to 462 wells and a daily production of 53,078 barrels from sixteen fields nine months later, and it continued to grow. To facilitate development of the trend and the supervision of operations, the Railroad Commission decided in August 1951 to grant discovery allowables to any well in the Spraberry completed at a distance of three miles or more from known Spraberry production, and to adopt blanket spacing and production allocation rules. Development continued with gas production becoming far in excess of capacity to move it until all wells were ordered closed in, effective on April 1, 1953, at which time it was estimated that the amount of such gas being flared amounted to nearly a quarter of a billion cubic feet per day—enough to serve a good-sized pipeline. This order of the Railroad Commission was a pioneer one in that it not only shut down the wells from which the gas was being flared but also shut down the other wells to protect correlative rights in the fields affected. The order was held void on June 10, 1953, by the Supreme Court of Texas, which pointed out that the statutes permitted the shutting down of wells in order to prevent waste but not to protect correlative rights. A new order, effective July 16, was issued immediately by the Commission permitting the production of a quantity of oil such that the amount of gas produced with it would not be in excess of facilities to handle it. Although many of the wells were off production for several months, such order and the completion shortly afterward of more ample facilities to handle the gas had reduced materially the waste of gas formerly attendant upon the production of oil from this great area.

Another excellent illustration of the effectiveness of conservation is shown by the unitization agreement for the Canyon Reef production of the Scurry County area, which was approved by the Commission on January 25, 1954, more than a year after the field had been unitized and after extensive hearings at which about three thousand pages of testimony had been taken in addition to many briefs by attorneys and engineers. The SACROC agreement, as it is commonly referred to, is a coordinated gas and water injection pressure regulation program for the entire unitized area of some 47,000 acres, and it is estimated by some engineers that it will result in the recovery of approximately 720,000,000 barrels more oil. This is an achievement of material significance to producers, to royalty owners, and to the state generally.

Additional steps in the program of gas conservation were taken by the Commission in April 1952, when it acted to require that reports be furnished on the amount of gas burned from every well in the state, and again on August 1 when it amended existing rules, adopted certain uniform terms respecting gas and its production, and ordered into effect new provisions designed to insure that the production and disposition of all gas, regardless of type, produced in the state would be reported regardless of whether it was actually used or whether it was flared.

Other phases of regulation and conservation enacted, adopted, or promulgated by agencies of the state during this period include: the creation by the Legislature of a separate Liquefied Petroleum Gas Division of the Railroad Commission to regulate the distribution, storage, and sale of liquefied petroleum gases, which regulatory power had been handled by the Gas Utilities Division prior to 1951; additional legislation in 1955 (Article 6029-a) with respect to pollution of fresh water sources by drilling and other operations; Rule 55 of the Railroad Commission, adopted on May 19, 1955, requiring the furnishing of the same information and reports with respect to such exploratory wells as slim holes and core holes as is required with respect to wells drilled for oil or gas; restriction of production from certain fields such as Fort Chadbourne, McElroy, Jigger Y, and others until facilities were adequate to handle increased casinghead gas resulting from intensive exploration, formation fracturing, and the like; and adoption by the Commission, as Statewide Rule 24 (b), of the requirements of Senate Bill 431 of the Fiftieth Legislature with respect to balancing periods to adjust over and under production of gas from the fields of the state.

Another phase of regulation during this period was the ruling by the United States Supreme Court on June 7, 1954, that the Federal Power Commission had the power and authority to regulate sales of gas in interstate commerce. This was followed on July 16 by Order Number 174 of the Federal Power Commission blanketing all producers selling gas into interstate commerce, which order was supplemented by Orders 174-A and 174-B on August 6 and December 17, respectively. The future of the independent producer whose gas may find its way into interstate commerce is uncertain at this time, particularly following the veto of the Harris-Fulbright Bill in February of 1956.

Pipeline expansion during the past six years has not been confined to gas lines, although there has been considerable expansion and extension of such facilities, including those projected for the importation of gas into Texas from Mexico and for the delivery of additional gas to eastern areas. Oil pipelines have been looped and extended to increase outlets for both old and new areas, and new lines of importance have been constructed, including the West Texas Gulf 466-mile line from Canyon City to Sour

Lake and the Rancho 457-mile line from McCamey to Houston. These two lines increased the pipeline capacity for transporting oil from West Texas to the Gulf Coast by over 600,000 barrels per day when they were placed in service during the first quarter of 1953. Facilities for the transportation of oil, however, are not yet extensive enough to enable the movement of all oil from lease tanks by pipelines, as was well illustrated at a hearing before the Railroad Commission early in April 1957, but that is merely one of the many problems that are perennial with the oil industry.

Although generally thought of as the foremost producer and exporter of gas to other states, as indeed it is, Texas actually ranks first among the states in the nation in the quantity of gas it consumes. It is this convenient and clean fuel which heats more than a million Texas homes, accounts for the clean, new look of the buildings in Texas cities, and is a primary factor in industrial growth throughout the state.

Texas continues undisputed in first place in the oil industry of the United States. It produces oil or gas in 204 of its 254 counties; it has about 7,000 oilfields and 1,900 gas fields, and new ones are being discovered at the rate of about 45 per month; it has over 171,500 oil wells and 17,300 gas wells; and it has produced a total of 19,720,689,338 barrels of oil since 1886, which is about 36 per cent of the total production in the United States since 1859. Within the state there are currently 85,000 miles of pipeline, exclusive of gas distribution lines, 57 operating refineries, 205 gasoline plants, 30 cycling plants, 150 pressure maintenance plants, and more than 6,000 individuals and companies are operating more than 42,000 leases.

The state is currently producing approximately 3,250,000 barrels of oil every day, with the major oil producing capacity being restricted to about sixteen allowable producing days per month, and its proven reserves are estimated at approximately 15,000,000,000 barrels of crude oil, 3,000,000,000 barrels of natural gas liquids, and 113,000,000,000,000 cubic feet of gas. In connection with these estimated recoverable reserves, however, it should be pointed out that the results of exploration and development in Texas during the past five years have been able barely to maintain the reserves of liquid hydrocarbons at their previous level and to increase the reserves of natural gas only about 10 per cent. This is significant indeed, in view of the constantly increasing demand for oil and gas and their products and in view of the fact that such reserves constitute less than a twenty-year supply at present rate of production.

In the fifteen years since Pearl Harbor, the oil industry in Texas has made outstanding progress in gas conservation and the development of the liquefied petroleum gas industry and in the fields of well completion technique and secondary recovery; it has adopted such new methods as mud acids, miscible displacement "fracking," jet perforating, and lease automatic custody transfer of oil; and it has witnessed an increase in its producing depth record from approximately 11,500 feet to 15,000 feet. During this fifteen-year period, Texas has produced some 12,641,013,287 barrels of oil, an amount equal to the total production of the United States from the time of the Drake well in 1859 until shortly before the discovery of the great East Texas oilfield. The Texas oil industry is now practicing and will continue to use the most advanced processes in its exploration for production, refining, and marketing of oil and gas to the end that coming years will witness the fullest utilization of the maximum recovery of these Godgiven resources.

GEOLOGIC FORMATIONS PROVEN PRODUCTIVE IN VARIOUS COUNTIES SINCE JANUARY 1, 1942

Oligocene	Frio and Vicksburg	Bee, Newton
Eocene	Cockfield and Yegua	DeWitt, Jasper, Lavaca, San Jacinto, Starr, Walker (1946)*
	Cook Mountain	Austin
	Mt. Selman	Atascosa, Frio, Houston, Karnes, McMullen
	Wilcox	Atascosa, Austin, Bee, Brazos, Fayette, Goliad, Gonzales, Grimes (1951), Hardin, Karnes, LaSalle, Lee, Liberty, Live Oak, Madison (1946), McMullen, Newton, San Jacinto (1942), Waller, Washington, Wilson (1942)

*Discovery also constituted first commercial oil production for the county.

GEOLOGIC FORMATIONS PROVEN PRODUCTIVE IN VARIOUS COUNTIES SINCE JANUARY 1, 1942—Continued

Cretaceous	Navarro		Burleson, Cherokee, Robertson (1944)
	Austin		Atascosa, Wilson
	Eagle Ford		Anderson, Camp, Cherokee, Hopkins, Houston, Wood
	Woodbine		Hunt (1942), Kaufman, Madison, Trinity
	Washita	Buda	Bastrop, Bell, Falls, Gonzales, Madison, Maverick, Trinity, Wilson
		Georgetown	Falls, Houston, Madison
	Fredericksburg Edwards		Atascosa, Bastrop, Falls, Gonzales, Harrison, LaSalle, Lee (1948), Madison (1946), McMullen, Trinity
		Paluxy	Bowie, Hunt, Kaufman, Red River (1949), Trinity, Wood
	Trinity	Glen Rose	Angelina, Cherokee, Edwards, Franklin, Gregg, Hopkins, Hunt, Kaufman (1948), Leon, Limestone, Maverick, Nacogdoches, Navarro, Panola, Red River, Robertson, Rusk, San Augustine (1947), Shelby, Van Zandt, Wood
		Travis Peak	Cass, Franklin, Freestone, Gregg, Harrison, Henderson, Leon, Marion, Nacogdoches, Navarro, Panola, Rusk, Smith, Upshur, VanZandt, Wood
Jurassic			Bowie (1944), Franklin, Limestone, Marion
Permian	Undifferentiated		Borden (1948), Callahan, Crosby, Culberson (1948), Cottle, Dickens, Floyd (1948), Hale (1946), Hansford (1951), Haskell, Kent, Knox, Lamb (1944), Martin (1944), Midland, Schleicher, Sterling (1948), Sutton
	Spraberry		Borden, Dawson, Glasscock, Howard, Martin, Midland, Reagan, Sterling, Tom Green, Upton
Pennsylvanian	Undifferentiated		Andrews, Hale, Hansford (1951), Martin, Midland, Ochiltree (1951), Sherman (1949), Upton
	Cisco-Canyon-Strawn		Borden, Coke (1942), Crane, Dawson, Ector, Floyd, Gaines, Garza, Hale, Hansford, Hardeman (1944), Hockley, Howard, Irion, Kent, King (1943), Knox, Lynn (1950), Midland (1945), Mitchell, Scurry, Sterling, Sutton (1948), Terry, Tom Green, Upton, Wise
	Bend		Baylor, Brown, Callahan, Cochran, Coke, Concho, Foard, Grayson, Haskell, Knox (1946), Reagan, Stephens, Wise (1942)
Mississippian			Archer, Baylor, Borden, Brown, Callahan, Comanche, Eastland, Gaines, Glasscock, Haskell, Howard, Jack, Lynn, Roberts (1949), Shackelford, Stephens, Sterling, Taylor, Throckmorton, Wilbarger, Winkler
Devonian			Andrews, Cochran, Crane, Crockett, Dawson, Ector, Gaines, Martin, Midland, Runnels, Terry, Upton, Ward, Winkler, Yoakum
Silurian			Andrews, Crane, Crockett, Dawson, Ector, Gaines, Howard, Midland, Pecos, Reagan, Terry, Upton, Winkler
Ordovician	Viola		Montague
	Simpson		Clay, Cooke, Crane, Ector, Grayson, Montague
	Ellenberger		Andrews, Archer, Borden, Callahan, Clay, Coke, Coleman, Crockett, Eastland, Ector, Fisher, Gaines, Gray, Grayson, Irion, Jack, Jones, Kent (1946), Martin, Midland, Mitchell, Montague, Nolan, Palo Pinto, Scurry, Shackelford, Schleicher, Stephens, Sterling, Stonewall, Taylor, Tom Green, Upton, Ward, Winkler, Wise
Cambrian			Coke, Nolan, Stonewall

TOTAL PRODUCTION OF OIL IN TEXAS*
(In thousands of barrels)

Year	East and E. Central	Gulf Coast	North	Pan-handle	South-west	West	Texas Total	Cumulative	Allowable Producing Days†
To 1-1-42	2,204,215	1,395,798	1,115,518	407,384	758,924	1,197,837	7,079,676		
1942	152,117	91,190	50,318	30,747	72,270	81,186	477,828	7,557,504	243
1943	171,800	139,174	50,592	33,352	94,875	98,096	587,689	8,145,193	249
1944	184,562	178,302	53,433	33,442	131,343	160,103	741,185	8,886,378	281
1945	179,573	174,396	54,478	31,436	135,379	175,406	750,668	9,637,046	277
1946	172,195	167,248	57,345	30,470	138,495	190,888	756,641	10,393,687	292
1947	173,063	175,555	62,303	31,347	153,932	220,421	816,621	11,210,308	324
1948	174,117	182,610	69,569	30,795	165,546	276,122	893,759	12,109,067	366
1949	139,547	139,312	70,235	33,034	126,807	227,692	736,627	12,845,694	238
1950	143,550	143,873	78,868	33,057	134,018	284,476	817,842	13,663,536	230
1951	160,358	171,690	87,485	30,977	163,624	377,848	991,982	14,655,518	278
1952	159,926	164,031	98,925	29,018	161,857	396,038	1,009,793	15,665,311	259
1953	152,624	161,205	109,841	27,260	161,647	387,001	999,578	16,664,889	236
1954	138,009	149,586	114,235	30,910	150,314	371,381	954,435	17,619,324	194
1955	140,931	155,212	126,593	33,015	158,021	408,708	1,022,480	18,641,804	194
1956	138,542	157,477	135,433	36,155	160,460	450,818	1,078,885	19,720,689	190
Total	4,585,129	3,746,659	2,334,971	882,399	2,867,512	5,304,019	12,641,013	19,720,689	

*Data are compiled from published reports of U. S. Bureau of Mines and Railroad Commission of Texas and from unpublished private files and reports.
†Statewide—for all fields not exempted or covered by special order.

WELLS COMPLETED IN TEXAS

Year	TOTAL (INCLUDING WILDCATS)				WILDCATS			
	Oil	Gas	Dry	Total	Oil	Gas	Dry	Total
1942	3,041	186	1,461	4,688	55	12	780	847
1943	2,373	140	1,908	4,421	135	17	1,021	1,173
1944	3,526	268	1,935	5,729	170	33	1,072	1,275
1945	4,036	714	2,445	7,195	228	44	1,280	1,552
1946	4,720	499	2,582	7,801	247	34	1,310	1,591
1947	5,814	537	2,950	9,301	355	80	1,460	1,895
1948	7,619	542	4,090	12,251	377	104	2,087	2,568
1949	8,613	746	4,306	13,665	440	112	2,239	2,791
1950	10,665	647	5,273	16,585	575	113	2,755	3,443
1951	10,086	726	5,843	16,655	802	133	3,473	4,408
1952	9,682	778	6,385	16,845	823	126	3,902	4,851
1953	9,380	978	6,648	17,006	904	169	4,172	5,245
1954	11,068	912	6,885	18,865	823	163	4,204	5,190
1955	12,476	603	6,902	19,981	883	132	4,109	5,124
1956	13,082	894	7,543	21,519	766	205	4,639	5,610
Total	116,181	9,170	67,156	192,507	7,583	1,477	38,503	47,563
%	60	5	35	100	16	3	81	100

COMPARATIVE DATA

	1942	1956
Field Activity		
Total Wells Drilled	9,827	21,519
Wildcat Wells Drilled	847	5,160
Total Footage Drilled	57,317,700	92,620,000
Production		
Number of Oil Wells	99,185	171,500
Statewide Producing Days	242	190
Oil Production (Millions Bbls.)	478	1,079
Number of Gas Wells	3,685	17,339
Gas Production (Billions cu. ft.)	1,916	6,005
Reserves (Estimated)		
Oil (Including gas liquids)	11,756 Millions Bbls.	18,163
Gas	78* Trillions cu.ft.	113

*As of December 31, 1945 (first available).

Oilfield workers at Kilgore in 1939 by Russell Lee.
Courtesy of Library of Congress

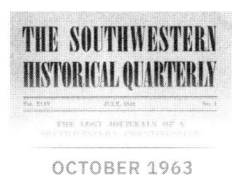

OCTOBER 1963

Texas Petroleum History: A Selected Annotated Bibliography

WALTER RUNDELL JR.

THIS BIBLIOGRAPHY ATTEMPTS to evaluate selected literature dealing with the history of the petroleum industry in Texas. The list of books treated is by no means comprehensive; it is merely an effort to comment on some of the significant volumes dealing with the Texas oil industry. Interested readers may add to the list as they see fit. The preparation of the bibliography has revealed that only one of the four major phases of this industry has been dealt with extensively. That phase is production. In this respect, the literature on Texas oil exhibits the same characteristics as that dealing with the industry on a national basis. Since production is easily the most exciting and spectacular part of the industry, it is perhaps natural that it would be the first to be awarded a thorough historical treatment. Some scholarly effort has recently been devoted to transportation and refining, but marketing has been notably lacking the attention of historians.

As a result of the early monopolistic control of the industry by John D. Rockefeller's Standard Oil combination and the continued importance of the "majors," a great deal has been written about the economic structure and implications of the industry. Since the history of industry is, after all, a phase of the more comprehensive field of economic history (where the dividing line between the two disciplines sometimes grows dim), these economic approaches take their place as important adjuncts to the body of literature dealing with the industry's history. Consequently, significant books on the economics of Texas oil are dealt with here. The plentiful economic scholarship devoted to Texas oil is indicative of that devoted to the industry nationally. Since Texas oil inevitably figures in any general economic analysis of the industry, important volumes of this nature are likewise discussed.

Notable vacancies exist in the historical treatment of the Texas petroleum industry. Some major companies of the state, such as Gulf, Magnolia, and Texaco, have not been subjects of serious historical scholarship. Little of significance has been done in the specialized phases of refining and marketing. The derivative industries, which presently have assumed a place of real importance in the Texas industry, are relatively untouched. Since most of these derivative industries date from World War II, it is not too early to expect serious historical coverage. This is also a field an economic historian could investigate profitably.

In the last dozen or so years, much of the serious historical research and writing on the industry has been done with grants from major oil companies. The gratifying feature of this program is that competent historians have been awarded the grants. The results have not been public relations blurbs, but scholarly, objective investigations. It is hoped that further substantial grants will be made available to those who would fill the gaps in the history of the Texas oil industry.

BADEN, ANNE L. (comp.), *The Petroleum Industry: A Selected List of Recent References* (Washington: The Library of Congress, Division of Bibliography, 1942). 60 pp.

For the serious student of the petroleum industry, this bibliography is an invaluable aid. It contains all the important publications in the

Library of Congress on oil. Many of the items listed are of no interest to the historian, since the bibliography contains a complete coverage of all phases of the industry. An excellent index further enhances the value of this publication.

BARTLEY, ERNEST R., *The Tidelands Oil Controversy, A Legal and Historical Analysis* (Austin: University of Texas Press, 1953). 312 pp.

The conflict between the legal rights of states and the federal government is thoroughly examined by the author. He puts this controversy in its historical setting from Roman times to the present, giving special attention to the Texas case. This well-written and extensively documented volume makes an invaluable contribution on a vital issue.

BOATWRIGHT, MODY C., *Gib Morgan, Minstrel of the Oil Fields* (Austin: Texas Folklore Society, 1945). 104 pp.

Morgan, an oil well driller, created and disseminated a great body of folklore about the oilfields. The author, an English professor at the University of Texas, ably records the minstrel's life (1841?-1909), with special emphasis on that part of it spent in the West Texas oilfields. Half the book is devoted to the tales Morgan told—some fifty-odd.

BRYAN, BARNABAS, JR., *Petroleum Control in the United States* (New York: American Council, Institute of Pacific Relations, 1933). 36 pp.

Methods of controlling production of oil are investigated in this work. The author pays special attention to prorationing, the unit plan, the Yates plan, and the Kettleman Hills plan.

CARL, ELLA LANE, *Letters of a Texas Oil Driller's Wife* (New York: Comet Press, 1959). 222 pp.

These letters were written between 1927 and 1931. They deal with life in the West Texas oil towns of Borger and Pampa, but contain negligible information about the petroleum industry.

CLARK, JAMES A., *Three Stars for the Colonel*
(New York: Random House, 1954). 265 pp.

Clark, a Houston public relations executive, has written an uncritical account of the public career of Ernest O. Thompson, the highly influential chairman of the Texas Railroad Commission. The Commission is the regulatory body for oil production in the state.

CLARK, JAMES A., and **MICHEL T. HALBOUTY**, *Spindletop*
(New York: Random House, 1952). 306 pp.

Here is an exciting, dramatized history of Texas' first big oil strike. The authors use fictitious dialogue to capture the vigor of the oil boom. All the big names of oil production in Texas are sprinkled through the pages of this book. The authors trace the development of four major companies from this field-Gulf, Texaco, Magnolia, and Humble. The book contains no attempt at economic analysis, except to state "the Standard Oil Company monopoly never hurt the general public." This glorification of oil pioneers makes most interesting reading.

COOK, ROY C., *Control of the Petroleum Industry by Major Oil Companies, Monograph No. 39, Temporary National Economic Committee*
(Washington: Government Printing Office, 1941). 101 pp.

Cook's economic study in the monopoly conditions existing in the oil industry has much the same tenor as Kemnitzer's earlier *Rebirth of Monopoly*. Control by the majors in the fields of production, transportation, refining, and retailing has tended to squeeze out the independents. Cook's solution to the problem is governmental control of the industry as a public utility.

COTNER, ROBERT C., *James Stephen Hogg: A Biography*
(Austin: University of Texas Press, 1959). 617 pp.

As a comprehensive biography of the popular Texas governor, this volume treats Hogg's involvements in the petroleum business. He was a central figure in the speculation at Spindletop, and much of his fortune resulted therefrom. The author is a history professor at the University of Texas.

DEGOLYER, E., and **HAROLD VANCE** (comps.), *Bibliography on the Petroleum Industry* (College Station: Bulletin No. 83 of the Agricultural and Mechanical College of Texas, 1944). 730 pp.

At the time of its publication, this was the most exhaustive bibliography on the technical aspects of the subject. As yet, it has not been superseded. The volume consists of a combination of DeGolyer's personal bibliography of some 12,000 entries with the bibliography of the Petroleum Engineering Department at Texas A.&M. Subjects covered include geographical distribution, physical and chemical properties, exploration, production, transportation, refining, utilization, and economics of petroleum. There is no annotation. DeGolyer was a leading Texas geologist and bibliophile.

ELLISOR, ALVA C., *Rockhounds of Houston: An Informal History of the Houston Geological Society* (Houston: Houston Geological Society, 1947). 99 pp.

A discussion of pioneer Texas geologists is in this booklet, as well as a brief, informal history of the society from its founding in 1923.

ENGLER, ROBERT, *The Politics of Oil* (New York: Macmillan, 1961). 565 pp.

Whereas most basic criticism of the petroleum industry in the United States has been economic, this volume attacks the industry from the standpoint of political control. Engler is concerned with the fundamental inroads the industry has made against democratic processes in this country. His thesis is that the industry has capitalized on the people's preoccupation with material well-being. This preoccupation has led them to an uncritical acceptance of the economic and political status quo. Hence the giant corporation is able to manipulate affairs to its own benefit. Since oil has been an important factor in Texas politics since Spindletop, Engler appropriately devotes a large portion of his volume to the impact of petroleum interests on Texas and national politics.

FANNING, LEONARD M., *The Rise of American Oil*
(New York: Harper, 1948). 178 pp.

The author's purpose in this book is to demonstrate how oil has been responsible for major developments in other fields of American industry—aviation, automotive manufacturing, farming, road building, heating, and heavy tooling. Fanning goes into the historical background to show the setting and context of American innovations. This is an important book in that it essays an analysis of the interrelation of heavy industries. On the other hand, the book is an unquestioning statement of admiration for the American petroleum industry. It makes no inquiry at all into the economic consequences of the monopolistic control of the early industry.

FARISH, W. S., and **J. HOWARD PEW**, *Review and Criticism on Behalf of Standard Oil Company (New Jersey) and Sun Oil Company of Monograph No. 39 with Rejoinder by Monograph Author, Monograph No. 39-a, Temporary National Economic Committee* (Washington: Government Printing Office, 1941). 96 pp.

This reply to *Monograph No. 39* is an attempt by the majors to refute every point made by Cook. The burden of their defense rests upon testimony given before the Temporary National Economic Committee by other members of the American Petroleum Institute. Frequently, rather than face Cook's charges directly, Farish and Pew launch out on another topic such as the contributions of the petroleum industry to the American way of life. On the whole, Cook's contentions stand up well in the face of this rebuttal.

FORBES, GERALD, *Flush Production*
(Norman: University of Oklahoma Press, 1942). 255 pp.

Oil production in Texas, Oklahoma, Louisiana, and Kansas is the subject of this intensive study. It contains some impartial inquiry into the economic effects of the regulation of production. The conclusions are that prorationing and the unit systems tend to promote monopoly and that it is to the interest of the majors to control production. Forbes studies the social effects of controlled production.

GARDNER, FRANK J., *Ira Rinehart's West Texas Oil, a Study of the Petroleum Industry in Fifty-five Counties of the West Texas Permian Basin*
(Dallas: Rinehart Oil News Co., 1949). 499 pp.
Rich in technical data, these two loose-leaf volumes contain little conventional historical analysis.

_____, *Reference Report on Oil and Gas Fields of the Texas Lower Gulf Coast, Railroad Commission District Two*
(Dallas: Five Star Oil Report, 1951). 240 pp.
Like other publications of Gardner, this work is primarily technical; yet it, in common with the others, contains information of some historical importance.

_____, *Reference Report on the Oil and Gas Fields of the Texas Upper Gulf Coast, Railroad Commission District Three*
(Dallas: Five Star Oil Report, 1952). 484 pp.
A sequel to the foregoing, this volume has a brief history of prorationing and conservation.

_____, *Rinehart's North Texas Oil*
(Houston: Rinehart Oil News Company of Texas, 1941). 342 pp.
Burkburnett is the focal point of this study, which contains a historical introduction to the North Texas oilfields during the period 1870 to 1941. The volume is filled with valuable statistics.

_____, *South Texas Oil, a Study of the Petroleum Industry in Thirty-one Counties of the Rio Grande Embayment*, 2 vols.
(Tulsa: The Rinehart Oil News Company, 1947). 398 pp.
While this work contains only a brief historical introduction to the South Texas petroleum industry up to 1947, it has a wealth of technical data on specific fields.

_____, *Texas Gulf Coast Oil*

(Dallas: The Rinehart Oil News Company, 1948). 311 pp.

The historical value of this volume lies in the chronology of production activities in the Gulf Coast region.

GARDNER, FRANK J., and ROBERT L. PHIFER, *The Oil and Gas Fields of West Texas, Part I: Railroad Commission District 7-C*

(Houston: Five Star Oil Report, Inc., 1953). 304 pp.

The book has no historical information as such but contains a great deal of technical data on West Texas fields.

GLASSCOCK, LUCILLE M., *A Texas Wildcatter; a Fascinating Saga of Oil*

(San Antonio: Naylor, 1952). 126 pp.

A dutiful wife tells the story of how her husband struck black gold in East Texas.

GRAHAM, LLEWELLYN (pseud.), *The Romance of Texas Oil*

(Fort Worth: Tariff Publishing Co., 1935). 126 pp.

The book is an informal, chronological account of oil production in Texas. It contains no documentation and could scarcely be considered reliable.

HAMILTON, DANIEL C., *Competition in Oil, The Gulf Coast Refinery Market, 1925–1950* (Cambridge: Harvard University Press, 1958). 233 pp.

A "modest revision'" of a Columbia University doctoral dissertation, this scholarly study of regional market structure and operation focuses chiefly on the present but contains historically valuable statistics and useful trend observations. While pointing to the presence of "moderate but persistent oligopoly," the author concludes that competition in the area studied has been an effective market influence.

HARDWICKE, ROBERT E., *Antitrust Laws, et al., v. Unit Operation of Oil or Gas Pools* (New York: American Institute of Mining and Metallurgical Engineers, 1948). 300 pp.

In this treatise, Hardwicke, a Fort Worth attorney who is one of the nation's leading scholars in the field of oil and gas law, presents the historical background of antitrust legislation aimed at the production of oil and gas. Many of the important cases developed in Texas, e.g., the discovery of the East Texas field by Dad Joiner on October 3, 1930.

_____ (comp.), *Petroleum and Natural Gas Bibliography* (Austin: The University of Texas, 1937). 167 pp.

The conservation law specialist has prepared this monumental bibliography including listings on the following topics: history, prospecting, production, transportation, storage, refining, marketing, utilization, statistics, legal references, hearings, investigations, reports, accounting, and finance. A mimeographed supplement was issued by the American Petroleum Institute on May 1, 1940.

HARTER, HARRY, *East Texas Oil Parade* (San Antonio: Naylor, 1934). 220 pp.

The author gives a detailed but informal account of the problems connected with controlling production in the East Texas fields. He puts special emphasis on the results of martial law being declared in the fields in 1931.

HORLACHER, JAMES LEVI, *A Year in the Oil Fields* (Lexington: The Kentucky Kernel Press, 1929). 68 pp.

These are the interesting recollections of a roughneck in the West Texas fields. The author makes some intelligent observations on oilfield labor problems, methods, and mores.

HOUSE, BOYCE, *Oil Boom* (Caldwell, Idaho: Caxton Printers, Ltd., 1941). 194 pp.

House treats the strikes at Spindletop, Burkburnett, Mexia, Smackover, Desdemona, and Ranger superficially and without literary appeal. The author was a Texas journalist.

_____, *Oil Field Fury* (San Antonio: Naylor, 1934). 142 pp.

Corruption and oil ran together in Eastland County in the 1920's. Like House's other volumes concerning the Texas petroleum industry, this one is of scant value to the serious student.

_____, *Roaring Ranger* (San Antonio: Naylor, 1951). 122 pp.

This volume retreads the author's *Were You in Ranger?* but makes no improvement.

_____, *Were You in Ranger?* (Dallas: Tardy Publishing Co., 1935). 210 pp.

Written in a telegraphic style, this book is a breezy, undocumented social history of the Ranger field.

ISE, JOHN, *The United States Oil Policy* (New Haven: Yale University Press, 1926). 547 pp.

This solid piece of scholarship is an economic investigation into the condition of the United States' oil policy. It contains an excellent analysis of all types of waste found in the petroleum industry—waste in production, in capital, and of energy. Ise shows how oil tends to be a natural monopoly and how the Standard Oil Company took advantage of this phenomenon. His conclusion is that the United States' oil policy should not echo the sentiment on the face of our coins, but rather that the government should take positive steps to control our remaining resources.

JAMES, MARQUIS, *The Texaco Story* (Houston: The Texas Co., 1953). 118 pp.

The biographer of Sam Houston tells a brief but interesting story of the Texas Company's first fifty years, which began with Spindletop. He explains with ease the important technological developments that revolutionized the business, such as the Burton and Manley-Holmes processes of distillation. The writing is simplified so that the lay reader can easily follow the story. A good bit of emphasis is placed on the founders of the company, especially J. S. Cullinan.

KEMNITZER, WILLIAM J., *Rebirth of Monopoly*
(New York: Harper, 1938). 261 pp.

Rebirth of Monopoly is a book that strongly reflects the impulse for economic reform and regulation that has periodically penetrated the American conscience since the 1890's. This impulse ran with special vigor during the 1930's, so the book is in part a reflection of the time when it was written. This economic history of monopoly in the oil business is permeated with a sense of social and economic justice. Kemnitzer's thesis is that monopoly was rebuilt by devious means after the dissolution of Standard Oil in 1911. Conservation has actually been a device of the majors to restrict the activity of independent producers and refiners. The majors want a controlled supply in order to control refining and marketing. With conservation, they can, by using patented processes, get a greater percentage of gasoline from crude oil than the smaller refiners. The author shows how patents are a means of extending monopolistic control and how prorationing limits competition. The fact that the pipelines are largely controlled by the majors forces independents to use more expensive means of transportation. The government, by allowing these practices, merely perpetuates monopolistic control in the petroleum industry, contends Kemnitzer.

KILMAN, ED, and **THEON WRIGHT**, *Hugh Roy Cullen: A Story of American Opportunity* (New York: Prentice-Hall, 1954). 376 pp.

According to a reliable report, Cullen gave away at least 100,000 copies of this public-relations account of his life. The authors make no attempt to treat the Houston oilman-philanthropist objectively. At the time the book was published, Kilman was the editor of the *Houston Post*'s editorial page.

KING, JOHN O., *The Early History of the Houston Oil Company of Texas, 1901–1908* (Houston: Texas Gulf Coast Historical Association, 1959). 100 pp.

The origin of the Houston Oil Company was closely interwoven with that of the Kirby Lumber Company. King relates in a readable and scholarly manner the negotiations that led to the founding of these two important Texas businesses. The negotiations involved Patrick Calhoun, grandson of John C. and moving spirit behind the oil company, and John Henry Kirby, lumberman. During the period covered in this publication of the *Texas Gulf Coast Historical Association* (Volume III, Number 1, April 1959), the oil company was almost exclusively concerned with marketing the timber on its land. After 1908, when the two businesses were separated by litigation, the oil company engaged in the highly successful production of petroleum in East Texas. The oil company was liquidated in 1956 for $243,000,000.

KNOWLES, RUTH SHELDON, *The Greatest Gamblers, The Epic of American Oil Exploration* (New York: McGraw-Hill, 1959). 347 pp.

Written by a veteran oilwoman, this book considers the "art of oil exploration" and deals with the most dramatic discoveries of petroleum in the United States. The volume, presented in a lively, popular style without documentation or bibliography, contains an abundance of information on such oilmen as Benedum, Sinclair, Doheny, Marland, Rockefeller, and the Texans Joiner, Hunt, Pratt, and DeGolyer. The chief weakness of the book is the episodic nature of its topical organization around the activities of the various oilmen.

LARSON, HENRIETTA M., and **KENNETH W. PORTER**, *History of Humble Oil and Refining Company: A Study in Industrial Growth* (New York: Harper, 1959). 769 pp.

Texas' largest producing and refining company is the subject of this thorough, scholarly study. The book is organized so that separate chapters are devoted to administration, marketing, transportation, production, and technology. Chapter 18 on prorationing is of particular interest to students of Texas government. The authors lead the reader through a vast maze of facts with skill. Each chapter concludes with a summation of its importance and a transition showing how subsequent information relates. While the treatment of Humble from 1917 to 1950 is exhaustive, the authors do not set their history within the perspective of the industry as a whole or the Texas milieu. The reader sees Humble from the inside, but never from without.

Legal History of Conservation of Oil and Gas, A Symposium
(Chicago: American Bar Association, 1938). 302 pp.
The Texas section of this symposium was written by Robert E. Hardwicke (oil) and Maurice Cheek (gas). Eight other states are considered.

LEVEN, DAVID D., *Done in Oil* (New York: The Ranger Press, 1941). 1,084 pp.
Although this book is primarily an encyclopedia of oil terms, it contains useful historical material.

MARCOSSON, ISAAC F., *The Black Golconda* (New York: Harper, 1924). 369 pp.
Subtitled "The Romance of Petroleum," the book is an essay in the social history of oil production. It presents striking and unusual facts about oilfields and people who own or work in them. There is no documentation. Consequently, the author's facts are frequently open to question. Of greatest interest are the discussions of the effects of oil on the Oklahoma Indians and the growth of four major oil companies from the Spindletop field.

McDANIEL, RUEL, *Some Ran Hot* (Dallas: Regional Press, 1939). 252 pp.
East Texas oil troubles are explored in this volume. Hot oil was that produced in violation of the prorationed allowances. McDaniel examines the necessity of martial law in the oilfields. The author is also a biographer of Judge Roy Bean.

MURPHY, BLAKELY M., *Conservation of Oil and Gas, A Legal History, 1948*
(Chicago: American Bar Association, 1949). 754 pp.
A supplementary volume to that published by the American Bar Association a decade earlier, this work is far broader in treatment,

though it deals only with the 1938-1948 period. In addition to the chapter on conservation practices in Texas, this book treats thirty-four other states.

PARKER, GEORGE (pseud.), *Oil Field Medico*

(Dallas: Banks Upshaw and Co., 1948). 139 pp.

The author was a practicing physician at Spindletop, Batson, and Saratoga. He describes some grisly cases treated on the "oil frontier."

PETTENGILL, SAMUEL B., *Hot Oil* (New York: Economic Forum, 1936). 308 pp.

While a Member of Congress, the author wrote this inquiry into governmental control of the petroleum industry. The book is superficial and loose-jointed.

POPPLE, CHARLES S., *Standard Oil Company (New Jersey) in World War II*

(New York: Standard Oil Co. [NJ], 1952). 340 pp.

Popple, a former member of Harvard University's Business History Foundation, has written a detailed history of Standard's activities in World War II, with full attention given to the role played by subsidiary companies, such as Humble. There are many technical data, charts, and scientific explanations of the intricacies of the industry. The treatment of the company seems factual and fair. This is one of the few works that has attempted any historical coverage of petroleum's derivative industries, such as the manufacture of explosives, butadiene, and petrochemicals.

REDWOOD, BOVERTON, *Petroleum*

(London: Charles Griffin and Co., Ltd., 1922). 1,317 pp.

Volume III (pp. 1,155-1,317) of this technical study contains a bibliography with some 8,800 entries. The unannotated bibliography deals with the petroleum industry on a worldwide basis. Redwood published the first work in this series (same title) in 1896. Subsequent editions appeared in 1906 and 1913.

RISTER, CARL COKE, *Oil! Titan of the Southwest*
(Norman: University of Oklahoma Press, 1949). 467 pp.

Rister's volume is the most comprehensive and scholarly study yet made of production in the Southwest states of Texas, Oklahoma, Louisiana, Arkansas, and Kansas. It becomes a bit repetitious as one oilfield after another is brought in. The author misses much of the excitement inherent in the oilfield. Slight attention is given to transporting, refining, or marketing functions. The well-documented book was written on a grant from the Standard Oil Company (New Jersey) and the University of Oklahoma. The author's attitude is one of complete impartiality.

SCHWETTMANN, MARTIN W., *Santa Rita: The University of Texas Oil Discovery*
(Austin: The Texas State Historical Association, 1943). 43 pp.

The author presents a highly readable account of the initial oil strike at the Santa Rita rig on the West Texas lands of the University of Texas. Tom Lea, who later won renown with *The Brave Bulls* and *The King Ranch*, illustrated the volume.

SPRATT, JOHN S., *The Road to Spindletop: Economic Change in Texas, 1875–1901* (Dallas: Southern Methodist University Press, 1955). 337 pp.

The petroleum industry's impact on the Texas economy during the last quarter of the nineteenth century is thoughtfully analyzed in this volume. Spratt is an economics professor at Southern Methodist University.

STOCKING, GEORGE WARD, *The Oil Industry and the Competitive System*
(New York: Houghton Mifflin Co., 1925). 323 pp.

The thesis of this book by a former economics professor at the University of Texas is that competition in all phases of the oil industry means waste. Economic demand for the products has led to overdevelopment in production, transportation, refining, and retailing facilities. The plethora of oil to be refined has meant incomplete utilization of the crude available. The patent monopoly has discriminated against independent producers and has made them produce and refine with incomplete recovery from the crude. But the greatest waste has been in retailing. Competition in production has led to early depletion and ruination of good fields through careless, frenzied methods of getting the maximum out of the ground in the quickest possible time. The results have been that gas pressure has been dissipated and oil sands have been flooded with water. Stocking's solution to the problem of waste in the oil business is government control at all levels in the public interest. Originally a Columbia University doctoral dissertation, the book was also a Hart, Schaffner and Marx prize essay.

SWANSON, EDWARD BENJAMIN (comp.), *A Century of Oil and Gas in Books, a Descriptive Bibliography* (New York: Appleton-Century-Crofts, Inc., 1960). 214 pp.

Easily this is the most up-to-date bibliography of books in English relating to the petroleum industry. Prepared with the assistance of a grant from the American Petroleum Institute, it contains over 2,000 entries. Bibliographical details are complete and the comments helpful. The compiler, a widely recognized petroleum authority, was for many years with the Bureau of Mines.

TAIT, SAMUEL W., JR., *The Wildcatters; An Informal History of Oil Hunting in America* (Princeton: Princeton University Press, 1946). 218 pp.

The author presents in a matter-of-fact manner the accounts of such famous oil scouts as Colonel Drake, John Galey, Captain Lucas, and Dad Joiner. The latter two discovered the Spindletop and East Texas field respectively.

THOMPSON, CRAIG, *Since Spindletop; A Human Story of Gulf's First Half Century* (Pittsburgh?, 1951?). 110 pp.

This is Gulf's story, told largely in terms of Gulf personnel, from its beginnings in Texas in 1901 to 1951. The appendix lists important statistics for each year of the company's life.

U. S. TEMPORARY NATIONAL ECONOMIC COMMITTEE, *Investigation of Concentration of Economic Power, Hearings, Parts 14-17a, Petroleum Industry* (Washington: Government Printing Office, 1940). 590 pp.

These investigations were primarily of an economic nature. The reports contain excellent source material for an economist or historian doing a specialized study. There are statements by important figures in the oil business, leading American Petroleum Institute members, John Ise, et al. The body of the hearings consists of questioning by the committee.

WARNER, C. A., *Texas Oil and Gas Since 1543* (Houston: Gulf Publishing Company, 1939). 487 pp.

This is the classic history of Texas oil. There is a general history and topical treatment of the following areas: East Texas, Gulf Coast, North Texas, Panhandle, Southwest Texas, and West Texas. There is also a serviceable selective bibliography. Warner has followed his account with two additional articles in the *Southwestern Historical Quarterly*, July 1946 and January 1958. A Houstonian, the author is a trustee for the Texas Gulf Coast Historical Association.

WATKINS, MYRON W., *Oil: Stabilization or Conservation?* (New York: Harper, 1937). 269 pp.

Watkins' book is one of the leading economic studies of the problem of control in the petroleum industry. The author examines the aspects of control from all angles, with particular attention to the New Deal's attempts through NRA codes. As of 1937, Watkins thought the problem was still unsolved; the petroleum industry was still calling the tune. Two major groups, labor and the consumer, were outside the realm of those planning policy concerning the control of oil.

WEBER, DICKINSON, *A Comparison of Two Oil City Business Centers (Odessa-Midland, Texas)* (Chicago: University of Chicago Press, 1958). 239 pp.
While analyzing these cities of the Permian basin from the standpoint of urban geography, this monograph furnishes useful collateral historical data. The book, which is the University of Chicago Department of Geography *Research Paper No. 60*, deals with the way oil has determined the development of these cities.

WILSON, CHARLES M., *Oil Across the World*
(New York: Longmans, Green and Co., 1946). 318 pp.
Although this story of pipelines is primarily concerned with oil transportation, it does not limit itself to that commodity. The book fills a gap in the history of one of the major areas of the petroleum industry. The discussion of the use of pipelines during World War II is particularly good. The Big and Little Inches, originating in Texas, are covered in ample detail. This story of pipelines is not limited to America, but stretches across the world, as the title indicates.

WOLBERT, GEORGES, *American Pipe Lines*
(Norman: University of Oklahoma Press, 1952). 179 pp.
This is an economic study of pipeline organization with a brief historical background. Texas pipelines are awarded appropriate consideration.

ZIMMERMANN, ERICH W., *Conservation in the Production of Petroleum, A Study in Industrial Control* (New Haven: Yale University Press, 1957). 417 pp.
With this exemplary monograph, the late Professor Zimmermann, the University of Texas' distinguished authority on world resources, offers a most comprehensive and objective statement on the subject of conservation in the petroleum industry. The author develops his subject with rare skill, taking pains to set conservation in its proper historical perspective.

Although this book was made possible by a grant from the American Petroleum Institute, it appears to be free of any pro-industry bias. Indeed, Zimmermann has achieved a high degree of scholarly impartiality. He concludes that conservation has been in the best interests of American society because it has reduced waste, enlarged reserves, and contributed to price stability. Of course, the industry has profited from conservation, but not unduly. The author points out that between 1938 and 1953 leaders of the petroleum industry earned 12.9 per cent on net worth—"almost exactly the same rate as the average earnings for manufacturing or trading corporations." (p. 199)

A real contribution of this work is its analysis of traditional arguments against conservation. The author explains the positions of such economists as Watkins and Stocking, and then exposes what he considers their defects. Another strength of the volume is that the writer makes manifest that his judgments, as must be those of any scholar, are largely personal and subjective. The fact that these judgments are supported by an impressive array of facts, presented with extraordinary literary ability, gives the student ample basis for confidence in the integrity of this work.

Oilfield at Gladewater in East Texas during the 1930s.
Courtesy of DeGolyer Library, Southern Methodist University

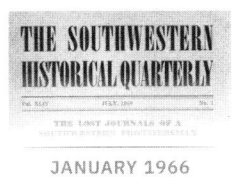

JANUARY 1966

Chaos in the East Texas Oil Field, 1930-1935

ROBERT D. BOYLE

THE MANY-FACETED STORY of oil in Texas has been told well by the scholarly Carl Coke Rister, the late Boyce House, the irrepressible George Sessions Perry, the dignified Fritz Lanham, and many others. But in a field so large, there is still room to add a few sidelights and human interest stories of "might have beens" and skullduggery connected with the East Texas Joiner discovery and its consequences.

The Joiner Test Number 3 spudded in in early October 1930 at Henderson,[1] with some estimates placing its production as high as 10,000 barrels per day, and "All hell broke loose in East Texas." Persons from all sections rushed to the new field. There was brisk trading in leases and royalties. Properties that could have been bought for ten dollars an acre a short time before, sold for eight hundred to one thousand dollars per acre.[2] Drilling went on at a dizzy pace, and within a few months a forest of derricks had risen around the Joiner discovery well.

While a man might not have oil under his own land, at least he well might feel secure in the ownership of the property. But was he? The era of lawsuits and cloudy titles began. Stories concerning them are varied and numerous. For instance, an elderly woman had 700 acres of good farmland in an area floating on oil. Lawyers came representing an unknown client. It seemed that back in the late 1880's her half-brother, while camping out on a fishing trip with some friends, engaged in horseplay with one of them over the possession of a gun. There had been some drinking and the play developed into a real battle in which the halfbrother gave the friend quite a beating. Still enraged the next day, the friend went to town and before a judge demanded that a "peace bond" be put on the half-brother to ensure his keeping the peace in the future. A portion of the 700 acres was put up to guarantee the keeping of the peace. The bond had never been cancelled and, therefore, said the plaintiffs, the title was cloudy. With the half-brother long dead, however, the woman's son-in-law explained the whole story to the county attorney, who simply went to the courthouse and wrote "Cancelled" across the peace bond, which saved the case from even going to court.[3]

A man whose farm, owned since 1905, was also well situated in the new oilfield, was approached by the agent of an oil company who paid him a dollar an acre for a lease. The company's legal department, however, in tracing title could find no record of the man's ownership of the farm in the county records. The worried owner hastily reminded the county clerk (who had been in office for almost a lifetime) that way back in 1905 the deed to the then newly purchased farm had been presented for recording. The old clerk replied that if the owner said it was so then it must be, but that he had absolutely no recollection of it. A search was begun at once, but no deed was discovered. The landowner then traveled to West Texas, where the former owners of the farm lived. "Yes," said the man and his wife, "we sold you the property and gave you the deed, but we distinctly remember reserving all the mineral rights." The landowner was shocked and even more confused, for he had no recollection of any mineral rights being reserved by the former owners. "Who drew up the deed?" asked the county clerk after the owner returned to East Texas.

Judge J. M. Campbell had drawn it, and he recalled that "I wrote it out in long-hand, and I don't remember anything about mineral rights in it." Everyone knew Judge Campbell's left-handed writing, but still the deed remained lost. "I've looked everywhere," said the old county clerk, "and I can't find it."

The night before the case came to trial, with the former owners claiming mineral rights, the county clerk sat before his old roll-top desk making a final search for his friend's deed. He went through every cubby-hole time and again. Finally, about two o'clock in the morning, he said to someone who was helping him, "Help me move this desk." As the desk was moved from the wall there was a faint "plop." It was the deed, containing no reference to any reservation of mineral rights.[4]

No stone was left unturned by men who wanted to make a dollar in any way. Often, however, any loss sustained was because of naivete or downright carelessness on the part of the owners themselves. Major companies eager to obtain leases began bonus payments. An old farmer was offered a half-million-dollar bonus if he would lease his substantial acreage to a major company. Naturally, he agreed. Then the agent, as if by second thought, appealed to the old man's sense of generosity and cooperation. He said, "You would not want us to drill and find no oil and lose a half a million dollars, would you?" "Why of course not," said the farmer. "Well then," said the agent, "suppose I pay you five thousand dollars to run a test, and if we find oil you'll get your half million anyway." The old man agreed, and he got his five thousand dollars; but the test was a dry hole, and he lost his half million.[5]

Then there was Uncle Joe B. of Gladewater whose forgetfulness years before cost him wealth later on. In 1918, he had sold 200 acres of land that his father had left him and forgot to reserve the mineral rights. Twelve years later, the man to whom he had sold the property was receiving up to $30,000 a year from royalties on that 200 acres, while Uncle Joe operated a barber shop. As trade increased, he was able to buy land in town on which he built about fourteen small homes, which he leased. During the height of the Gladewater boom, his net income was about $500 per month. Taxes were low, and he experienced mild prosperity. But taxes increased. So did the seepage of water into the western end of the great East Texas field. Business died off. Oil workers moved out. Gladewater in the height of the excitement had failed to attract major industry. Uncle Joe found times harder. He opened up a cabinet and carpenter shop, illustrating that the touted inventive New England mind has nothing on East Texas for ingenuity when the chips are down. For a while he did well making outdoor swings and benches for townspeople; but eventually air conditioning changed that. Persons do not sit outside much anymore. Uncle Joe fell on hard times. An old real estate friend, however, remembered that the deed conveying the 200 acres in 1918 had read "200 acres more or less." He ran a survey, then said, "Uncle Joe there's a few acres around that corner that belong to you. It's yours. No doubt about it." Uncle Joe, being a thoughtful man, called on the one who had purchased his 200 acres in 1918 and told him about the extra acreage. "It's all yours Uncle Joe. I won't claim it. I've had plenty out of that acreage I bought from you." So, Uncle Joe found himself the owner of a plot big enough for a well. Oil came in, and he received $180 monthly until prorationing cut the allowable to eight days. In 1961, he received $65 in his monthly check. His wife was ill; taxes were higher on the small houses he built; rents were lower, and many were vacant. He said a lot he sold some years ago for $1,500 would not bring $50. Uncle Joe, in his eighties, sat on the porch of his little workshop off the main street. Once in a while, someone came around and placed an order, but not often.[6]

All that glitters is not gold. Likewise, all is not wealth and prosperity even in an oilfield boom. Jack Cannon was a roofer and metal man in Shreveport, Louisiana, who heard of the big activity in East Texas. He borrowed a hundred dollars from his father and left for Longview early in 1931 with a partner who had a few hundred dollars. On their first trip, they looked for a place to work and a place to live. The only thing that looked usable from any standpoint was an old blacksmith shop about sixty feet by sixty feet in an alley half a block from the main street of Longview. The blacksmith ignored their pleas to rent half of his space. Everything in town was jammed, and they had to return to Shreveport. The following week they returned and all day fared no better. Just before leaving for Shreveport at the end of the day, they decided to make one more try at the blacksmith shop. Fortune favored them. The landlord had just raised the blacksmith's rent from $13 a month to $35. When they sought space, the old man took a stick and drew a line on the dirt floor about thirty-five feet in from the open doorway. "You can have it for $35 a month," he said. So they moved in. The dirt-floored blackmith shop was their office, workshop, and home. In addition to Cannon and his partner, there was a work crew of six men. They bought iron beds and mattresses and set them against the walls. They attached pulleys to the beams overhead, and when they got up in the mornings, they would hoist the beds up to the ceiling to have room to work. At night, after letting the beds down, they would brush away the day's accumulation of soot from the forge. Cannon and his crew lived that way for two months. Then a woman who ran a boarding house with three bedrooms told them one room was vacant, with a double bed in each corner. Into that paradise they moved. In one of the other two rooms there were eight barbers; in the other, eight electricians.

Meanwhile, the landlord again raised the blacksmith's rent, that time to $60. He moved out, and Cannon occupied the whole space. His memories include working from dawn to midnight to finish a roof under a string of lights; making all-purpose sinks out of washtubs and rubber hose; a maid whom Cannon and his wife drove to Shreveport for a holiday, only to find she had returned and robbed their apartment in their absence; the noise; the grime; the eternal restlessness; and the humor of it over all. Across the alley from their first quarters in the smithy, contractor Lawrence Birdsong was erecting a two-story building. At night, a Negro with a mule on the end of a hoist lifted materials up to the second story. Just as the roofing crew dozed off in that exquisite first sleep, there would begin: "Get up; whoa; back up," all night long. They kept their clothes on a table moved into the center of the bed space at night. One night, Cannon awoke to find a big Negro casually sorting out the trousers to see which pair suited him best. With a yell, Jack jumped out of bed and chased the man down the alley. He said later that he did not know what he would have done if he had caught him. Returning from the chase, he found Jack Cook, a visitor from Dallas, frantically yelling, "He's got them! He's got them." The Negro had grabbed Cook's only pair of pants. Then there was the crosseyed cook at the boarding house who took orders for eggs twice each meal, once before cooking and once before delivery. She would look one way and point the other amidst wild hilarity.

Man's humanity to man also wove its way into the daily life. An independent driller named Snyder borrowed money from Cannon and brought in a dry hole. He tried again with the same luck. Finally, they went along with him a third time when he drilled at Hawkins. Failing a third time, Snyder gave Cannon's outfit the leases he had obtained. Feeling sure that there was no oil there, Cannon and his partner failed to renew the leases when they came due. They first learned of their mistake when an agent offered them $50,000 for one of those leases. Snyder had drilled only one thousand feet from the real strike at Hawkins.[7]

The other side of human nature was also present. Petty thievery was rampant. All kinds of individuals had come to East Texas from all parts of the country looking for work. A hundred or more slept on the courthouse lawn at Longview every night. Landlords renting rooms to boarders, who had free entry, would awake to find gold watches, rings, and other treasures missing. While they and the roomers slept, outsiders taking advantage of the general confusion would loot. Many sought amusement and relaxation in the nightlife along Highway 80 between Longview and Gladewater. Night spots were varied along a strip, in some respects as exciting as the "strip" in Las Vegas. They were: "The Barn," "The Salty Dog," "The Spotted Puppy," "The Red Rooster," "Texas Bud's," "The Black Cat," "Mamy's Kitchen," and " Mattie's Place." Food was cheap;

entertainment was varied, and the dance halls, taverns, and beer palaces thrived on the crowds. Through it all, a man tried to make a five-cent bag of tobacco last all week.[8]

The law, and the great principles it reflects, was in East Texas also, after a fashion, and with it, its representatives, the lawyers. There were women lawyers too, and women "lease-hounds." Many lawyers got rich.[9] After Joiner's Henderson well in Rusk County had come in in October 1930, the Bateman-Crim well was drilled in Kilgore on Christmas Day. The third well was in an eight-thousand-acre block many miles north of Joiner's, and many wondered if oil were there. In fact the drillers, a Fort Worth group, ran out of money at three thousand feet and propositioned the Arkansas Fuel Oil Company to see if it would pay past due bills and advance money for continued drilling in return for half interest in the eight thousand acres. The Arkansas Company did so, and in January 1931 the well, known as Lathrop Number 1, was brought in. The whole block turned out to be a producing area, and the Fort Worth group sold their interest, 4,000 acres, to the Yount Lee Company for three million dollars. Seventeen years later, Yount Lee in turn sold out its holdings to Stanolind Oil and Gas Company for $49,000,000, of which the Lathrop Block was a major portion. Lawyers were involved, of course, in the searching of titles and in preparation of all paperwork in these and other transactions.[10]

Not all investors were fortunate. A Shreveport man, reported to be sharp and known to be broke, leased two tracts in 1930, one of forty acres, situated thirty miles from the Joiner well, and the other of eighty acres less than two miles away. He paid the owners a dollar an acre for the leases. Of course, when the Joiner well came in in October, lease prices skyrocketed, and he sold the forty-acre lease and kept the eighty-acre one. In time, the eighty-acre tract proved dry, while the forty-acre leasehold, which he had sold, produced oil.

An interesting case involving East Texas land concerned old General T. M. Griffin of Mississippi. Before he died in 1885, the general had dictated his will, leaving 500 acres of land in Kilgore to his nephew T. M. Griffin for life and then to T. M.'s heirs and, if none, to his heirs-at-law. The nephew later sold part of the Kilgore property in 1905. A suit involving ownership in the early 1930's brought in what was known as "the Rule in Shelley's Case," which had been in effect for five hundred years, in a case involving the construction of a deed where life ownership and fee ownership were in question. Because of the peculiar language of the will, which clouded the meaning of the case, the Texas Supreme Court applied "the Rule in Shelley's Case" and found for T. M. Griffin, the nephew who took the fee simple title and not a mere a life estate.[11]

Before the discovery of oil in East Texas, land was selling at about a dollar an acre, and even at that price a farmer found it hard to make a living. With land cheap, persons bothered little about registering titles. Often deeds were prepared by notaries and brokers to save lawyers fees, and thus a fertile field for errors was created that could and often did affect the validity of titles later. In general, land was cut up into small farms, some of them with considerable timber. Many owners found it easy to sell land on credit at a price far above the cash market price, taking a vendor's lien for the full sale price, which in some instances is known to have run as high as ten dollars per acre, with interest on the lien often as high as ten per cent. Because of the high lien and the high interest rate, it often happened that the purchaser had little possibility of paying. In order to avoid eventual litigation and expense, the owner might sometimes try to have the new purchaser deed the property back to him at the time of the sale, with the understanding that if, after a lapse of time, the new purchaser had not paid his interest and taxes, then the old owner would simply file the deed and become owner of record again. Many Negroes as well as whites were involved in that type of sale. When oil was discovered, major company agents as well as independent operators would approach the occupant of a farm, inquire if he was the owner of record, and obtain a lease from him. Then if oil was discovered on the particular farm, the occupant would start collecting royalties and in some instances would pay off back taxes and interest and stand in the clear. Sometimes an unscrupulous former owner, as soon as oil came in and royalties started, would file the deed which the new purchaser had given back to him or start suit before old taxes and interest were paid. Sometimes in cases where the new owner had failed to file the original deed given him, an unscrupulous owner would claim that there never had been a deed. It should be said in justice, however, that an all-white jury more often than not would find for an honest, hard-working Negro.[12]

One of the most far-reaching cases at law involving hundreds of East Texas investors was that of the Virginia Oil and Refining Company. Gaines B. Turner, formerly of East Texas, had gone to the Ranger field in 1917 and had created the Virginia company. Turner came back to Longview, having sold three and a half million shares of stock in the Virginia Oil and Refining Company to investors all over the United States, and began taking leases on East Texas property at $2.00 per acre for stock instead of cash as payment. Before the East Texas field had come in, however, the Virginia Oil and Refining Company had gone into bankruptcy, and in the bankruptcy the trustee was unable to sell any of the leases which the Virginia company had obtained in East Texas. The usual type of lease required the payment of rentals of a dollar per acre each year. As usual, no one paid any attention to reading the details of the leases, and the Virginia Oil and Refining Company was forgotten until new activity in East Texas led those who wanted to lease these tracts to discover that the leases contained a clause showing them to have been paid up for twenty years. Then Turner came to life again and asked to be appointed receiver by the state courts because of the existence of unadministered assets, and the old creditors filed suit in the federal courts to reopen the bankruptcy proceedings for the same reason. The courts, however, reopened the bankruptcy, whereupon the old creditors and the stockholders as well, filed claims. At the trustee's sale, only the major companies could buy up the leases, which by then had a value of around $10,000 per acre. The creditors were paid about double on their claims and the old stockholders got a few dollars per share for their former holdings which had been considered worthless. Also, Dr. Fred A. Cook, of polar fame, owner of the Puritan Oil Company, had obtained the "sucker list" of the old Virginia Oil and Refining Company and attempted unsuccessfully to get in on the "kill." His manipulations added to the vast amount of litigation and confusion.[13]

One of the leading cases in administrative law in East Texas goes back to the days of the National Recovery Act and may be said to foreshadow the decease of that agency. The National Recovery Act required codes in all industries, and oil was no exception. A Petroleum Code was drawn up in Washington to eliminate chaotic conditions in the oilfields and to see that production was kept in line with state allowables. Employees of Chairman Joseph Ryan of the Petroleum Code Commission jailed the officers of the Amazon Petroleum Company for running hot oil. The case, known as Ryan vs. Amazon Petroleum Company, reached the United States Supreme Court. The attorneys for Amazon contended that the Petroleum Code Commission had taken it upon itself to legislate, by making it a federal crime to violate a state law. This was the first case to reach the Supreme Court testing the rulemaking power of the federal agencies established under the NRA codes. The Amazon attorneys attacked the conviction from two angles. J. N. Saye presented the argument that the principle involved was the unauthorized delegation by the United States Congress of legislative power to federal agencies. Attorney "Big" Fisher attacked from the more practical angle that his client, Amazon, was arrested on the charge of violating a law of which the client was unaware.

At that point, Justice Louis D. Brandeis asked Fisher how he himself had become aware of the law, to which Fisher is supposed to have replied in substance: "Your honor, the only place that law existed was in the hip-pocket of the Federal Commissioner!" Thus is supposed to have originated the expression "trial by hippocket law." The United States Supreme Court found for the Amazon Petroleum Company, and that decision began to toll the death-knell of the National Recovery Act by knocking out the Petroleum Code.

Another factor in the development of the East Texas Oil Field was "hot oil." The term is broad. After the first hundred Texas wells had been brought in, the Texas Railroad Commission set a limit on production which might apply to any field, because already wells were being drilled at a prolific rate, with many bringing in as much as a thousand barrels an hour. When no one had paid any attention to the order, Governor Ross Sterling declared martial law, called out the National Guard, and placed at least one soldier at each well to watch the oil flow. That action led to much ingenuity on the part of producers, who might run by-pass pipes to storage tanks located far from the well itself. One man built a wolf-proof fence around his well and kept everyone out, including state officials, so that he could neither be served with a summons nor have his well inspected. Eventually he was served, but meanwhile he had been able to pump much extra oil. Another producer built a house around his well and claimed that a man's home was his castle and therefore inviolate. He likewise gained time to draw added oil out of his well.[15]

The purpose of proration was, of course, to prevent waste, but the railroad commission could not always prove that what it called overproduction was actually waste—a condition precedent to any action it might take. Eventually, the Texas legislature passed a law by which "waste" or "overproduction" was to be determined by the railroad commission on the basis of market demand. That is the present Texas system. For instance, in setting a nineday-per-month allowable, the Texas Railroad Commission is permitted to obtain from the Federal Bureau of Mines the estimated national oil requirement for a particular period. That figure, then broken down into states, and applied mathematically by the Texas Railroad Commission to the number of wells in the State of Texas, enables the commission to determine the allowable for the month. This description is, of course, an oversimplification, but it does suggest the present method.[16]

Still another aspect of the railroad commission's actions producing litigation is Rule Number 37 of the commission's oil and gas regulations. To drill a well, the driller must obtain a state permit. In the case of a wildcat or big block area such a permit may be easily obtained by almost anyone. But when a field has already been developed, the problem of waste is important. Therefore, the commission set up Rule Number 37, which provided that in an established field only one well could be drilled for every twenty acres. The rule was formulated quite early in Texas oil history, but the number of acres per well varied in the different oil and gas fields. Still, one may drive through the Kilgore field and find wells almost overlapping one another because of exceptions granted to prevent confiscation or waste. For instance, if one had purchased a lot, even a lot small enough to build a home on, and it could be shown that the lot had been purchased before 1918 and had been separated from a larger tract at the time of purchase, then that was automatically an exception, because one could claim that he was drilling in order to prevent his own property from being drained. Thus, in the whole East Texas field, which at its greatest extent contained approximately 25,000 wells, about two-thirds of those wells were exceptions at the time of drilling. Each time an exception was granted by the railroad commission, the adjoining owners would generally file suits of protest; but the practice of granting exceptions was based on an early Pennsylvania case which declared that oil was fugitive and subject to capture.[17]

A recent Gulf Coast case, the Normanna Case, decided by the Texas Supreme Court in the spring of 1961, however, upset the tranquility of the small-plot drillers. Specifically, the owner of a 3/10-acre tract in a large gas field, where the ratio had been set by the railroad commission at one well to every 320 acres, drilled a well on his small plot. That, of course, tapped the whole field, which had already been discovered and was being developed. An owner of a large tract in the field sued, and the allowable production based 1/3 on acreage and 2/3 on the wells in the field was not granted by the courts. Thus a new formula was established, namely, that proration by the Texas Railroad Commission was to be made on the basis of the amount of acreage owned. That formula, established by the Normanna Case, was considered an attempt to prevent another Kilgore.

The Normanna Case, however, is still subject to further examination by the courts.[18]

Finally, a glimpse at the "behind-the-scenes" office work during the East Texas boom days is quite revealing. The secretary in the Rusk County Clerk's office was a good hard worker who felt responsible for all the work herself. She kept the books on all the land transactions and, in recording a deed, she left a little space for the field notes to be filled in later. As the boom developed and the field notes grew bulkier, the secretary typed the overflow on a piece of onionskin paper and pasted it over the old notes. As the rush grew worse, she typed new information over the old notes already entered. Eventually, it took a crew of clerks two solid months from eight in the morning until eleven at night to straighten out the chaos.[19] Yet East Texas is presently so peaceful, it is hard to imagine the chaos of the oil boom only thirty years ago.

Natural gas flare in Texas.
Courtesy of Texas Railroad Commission

JANUARY 1981

The Texas Railroad Commission and the Elimination of the Flaring of Natural Gas, 1930-1949

DAVID F. PRINDLE

FROM THE 1930s to the 1970s, the Railroad Commission of Texas was one of the most important regulatory bodies in the United States. Its decisions determined how many oil and gas wells could be drilled, where they might be located, and the quantity of petroleum that they might produce. By regulating the drilling, operation, and plugging of wells, and the transportation and storage of both oil and gas, it protected the ecological environment of Texas and the safety and health of the state's citizens. By suppressing ("prorating") the rate of production of the state's oil, it placed a floor under the price of that commodity. Because Texas looms so large in the nation's domestic petroleum picture, the Railroad Commission's control over the oil and gas industry within the state's boundaries had a decisive effect on that industry in the rest of the country, and, as a consequence, on the supply and price of petroleum to consumers in every other state.[1]

One of the most animated and important episodes in the history of the Commission involved its successful attempt, in the 1930s and 1940s, to prevent the destruction of the state's natural gas reserves. An account of this episode illustrates both the historical importance of the Commission, and the interaction of technology, economics, and politics in twentieth-century Texas history.

From the earliest days of oil production, the industry had problems with natural gas. The difficulties all rested, at bottom, on a fact that seems incredible to our gas-hungry age: the stuff was practically worthless. Unlike oil, which can be temporarily stored and easily transported, gas is a difficult substance to handle. It is hard to store and transport, dissipates quickly, and is likely to ignite and explode.[2] Moreover, although both oil and gas can be used for heating, gas is useless as a lubricant and auto fuel.

Because of these problems, there was in the 1930s very little market for natural gas. The lack of a market made the monetary value of gas quite low by today's standards. In 1930, when oil sold for almost a dollar a barrel, the price of natural gas was 3.6 cents for a thousand cubic feet ("MCF"). At a heat equivalency of six MCF of gas to one barrel of oil, this meant that oil was five times more valuable than gas in terms of its available energy.[3]

As a result, gas fields were not then considered by most citizens to be the great natural resources that they would be today. When Amarillo, situated near an ocean of gas in the Panhandle, spent $60,000 advertising its abundance nationally, it found not a single buyer. The city administration then offered free gas for five years to any industry that would move to Amarillo and employ fifty or more people but still found no takers.[4] This example illustrates the situation of the petroleum industry in general for its first eighty years. Most producers regarded oil as the only hydrocarbon worth searching for.

For the leaseholder who owned a well over the 70 percent or so of natural gas that occurs "unassociated" with oil, the low price was at worst an annoyance. In the early days of the industry, discovery wells in gas fields were often simply capped and forgotten.[5]

There were, however, a few uses for gas. A small number of industrial concerns burned it for boiler fuel, and a few cities (such as Amarillo) used gas in public utilities. Gas could be burned to produce the "carbon black" that was employed by the rubber industry, and, as the 1930s progressed, some companies learned to use it to make other chemicals.[6] During the 1930s, however, the major conservation problem caused by the exploitation of unassociated gas arose from the fact that it was used to produce a liquid known as "condensate" gasoline.

When natural gas is allowed to expand suddenly, as it does when let out of a well-bore, somewhat less than 10 percent of its contents will condense into a liquid almost indistinguishable from refined gasoline. This process is called "stripping" gas. Condensate gasoline could be used like the refined variety to power automobiles. Companies could make a profit by setting up over a gas field, marketing the stripped condensate, and simply releasing ("venting") the nine-tenths remainder into the atmosphere.[7]

As it was soon discovered that natural gas in the air poses a deadly hazard, producers began to run it up pipes and burn it at the top. The flames from these pipes are known as "flares." The practice of retrieving the 10 percent of stripped condensate and flaring the rest became the object of a legal and political struggle in Texas that lasted for the first five years of the 1930s.[8]

Stripping and flaring of unassociated gas clearly presents a waste of natural resources. For a second type of gas production, however, the conservation problem is more complex. This type of production involves what is known as "casinghead gas."

While gas may be found without oil, the reverse is not true. Oil-bearing rock formations often contain a "gas-cap" at the top, and oil in underground reservoirs always contains dissolved gas. When the oil is extracted, the dissolved gas is an inevitable by-product. There is no known method of producing oil without simultaneously bringing up large quantities of gas. About 30 percent of the gas that is produced is of this "associated" type.[9]

Within the well, the petroleum travels to the surface inside a metal tubing. The tubing is held in another set of pipes called the "casing." At the top of the well, a metal device called the "casinghead" connects the casing and the tubing. When oil arrives at the mouth of the well, the associated gas dissolved in it escapes into the casing and out of the casinghead. It is therefore called "casinghead gas."[10]

For the casinghead gas that was extracted with oil in the 1930s, the prospects for productive employment were even less than for unassociated gas. Its rate of production could not be controlled, for it was an inescapable by-product of oil extraction. Because its supply was dependent on the demand for oil, it was unattractive to industrial customers, who preferred to contract for a steady, predictable supply of unassociated gas. The market, which was weak for unassociated gas, was thus practically nonexistent for casinghead gas. To put it back into the ground was expensive. As a result, casinghead gas was almost invariably flared.[11]

The combination of low gas prices, the technology of condensation, and the uncontrollable nature of casinghead gas production caused a waste that staggers today's imagination. There are no reliable figures on the total volume of gas dissipation in the industry's first seven decades after 1859, but it must have amounted to dozens of trillions of cubic feet, as drillers in oilfield after oilfield vented or flared the entire accumulation of casinghead gas, and as stripping plants in unassociated gas fields utilized only a tiny proportion of the resource.[12]

The waste in the nation's petroleum fields in the 1930s and 1940s continued apace, especially in regard to casinghead gas. As Texas produced the most oil and gas, it was the scene of the greatest despoliation. According to many accounts, motorists could drive for hours at night in parts of the state in those years and never have to turn on their automobile lights, because the casinghead flares illuminated the countryside. Miles away from any major oilfield, newspapers could be read easily at night by the light of these flares.[13]

Historian Maurice Cheek estimated that in 1934 roughly a billion cubic feet of unassociated gas was stripped and flared daily in the Panhandle. Assuming that this total was matched by casinghead flares from oilfields then in production (especially East Texas), then roughly three-quarters of a trillion cubic feet were lost that year. The best estimate from the early 1940s is that one and a half billion cubic feet of casinghead gas was flared each day from Texas's larger fields; that would make the state total for all fields about two and a half billion a day, or over nine-tenths of a trillion a year. As the yearly consumption of natural gas in the entire United States was only about twenty trillion cubic feet a year in the mid-1970s, this means that a sizable proportion of the nation's potential energy supply vanished in a glow of prosperity in Texas in the two decades before 1949.[14]

The magnitude of this devastation was not lost on observers of the time. But, as might be expected, the effort to stop it was met with determined resistance from oil producers, who did not wish to lower their profits by spending money to preserve a substance that they considered valueless.[15]

The engineering staff of the Railroad Commission, however, joined by others of scientific training, argued that the waste of natural gas must stop. They made this argument for two reasons. First, they believed simply that gas flaring was an unforgivable destruction of natural resources. Second, they wanted to save casinghead gas in order to increase the state's recoverable oil reserves.[16]

In most reservoirs, the propulsive force that moves the oil to the wellbore is provided by gas pressure. The higher the pressure, and the longer it lasts, the more the oil that is ultimately recoverable. The faster the pressure is depleted, the smaller the proportion of the oil-inplace that can be brought to the surface, without using sophisticated (and expensive) recovery techniques.[17]

When a method of returning the gas to the producing rock formation ("pressure maintenance") was invented in the early 1930s, it meant that the life of oilfields could be greatly extended. But pressure maintenance was costly. Although in the long run it might quadruple the amount of oil extractable from a field, in the short run it cost producers money to no obvious advantage. Their perspectives dominated by short-run profit considerations, oil producers resisted suggestions that they should take the necessary steps to preserve gas pressure.[18]

As the agency charged with conserving the state's oil and gas resources, the Railroad Commission was at the center of the controversy over gas flaring. Throughout the 1930s and 1940s, the three commissioners and their engineering staff attempted to deal with the technological and political problems of gas conservation. This conflict placed the commissioners in a difficult political position. To have forced "uneconomical" conservation on the industry would have incited it to strong opposition. As politicians subject to electoral defeat, commissioners were not eager to provoke hostility from this, their basic constituency. Until 1947, consequently, the various commissioners treated the problem of gas gingerly. The Commission's engineers, however, worked for two decades to eliminate the waste of gas, and finally created a political momentum that succeeded in making the Commission move decisively to stop the flaring.[19]

In the 1930s, the Railroad Commission employed less than twenty engineers to oversee Texas's 75,000 wells in more than 500 fields. These men had many jobs relating to oil; in regard to gas, their chief task lay in trying to enforce the Commission's rules about "gas/oil ratios."[20]

In 1899, the state legislature had passed a comprehensive conservation law, later amended several times, in which the flaring of unassociated gas from a gas well was prohibited. In 1925 the legislature passed another law permitting the flaring of associated (casinghead) gas from an oil well. In theory, the Railroad Commission's task in enforcing these statutes was easy: it should prohibit the flaring of gas from gas wells but not from oil wells. In practice, however, the two laws created a regulatory nightmare. [21]

Even in a gas field, there may be traces of oil. Gas that is "unassociated" with oil in a practical sense may be "associated" with minute quantities in a literal sense. Furthermore, the amount of oil found in a "gas" field may vary widely, which must bring up the question: how much oil can be found in a well before that well stops being a "gas" well and becomes an "oil" well? With producers permitted to flare gas from one kind of well but not another, this technical problem of differentiating gas from oil wells became a political problem.

Moreover, gas expands, contracts, and changes its physical composition under differing pressures and temperatures; under some conditions, gas will change to a liquid, and vice-versa. These circumstances combine to create an uncertainty as to whether it is a "gas" or "oil" well that is under consideration. The task of regulating gas production is therefore subject to many technical ambiguities. Producers attempted to use these ambiguities to evade Commission regulations.

The statutory definition of a "gas well" was one that produced 100,000 or more cubic feet of gas for every barrel of oil. If the ratio was less than 100,000 to one, the well was classified as "oil," the gas was "casinghead," and could be flared. If the ratio was higher, the well was classified as "gas," and its product could not be flared. It was thus in the interest of operators who owned wells that produced both gas and oil to have as many of them as possible classified as "oil," producing at less than a 100,000-to-one ratio, so that they could flare unmolested. They played cat-and-mouse with the Commission's undermanned inspection staff to attain that goal.[22]

One of the critical junctures in this struggle occurred in 1934. A number of the fields of the time produced large quantities of a clear petroleum liquid known as "water-white oil," along with conventional oil and gas. Their operators treated this liquid as though it were oil. By doing so, they made the gas/oil ratios of their wells 40,000 or 50,000 to one, thereby causing them to be categorized as "oil" wells. This permitted the operators to flare a large amount of gas after they had retrieved a small amount of oil. If the water-white oil were to be classified as "gas," however, the ratio of the wells in question would rise above 100,000-to-one, the wells would be reclassified as "gas," and the flaring could be halted. The Railroad Commission hired Dr. Eugene P. Schoch, a chemist at the University of Texas, to investigate this waterwhite oil.[23]

Schoch instructed one of his students, Jack K. Baumel—later to be chief engineer for the Commission—to take samples of water-white oil from the Agua Dulce field near Corpus Christi. Back at the University of Texas laboratory, Schoch and Baumel put this liquid into a "highpressure separator," which allowed them to recreate reservoir conditions by raising the temperature to 247 degrees and the pressure to 3,700 pounds per square inch. When they did this, the water-white oil turned into a gas. The substance had been gas in the reservoir but had turned into liquid upon reaching the surface.[24]

With this evidence, the Commission's engineering staff recommended that hundreds of "oil" wells be reclassified as "gas" and ordered to stop flaring. The operators naturally objected to this order, but in a series of judicial opinions known collectively as "the Clymore case," the Texas courts backed the Commission to the hilt.[25]

Now the operators were in difficult circumstances, for they had to find something to do with the gas produced with the oil or shut in their wells. The Commission engineers suggested to them that they could both keep their oil wells flowing, and make further revenues from gas, by making use of a process called "cycling."

The Schoch-Baumel experiments had demonstrated that the gas in many fields like Agua Dulce was rich in condensable liquids. Why not, suggested the engineers, collect the ("wet") gas on the surface, extract the liquids, return the remainder of the gas (now "dry") to the reservoir, where its added pressure could aid in the production of more oil and wet gas, and so on? The condensate from the gas could be marketed, as could, of course, the oil.[26]

If they wanted to continue production, the operators had no choice but to begin cycling. The first commercial cycling plant began operating in the Cayuga field of Northeast Texas in March 1938. To everyone's relief, it proved profitable. By 1942 there were over twenty-nine cycling plants in Texas, processing over forty-four billion cubic feet of gas a year.[27] By losing a technical battle to the Railroad Commission, petroleum producers had improved their economic position.

One of the conflicts over gas flaring thus ended happily for all concerned. With superior technical imagination and a determination to take the long view, the Railroad Commission had finessed one of the problems of gas conservation. Other struggles, however, were more complicated.

One of the more difficult challenges concerned the flaring of unassociated gas in the enormous Panhandle field. One hundred twentyfive miles in length and an average of twenty-five miles wide, when discovered in 1918 it is estimated to have contained between fifteen and twenty-five trillion cubic feet of natural gas. Beginning in 1930, some operators began to attempt to acquire the right to strip and flare this gas. This desire brought them into conflict, however, with pipeline interests, who were simultaneously beginning to develop markets in northern cities. By 1933, there was a serious political struggle between strippers and pipeliners over the use of the Panhandle's resources. At the same time, the Texas public was becoming more conscious of conservation, largely due to the conflict over oil prorationing in the East Texas field that was occurring during the same years.[28] The fight between pipeline and stripping interests over gas, therefore, took on the mantle of an argument over the public interest, with the public at large and the Railroad Commission as interested spectators.

In 1933, under lobbying pressure from stripping interests, the legislature passed a law specifically permitting Panhandle operators to strip and flare gas under certain conditions. The same year, in the Canadian River case, a federal court placed severe restrictions on the Railroad Commission's authority to regulate gas. In combination, the 1933 law and court decision had the effect of repealing the 1899 conservation statute and freeing strippers from any restraints.[29]

The enormous volume of gas burned and vented under these conditions—over a billion cubic feet a day—caused both a public outcry and a lobbying campaign by pipeline companies to persuade the legislature to adopt a more satisfactory conservation policy. This effort succeeded in 1935 when House Bill 266 forbade the production of gas in any manner so as to cause underground waste (e.g. the stripping and flaring of unassociated gas). The Railroad Commission was empowered to enforce the act.[30]

Most portions of HB 266 were upheld in the courts, and the Commission swiftly put an end to stripping-and-flaring operations in the Panhandle and elsewhere.[31] Since 1935, therefore, there has been no problem in Texas with the destruction of unassociated gas reserves.

The waste of casinghead gas, however, increased during this period. Throughout the decade, the Texas industry continued to discover giant fields: Conroe in 1931, Tom O'Connor in 1934, Wasson in 1936, Levelland in 1938, Hawkins in 1940, and so on.[32] Every new field opened to development meant another great volume of casinghead gas doomed to vanish unproductively.

Without actually forbidding the flaring of such gas, commissioners of the late 1930s and early 1940s attempted to encourage its conservation. For example, they issued a statewide order establishing a permissible gas/oil ratio of 2,000 feet per barrel. If the flared gas amounted to more than 2,000 feet for every barrel of oil produced, the well was subject to having its oil allowable reduced.[33]

This and other Commission efforts at conservation were well-intended, but they made little impact on the problem of casinghead gas for two reasons.

First, the Commission had such a small staff that it could not enforce the order. In the case of oil regulation, there was an actual substance flowing in commerce, which could be monitored. In the case of gas, however, the substance in question was destroyed as soon as it was produced; there was no commerce to monitor. The only way to enforce the order was to keep testing the gas/oil ratios of many thousands of wells. The commissioners did not have anything like a staff adequate to this task, although they did what they could with the staff at their disposal.[34]

Second, even if there had been some means of ensuring that all oil wells were kept within the 2,000-to-one boundary, that would have eliminated only the most wasteful wells. The basic problem of the wanton flaring of "useless" gas was not touched by creating "acceptable" levels of destruction. Within the prescribed limit or not, the flared gas was gone forever. The only way to save this resource was to outlaw the flaring completely.

Fearing to provoke opposition from the industry, and reluctant to impose economic hardship on it, the commissioners of the 1930s and early '40s refused to take this step. They were happy to encourage conservation by approving schemes for repressuring fields with gas, but they would not consider compelling the industry to act responsibly. It would take the elevation of a petroleum engineer to the Commission to change this attitude.[35]

The engineer fated to play the role of effective conservationist was William J. Murray. Graduating with many honors from the University of Texas in 1936, he was employed for two years in private industry, then hired by the Railroad Commission. In 1939 he took a crew to South and West Texas, testing gas/oil ratios for the Commission. In the course of observing thousands of wells, and testing several hundred, he became appalled at the tremendous volume of gas that was being lost through casinghead flares. Most of this flared gas did not show up on Commission reports, for the operators were lax about keeping records, and the Commission did not have the staff to police them effectively. There was little that Murray could do to stop the waste, since most of the ratios were within the acceptable limit, but he nevertheless resolved to do something about it in the unlikely event that he ever got the chance.[36]

Murray worked for the Commission another two years, then left and was employed by the Federal Petroleum Administration for War until 1943. He then resigned and returned to Texas, where he again went to work for private industry.[37]

During this period, events were pushing Texans into a confrontation with the federal government. Some federal officials were concerned that the waste of casinghead gas in Texas was damaging potential oil recovery. Additionally, for several years some members of the Federal Power Commission had been contemplating an attempt to extend federal regulatory authority over the gas industry; the evident waste in Texas provided them with an excuse to move in that direction.[38]

Sitting on the Railroad Commission in the mid-1940s were Ernest O. Thompson, Olin W. Culberson, and Beauford H. Jester, all of them vociferous advocates of states' rights. They attempted to forestall federal meddling in Texas conservation policy by convincing the FPC that the state had the gas problem under control.[39]

In December of 1944, the Commission scheduled a special hearing to discuss the gas-flare problem, among other topics. The official figures showed that over four hundred billion cubic feet of casinghead gas had been produced in the state in 1943, of which only 3,690,787,000 cubic feet, or less than 1 percent, had been flared. Ernest Thompson argued that this volume was reasonable and posed no threat to conservation. But William Murray, attending the hearing as a private citizen, stood up and stated that he knew from personal experience that the received figures were gross underestimations, that from ten to twenty-five times the official estimates were being lost, and that this was indeed a serious conservation problem.[40]

This accusation drew some press coverage and embarrassed the commissioners.[41] Gas flaring is the sort of dramatic issue that is "news," for the unproductive burning of a natural resource is easily understood by a mass audience. In addition, of course, to refuse to take Murray's charges seriously would have looked bad in Washington. So, the Commission was forced to make at least symbolic gestures to solve the problem.

The commissioners appointed an industry-wide committee to "look into" the flaring problem, and asked Murray to chair it. But since Murray knew that some of the worst offenders were on the committee, he declined and asked instead to chair a smaller group, composed only of engineers, that would report to the larger body.[42]

The "Murray Committee Report," released in November of 1945, pulled no punches and caused a furor in the industry. Many of the most important members of the state oil industry— which included, of course, some of the most prominent citizens of Texas—were seen to be contributing to a waste of casinghead gas of almost a billion and a half cubic feet a day, or 57 percent of the state's total production.[43]

The big producers complained vigorously in private about this engineers' committee to their friends on the Commission. Publicly, they argued that an order to stop flaring the gas would ruin them. But because of the publicity created by the report, it would have been dangerous for the commissioners to ignore it. Instead, they stalled.[44]

Meanwhile, some members of the industry were awakening to the magnitude of the problem. The Murray Committee report, by compiling accurate figures on the volume of lost gas, forced the industry to confront its own profligacy, and those producers who were more farseeing became convinced that this resource must be conserved. In particular, Dan Moran, president of the Continental Oil Company and an active member of the industry committee, concluded that the flaring had to be stopped. Moran vigorously supported Murray and his fellow engineers within the industry.[45]

While the struggle over flaring was taking place, the petroleum industry was evolving in a direction that favored the conservationists. During the war, technical advances had been made in the process of cycling, and it became more feasible to employ that process with casinghead gas. Also during the war, the Big Inch and Little Inch oil pipelines had been built from Texas to the Northeast, to avoid the attacks of German submarines on tankers. With the war over and oil moving again by sea, the pipelines were capable of carrying gas, and people in the industry were discovering that they could sell it, once they had the means to move it. Finally, the war had given a great boost to the petrochemical industry, to which natural gas was becoming important.[46]

As a result of all these changes, the price of natural gas began to rise. Through the 1930s, the price had deteriorated, so that in 1940 it was only 1.8 cents per MCF. By 1947, however, it had more than doubled to 3.7 cents.[47] This was not enough to make gas conservation profitable for most operators, but it did tend to forestall panic in the industry at the thought of having to eliminate flaring.

Moreover, federal control threatened to overtake the industry if something was not done about the gas situation. In 1946 the Federal Power Commission held a series of hearings on gas waste; the obvious implication was that the FPC might resolve to extend its regulations over the state industry for reasons of conservation. At a hearing in February in Houston, six Texas officials, including two railroad commissioners, told the FPC that they were making great progress in eliminating waste, and that they did not need federal help. If the Murray Committee report was to be believed, however, they *were not* making progress, and that knowledge made figures in both public and private life in Texas nervous.[48]

All of these forces would have combined, sooner or later, to stop the flaring. But in January of 1947 a political act occurred that made it sooner. Commissioner Jester had been elected governor in 1946. One of his first acts as chief executive was to appoint William Murray, the crusading engineer, to serve out his own unexpired term on the Commission.[49]

As Murray had spent the previous two years disrupting the most important industry in Texas, the governor's choice of him as a successor may seem surprising. But Jester stated at the time that he thought the most important problem facing the industry was gas flaring, and that Murray was the best man to handle the problem; there is no reason to disbelieve him.[50] Jester must be given credit for possessing considerable political courage.

The confirmation of the appointment might have been stopped in the state senate, for in fact there was considerable opposition to Murray within the industry. But that opposition could only have succeeded in blocking the appointment if it had represented the unanimous sentiment of Texas producers. A small group of very active, influential independents, including Robert L. Foree and Glenn H. McCarthy, backed Murray vigorously and prevented any movement to contest the appointment. He was confirmed easily.[51]

With Murray's ascension, the tone of Railroad Commission activity altered abruptly. Because they had been worried about imposing economic burdens on the industry and political burdens on themselves, Culberson and Thompson had been halfhearted in their efforts to stop flaring. The arrival of a colleague committed to eliminating the waste, however, coinciding with rising gas prices and a nosy FPC, made it clear that they would have to move or lose their positions as leaders. The course of political expediency suddenly coincided with the path of political virtue. And so, faced with the inevitable, Thompson and Culberson jumped on the bandwagon with vigor.[52] The Railroad Commission became a conservation tiger.

On April 1, 1947, the Commission issued an order shutting in all 615 oil wells in the new Seeligson field in South Texas until a cycling and compression plant was completed, and the flaring of casinghead gas eliminated. To say the least, this order shocked the industry. Shell, Sun, and Magnolia (Mobil), big operators in the field, immediately filed suit. Former governor Daniel J. Moody was the attorney for Shell, and was confident of victory.[53]

But the Texas Supreme Court upheld the order.[54]

Having won its test case, the Commission proceeded to issue a series of orders shutting down seventeen fields for flaring.[55] These orders were also appealed to the courts. Despite the fact that for several decades the Commission had been accumulating constitutional and statutory power to compel the conservation of oil and gas, industry lawyers tried to convince the judges that the Commission did not have the authority to force operators to save gas if such savings were uneconomical.[56] The state supreme court, however, unambiguously endorsed the Commission's authority. In the Flour Bluff case, the court made it clear that it would do the industry no good to plead that saving gas was unprofitable:

> If the prevention of waste of natural resources such as gas is to await the time when direct and immediate profits can be realized from the operation, there would have been little need for the people of Texas to have amended their Constitution by declaring that the preservation and conservation of natural resources of the state are public rights and duties and directing that the Legislature pass such laws as may be appropriate thereto…for private enterprise would not need the compulsion of law to conserve these resources if the practice were financially profit able.[57]

More legal and political maneuvering followed, but it was only skirmishing.[58] The war had been won by 1949, with the Railroad Commission the unquestioned victor. Henceforward, with relatively insignificant exceptions, casinghead gas would go into a pipeline or back into the ground.

Carl G. Cromwell, who drilled Santa Rita No. 1, at the site with his wife, Luella, and daughter, Carlene. *Courtesy of Judy Boreham Dawson*

OCTOBER 1982

Oil and the Permanent University Fund: The Early Years

DAVID F. PRINDLE

IN THE NINETEENTH CENTURY, Texas was a state poor in commerce and industry but rich in land. As part of the 1845 treaty under which it entered the union, the state kept its public domain; unlike the situation in the other western states, the federal government was not a major landholder in Texas. For half a century after gaining its independence from Mexico, the Texas government used its public lands to accomplish state purposes otherwise beyond its capabilities. It put to use nearly 150 million acres to encourage railroads, attract settlers, reward soldiers, and educate citizens.[1]

The first land endowment for a university was voted by the Congress of the Texas Republic in 1838, but no surveys were authorized until eighteen years later. This land was sold without creating a university. In 1858 the original fifty-league (221,421 acre) grant was confirmed by the state legislature, and the future university was promised, in addition, one of every ten sections of land that had been reserved for the state in railroad grants.[2]

The Civil War and Reconstruction intervened at this point, and it was not until 1875 that the state government returned to the problem of creating a university. By that time, however, squatters had moved onto much of the hypothetical university's possessions. Fearing to incur the political opposition that would follow a confirmation of the university's title to these tracts, the authors of the Constitution of 1876 reneged on the one-in-ten section promise and substituted for it a million acres in the largely unsettled western half of the state. The legislature of 1883 added approximately another million acres in the same area, meanwhile dedicating a million or so to the public school fund.[3]

The apparent worthlessness of this two-million-acre consolation prize would be hard to exaggerate. It consisted entirely of parcels concentrated in arid, sandy, or rocky sections of nineteen counties in the Trans-Pecos and east of the Pecos. None of these parcels seemed suited to anything but grazing and perhaps some scattered dry farming. The parcels were thought so valueless that many of them had already been rejected as a grant by the Texas and Pacific Railroad.[4]

Worthless or not, the University had to be content with them. When the lands were finally accurately surveyed, they totaled 2,103,650 acres, or 3,281.3 square miles.[5]

To the bad luck of this land shuffle was added the bad luck of a restrictive constitutional directive. The University was forbidden to touch any of the income from the land. This was to go into a "Permanent University Fund," which would be invested. Income from the invested funds was to be deposited in an "Available Fund," which could be spent, but only for buildings. If this construction money was inadequate, the University would have no recourse, because legislative appropriations for buildings were expressly denied it. It must have seemed a cruel joke at the time: to force the University to rely on almost valueless properties for many of its funds, then to restrict the use even of those.[6]

Nevertheless, the University began functioning in 1883 and struggled along for nearly five decades in a financially crippled condition. The Permanent Fund consisted almost entirely of money garnered from grazing leases. This was but $40,000 in 1900, and still only $225,000 in 1925,

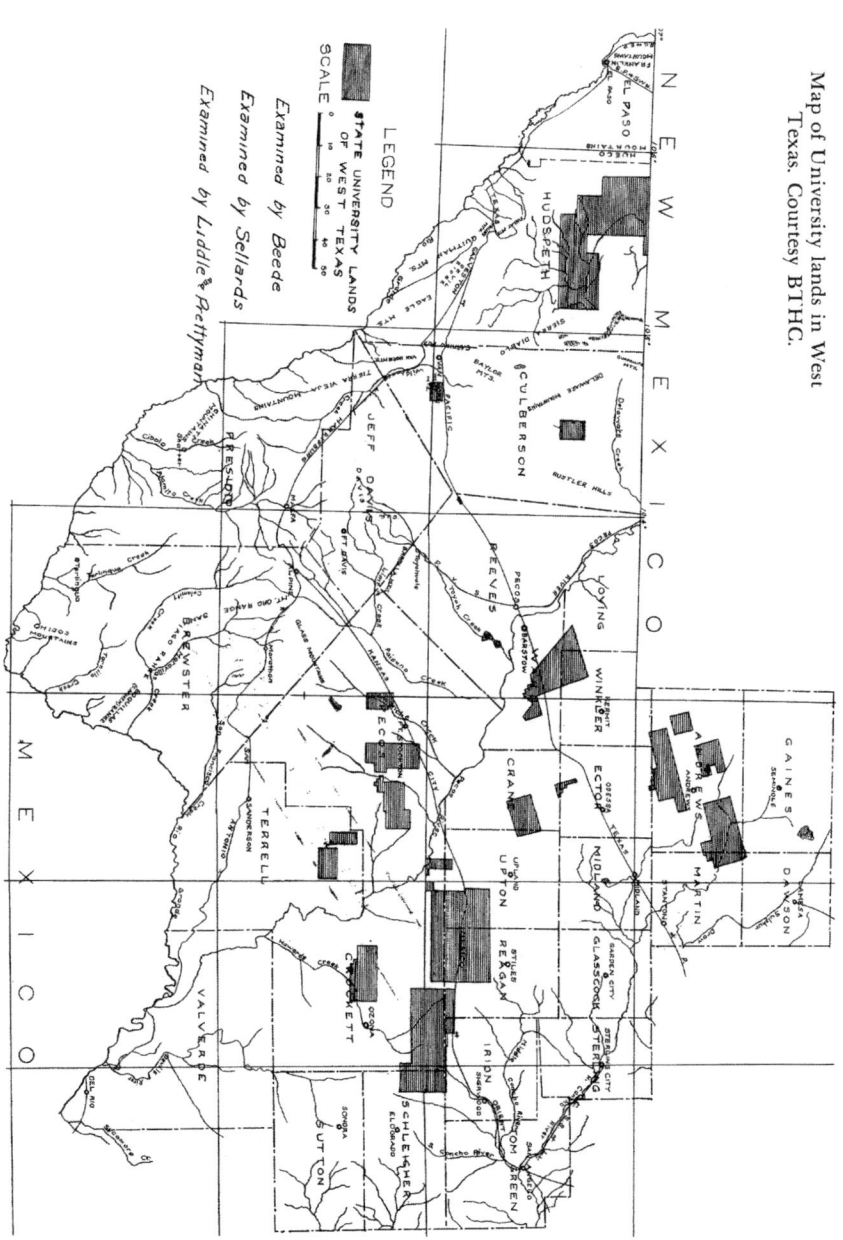

Map of University lands in West Texas. Courtesy BTHC.

hardly enough to provide a financial foundation for a respectable university. As a consequence, for decades most of the buildings on the campus in Austin were miserable shacks. Everyone agreed that these shacks were a humiliation to the University and an eyesore to the citizens, but no one could figure out a way to finance more appropriate structures.[7]

This situation would change, and the University itself would play a decisive, if indirect, part in the change. In June of 1916, Dr. Johan A. Udden, director of the University's Bureau of Economic Geology and Technology, wrote a letter to Major George W. Littlefield, chairman of the board of regents, suggesting cautiously that there might be oil in West Texas. A year later he published a paper concerning the Glass Mountains, pointing out somewhat more optimistically that parts of the Comanchean limestone of what is today known as the Permian Basin "are entirely impervious and would make an excellent cover for an oil pool."[8]

Despite Udden's research, however, wildcatters were not eager to go prospecting in western Texas. Exploratory borings had disclosed enormous buried salt deposits throughout the region, and it was at that time the conventional wisdom that oil could not be found below salt. As a result, that area of the state was known in the folklore of the industry as "the petroleum graveyard of Texas," and was avoided by all but the most audacious explorers.[9]

Udden's report was read, however, by just such a man, a rancher in Reagan County named Rupert P. Ricker. In late 1918, he and a group of investors filed in four West Texas counties 171 applications for exploration permits on 431,360 acres near his ranch. All of these were University property. The filing of the applications for permits was the first step in a process that Ricker hoped would lead to his acquiring oil leases. According to the 1917 Mineral Act, he then had to take the applications and file them with the General Land Office within thirty days, together with a filing fee of one dollar per application and an acquisition fee of 10¢ an acre. If all was in order, he would receive from the land commissioner the appropriate number of exploration permits. With these, he could apply

Johan A. Udden. *Courtesy of BTHC.*

to the land office for oil and gas leases.[10]

But Ricker was unable to raise the necessary $43,136 acquisition fee. With the allotted thirty days vanishing, he traveled to Fort Worth to try to find more backing. There he chanced to encounter Frank T. Pickrell, a former soldier he had commanded in World War I, in the company of Haymon Krupp, an El Paso dry-goods merchant. Pickrell and Krupp had been attempting to break into the oil business, and were journeying between two contemporary boomtowns, Burkburnett and Ranger. Ricker informed the two that he "currently had the hottest thing going that anybody ever heard of." This claim was, to say the least, an exaggeration, but he was able to convince Pickrell and Krupp of its truth. They bought his application on the 431,360 acres for 2,500.[11]

Upon arriving in West Texas, the two new partners discovered that the thirty-day limit on payment of the application fees had almost expired. No one had expressed interest in the land in the meantime, however, so at least there was no competition. Pickrell and Krupp completed new applications with their names instead of Ricker's, refiled, and paid the required $43,136. In March 1919, they were awarded oil and gas exploration permits. The next month, the partners formed the Texon Oil and Land Company.[12]

While Krupp minded his store, Pickrell took over the task of finding oil. This would not be easy. State law required that he commence drilling within eighteen months of acquiring a permit, but, because of the area's reputation as hopeless oil country, Pickrell found that he could not raise investment capital in Texas. With time running out, he finally persuaded some investors in New York to back the project and returned to West Texas just in time to begin drilling before the deadline. Some of the investors evidently had not been naive about the project's chances, and, being Catholic, had asked Pickrell to christen the drilling rig "Santa Rita," after the Saint of the Impossible.[13]

Having temporarily overcome his financial obstacles, Pickrell found, nevertheless, that his difficulties had not ended. Texon's geologist, Dr.

Hugh Tucker, had selected a spot fifteen miles west of the town of Big Lake, in Reagan County, to spud the well. The country was so desolate that Pickrell had difficulty keeping men on the job and was forced to employ some local cowboys to keep the drill running. Another well supplying water for the drilling operations went dry, and time was lost deepening it; meanwhile, drinking water had to be brought in from San Angelo, seventy-five miles away. Despite these and other problems, Pickrell persevered. University of Texas students can be thankful that he did, for on May 28, 1923, Santa Rita blew in, producing about one hundred barrels a day at 3,038 feet. With this small success, the partners were able to raise more money for further drilling in the area. On their ninth try, they hit a gusher two hundred feet to the east of Santa Rita that supplied five thousand barrels a day. Pickrell and Krupp, Texon, the Permian Basin, and the University were on the way to riches.[14]

In the long run, this Big Lake strike would become the foundation of the University's finances. In the short run, however, it created a series of problems. Never having owned an oilfield, the regents of the University were not prepared to manage one. When the first royalty payment from Texon arrived in August 1923, the regents possessed only the most rudimentary institutions to handle the new source of wealth. They had governed University lands since 1895, but, as the only income had come from grazing leases, they had no employees with knowledge of the oil business.[15]

It was imperative that management institutions be created, however, for almost as soon as the regents started to bank oil income, there were indications that they were not getting their full due. As the original discovery spawned others, as more companies began producing, and as it became clear that Big Lake was a major field, reports of shenanigans filtered to the board. Rumors circulated that the operators would sometimes neglect to report a well as flowing until months after it came in, that they understated production, that they misreported the oil's quality, and so on. Moreover, many more companies now wanted exploration leases, and pipeline operators desired easements across University lands. The regents thus began a difficult process of creating institutions that could manage University property so that they received a maximum of revenue. As they had no experience with this sort of thing, they made mistakes, and it was late in the next decade before orderly and satisfactory procedures and agencies were in place.[16]

During the first years after the Big Lake strike, the regents attempted both to create their own oil-lands agency and to persuade other bodies to give them help. In July 1924, they voted $750 for the Bureau of Economic Geology and Technology to look into allegations of irregularities by producers. Two months later, they asked the state land commissioner to check on producers in Reagan County. By August 1926, they were attempting to arrange with the railroad commission to look after conservation on University oil lands.[17]

None of these requests produced satisfactory results, so the board had to rely on its own resources. In October 1924, it authorized the president to appoint a royalty oil gauger to serve the University in the vicinity of the company town of Texon. In July 1925, it hired a counsel for possible litigation. By July of that year, it had authorized $4,000 for a house for the University oil inspector at Texon, and by September had bought him a Ford. Their suspicions growing, in March 1926 the regents hired the accounting firm of Ernst and Ernst to perform audits on the companies producing on University land. An office was established in 1929 in San Angelo, with a geological staff under Dr. Hal P. Bybee, and a surveying staff under the direction of Frank F. Friend. Five years later, the board hired an auditor-in-charge to work with the General Land Office supervising audits. This increasing institutional grasp of the oil lands led to a round of struggles with producing companies.[18]

The regents also had to contend with inadequate authority over oil and gas leasing. Under the Mineral Act of 1917, this power was vested in the General Land Office. Undoubtedly unhappy with this arrangement, the regents in 1926 asked the state attorney general to restrain the land

The Santa Rita oil rig. *Courtesy of BTHC.*

commissioner from leasing University property. Since the law was clear, they got nowhere with this request. They therefore asked the legislature to come to their rescue, and in 1929 received an acceptable compromise. Under chapter 282 of the acts of the 41st legislature, control over leasing was invested in a board for lease of University lands, consisting of the land commissioner and two regents. This act authorized the board for lease to sell petroleum leases on either a sealed-bid or open-auction basis. Two years later the legislature transferred authority to employ a surveyor, geologist, and mineralogist from the board for lease to the regents.[19]

The first sale of leases on University land under the new leasing board was held under the sealed-bid system on October 1, 1929. Thirty-eight tracts were offered in Crane, Ector, and Pecos counties. The royalty rate was set at one-eighth for the tracts in Crane and Ector, and one-sixth for those in Pecos. Companies bid $168,425 on twenty-eight of these tracts, an average of $63.80 an acre. As the land office average had been $22.23 per acre, the new arrangement was immediately pronounced a success.[20]

The average bid per acre on University lands subsequently fell dramatically, however, leading the regents to search for a still more lucrative system. It was not until 1935 that they found one, a topic to be discussed shortly.

The board of regents had already enhanced its ability to deal with oil questions by modifying the responsibilities of its University land committee. Originally charged with managing grazing leases, after 1923 the three regents on this committee quickly began to look after oil matters. In 1929, they started to consult with and advise the board for lease.[21]

By 1931, therefore, the board of regents had evolved a set of structures to oversee its new source of wealth. It had five members directly involved in governing the oil lands—three on the land committee, and two on the board for lease—plus a department of scientific inspectors in the field. These structures were not perfect, and they would be modified in the decade, but they were the basis for intelligent management of the University's good fortune.

This management was necessary, for the Big Lake oil strike had begun a series of problems for the regents that grew with the passing years. For the first decade of prosperity, they were constantly struggling with unfamiliar difficulties. The outcomes of these struggles created the context for the University's growth in the next half century.

A year after Santa Rita blew in, there were seventy-five wells on University property. The Permanent Fund's oil royalties for the first year totaled $16,611.75, expanded to $231,833.74 the second, and exploded to $3,853,257.60 in 1925. The University of Texas was clearly headed for prosperity, and the regents immediately began to chafe at the financial restrictions placed upon them by the Texas Constitution. When the Permanent Fund had consisted of insignificant contributions from grazing leases, no one minded the constitutional constraints, but as it expanded exponentially the regents began to cast about for a way to circumvent the constitution.[22]

In September of 1924, Regent Robert G. Story was requested by his colleagues to write a bill for submission to the next legislature that would authorize payments of oil royalties to the Available Fund. The regents' argument on this point was that royalties were "personal property" rather than income, and, as such, were exempt from the constitutional directive. They sold this to the legislature, which passed HB 246 in 1925, permitting oil royalties to be placed in the Available Fund, to be used only for buildings and other permanent improvements.[23]

Although she had some doubts as to the constitutionality of this legislation, Governor Miriam A. Ferguson signed it, because, as she wrote at the time, "to the average man who sees the miserable-looking buildings at the University it would appear that the state is making an effort to store up hay instead of to store up knowledge." Other state officials, however, were not so sympathetic. Treasurer W. Gregory Hatcher refused to accept the University oil royalties sent to him by Land Commissioner John T. Robison. Attorney General Dan J. Moody agreed with this position, and so the question was taken to the state supreme court.[24]

In March 1926, the court ruled against the regents, thus settling the question of the destination of the oil money. By this time, however, the members of the board of regents had evidently had second thoughts, for they expressed approval of the court's judgment.[25]

Even though the regents changed their minds about the constitutional question, they remained steadfast in their belief that the University was being cheated out of some of its rightful income. A discussion of all the controversies involving University lands and income would be tedious, but an examination of two of the most heated will give the flavor of the problem.

By the end of 1925, Texon was the fourth largest oil producer in the state. The company and its affiliates, the Group #1 Oil Company and the Big Lake Oil Company, were still expanding rapidly, and sending glowing reports to their stockholders. But the regents suspected that some of Texon's prosperity was gained at the University's expense. The Ernst and Ernst audit of 1926 confirmed their suspicions.[26]

In 1924, Frank Pickrell of Texon had contracted with E. W. Marland of the Marland Oil Company (now Conoco) for a pipeline to carry Big Lake's oil to Gulf Coast refineries. The contract called for the creation of the Reagan County Purchasing Company (RCPC), of which 51 percent was owned by Marland and 49 percent by Texon and the Big Lake Oil Company. This new gathering company would charge the producing companies 20¢ a barrel to transport the oil, and they would in turn deduct that charge from their University royalty payments. The University, of course, had no objection to this arrangement.[27]

Marland, however, had encountered financial difficulties, and was unable to construct a pipeline. Instead, the RCPC entered into an agreement with Humble Oil and Refining Company (now Exxon) under which Humble built its own pipeline and gathered Texon's oil. Apparently, the RCPC charged the University for Humble's gathering charge, but continued, in addition, to add its own 20¢ a barrel for services never rendered. In other words, the University had contracted to pay 20¢ a barrel for transportation but was being charged 40¢. When the regents disentangled this arrangement, they sued Texon, RCPC, and others for $2,750,000, the amount they believed they had been overcharged. This action went to court in September 1926.[28]

Evidently, Texon and the RCPC realized that they had been caught red-handed, for they did not contest the charges. Instead, they sent their lawyers to a board of regents meeting in November to suggest a compromise. The regents were receptive, but legal discussion is timeconsuming, and agreement was not immediate. After several more meetings and two years, however, an out-of-court settlement was reached. The companies agreed to pay the University one million dollars outright, increase its royalty to one-fourth, and refrain from assessing any more gathering charges.[29]

But this was not the end of the University's troubles with Texan and the Reagan County Purchasing Company. Through the 1930s, the regents continued to find instances of what they believed to be chicanery. Among other things, they accused the RCPC of paying exorbitant sums to its parent company and charging them against profits, and of incorrectly figuring the "average posted price" of its oil, in both cases creating artificially low royalty payments. Through the decade before the second world war, the regents were almost constantly embroiled in such lawsuits against the people who had made them rich.[30]

Although the regents were generally successful in these legal battles with the RCPC, they did not always win. In other areas, too, they failed to carry their point in court. Chief among their defeats was a dispute over a portion of land called the "Landreth Strip."

When the University lands had first been surveyed in 1879, 1884, and 1886, they were thought to be so worthless that the work had been haphazard in the extreme. The surveys were done in large blocks so as to avoid the expense of subdivision; impermanent markers were constructed; and field notes were scarcely taken. As a result, the boundaries of University land in the decades afterward were fuzzy. As soon as oil was discovered, of course, it became of great interest to many people in the state to locate boundary lines exactly. In 1929, the legislature ordered a resurvey of all University lands.[31]

Meanwhile, in 1929 the regents had discovered that they might own an extra oilfield. One of the sloppier surveys left a doubt as to whether a section of state land in Crane and Upton counties was University property. This area was resurveyed in 1925, with the findings accepted as official by the Land Office. At the time, it did not seem to bother anyone in the University that the resurvey had moved the southern boundary of its land 128 varas, or 355.5 feet, to the north.[32]

In 1926, however, two businessmen filed a claim for the newly created "vacant" land, were awarded title by the Land Office, and promptly sold oil leases to the Landreth Production Company, among others. As the Landreth Strip, as it was called, proved to be over a portion of the McElroy field, it soon contained sixteen producing wells. Under the laws of Texas, because this land had been officially vacant, onesixteenth of the royalty went to the public school fund. In a private suit, a state court confirmed the lines of the 1925 survey and hence the ownership of the Strip.[33]

Nevertheless, the regents soon claimed that the second survey had been inaccurate, and that consequently the sixteen wells should be considered to be on University property, with their (one-eighth) royalties accruing to the Permanent Fund. From 1929 to the eve of World War II, they asked each successive Texas attorney general to file suit on behalf of the University. As "true" survey lines did not exist, and as there was already a settled court judgment on the matter, every attorney general declined. The minutes of the board of regents contain references to numerous discussions of how to recover the lost strip, all futile. In 1940, the board tried again and again was turned down. It then gave up and contented itself with husbanding the royalties to which it had clear title.[34]

All of these problems and others occupied the board of regents in its defense of the University's wealth for many years after the Santa Rita strike. In these disputes, its antagonists were usually oil companies. The greatest controversy, however, occurred not with petroleum producers but with the Board of Directors of Texas A&M College (now University).

In the late 1920s, the Permanent University Fund was obviously on its way to becoming a truly substantial endowment. By December 1928, two hundred and twenty-eight wells had been drilled at Big Lake, 36½ million barrels of oil had been produced, and the field was still going strong. To Big Lake's royalties had been added those from the Church-Fields pool, discovered on University property in Crane County in 1926. Oil companies clambered for leases on University land. By 1927, the Permanent Fund was growing at the rate of $250,000 a month.[35]

All of this good fortune was heartening, but the regents found it difficult to turn it into tangible campus progress. Although the Permanent Fund was large and growing larger, it generated only about $100,000 a year for the Available Fund. "Shackeresque" architecture still dominated the campus.[36]

In 1930, therefore, the regents persuaded the legislature and the voters to amend the constitution, permitting them to invest four million dollars of the Permanent Fund in bonds, issued by themselves, for the construction of buildings. This was the only time during this period that the actual body of the Permanent Fund was spent directly. This provision was repealed in 1932, but by then it had done its good work. When the bond money was added to gifts from the Sealy and Smith Foundation, Littlefield family, and the Ex-Students' Association, among others, and to support from the federal government, it allowed the regents to embark upon a vigorous construction program. By 1935, they had spent $14½ million on buildings at Austin, the University medical branch in Galveston, and at McDonald Observatory near Fort Davis. Ten new structures stood on the main campus by 1933, and the shacks had disappeared.[37]

While they were gaining access to the Permanent Fund, however, the regents were also losing part of it. Although the Agricultural and Mechanical College of Texas had been established in 1871 as a federal land-grant college, it had been made a branch of the nonexistent University of Texas system by a statute that year, and by the Constitution of 1876.

Technically, therefore, the University and A&M should have been sharing the Permanent Fund when it began to become substantial. The wording of the constitutional provision associating the two schools, however, was ambiguous. The section creating the Permanent Fund was placed so as to leave some doubt as to whether it applied to A&M. Moreover, while the University was explicitly forbidden to receive legislative appropriations for buildings, it was unclear whether this prohibition applied to A&M. The ambiguity was such that it was possible to interpret the constitution as mandating a Permanent Fund for the University and legislative appropriations for A&M; alternatively, it might be interpreted so as to allow the Aggies to receive legislative appropriations the first year, but be restricted to the Available Fund thereafter.[38] This inexact wording created a financial uncertainty that bedeviled the two schools until 1930.

During the 1870s and 1880s, A&M had annually received a portion of the Available Fund. The Permanent Fund being so small, however, the Available Fund could barely support one school, let alone two. A&M therefore withdrew from participation in the endowment after 1887 and relied for its financial support on legislative appropriations. For years afterward, nevertheless, it received a nominal sum (usually $500) from the Available Fund each year as evidence that as a branch of the University it retained its rights to the money.[39]

Five months after the Big Lake strike changed the financial prospect of the University, Dean Charles Puryear of A&M wrote a letter to President William B. Bizzell urging him to press that institution's claims to the University endowment.[40]

The University board of regents and the A&M board of directors held their first post-oil-strike meeting in November 1924. Like several subsequent gatherings, this one was in executive session, and consequently there is no record of what the participants said to one another. From references and allusions in later minutes, newspaper accounts, and letters preserved in archives, however, it is possible to reconstruct the main lines of the argument.[41]

There was simply no doubt, urged the directors, that A&M was a branch of the University of Texas. The constitution was clear on that point. The board admitted that it had not been relying on the Permanent Fund for buildings, but the regents should be grateful for that restraint. Until now, it could not have supported two institutions. Since it was obvious that Big Lake would make the endowment large enough for both schools, the University could not in justice keep it for itself.[42]

On the contrary, answered the regents. For forty years the A&M directors had pretended that they were not related to the University and had gone to the legislature for buildings even though the regents could not. The campus in Austin was littered with shacks; not the campus in College Station. Now that the University had struck it rich, A&M wished to abandon its profitable fiction and associate with the University once again. Furthermore, the directors were unwilling to forswear legislative appropriations for construction. They seemed to want to have their cake and eat it too. The University felt no obligation to help them attain this ambition.[43] Needless to say, the first joint meeting did not end in agreement between the two schools.

The battle, however, had just begun. Through the rest of the decade, the A&M board of directors attempted to persuade the legislature to come to their aid, and the University board of regents maneuvered successfully with friendly legislators to forestall such an event. The directors even employed a full-time lobbyist at the capitol to argue their point of view, but all their efforts were in vain.[44]

By 1929, thoroughly exasperated, the directors had resolved to take the issue to the Texas Supreme Court. (They had for some years retained legal counsel on the oil revenues question.) Now, in April, they passed a resolution requesting the president of the board "to inform the President of the Board of Regents of the University of Texas, that the A&M College claims an interest in the University Land Funds."[45]

By that time, however, the regents were once again having second thoughts on an important policy stand. Not only A&M, but many other colleges in the state were asking for a slice of the Permanent Fund pie, and the regents were losing confidence in their ability to defend it. It began to seem to them that it might be better to make A&M an ally against the other schools by allowing it to share in the Permanent Fund.[46]

The regents therefore conceded A&M's theoretical right to the endowment money. But an agreement in principle is not a precise division of the wealth. The board of directors wanted to receive a third; the board of regents refused to go higher than a fourth. Each board appointed a committee of three to negotiate, and each committee refused to alter its position. The impasse was finally broken at a meeting of the two committees in College Station in 1930. According to Francis Marion Law, president of the directors at the time, he and two colleagues had argued all morning with three regents, including their president, Judge Robert L. Batts. At noon, when the bugle sounded for lunch, Batts stepped out on the porch and watched the A&M cadets marching to their meal. Upon returning to the table, he murmured, as if to himself, "What difference does it make; they are all Texas boys," and announced that he would favor acceding to the Aggies' request for one-third of the Permanent Fund.[47]

Despite Batts's sentiments, other regents were not eager to part with an entire third of the endowment. At a series of meetings on April 21, 1930, the regents, both with the directors and alone, debated the resolution vigorously. They passed it once four to three, under conditions of some confusion, which necessitated another vote. Prior to this final poll, the board of directors caucused and agreed to renounce any further intention to receive construction support from the legislature. This promise appears to have swung the balance decisively, for on its second test the resolution passed five to two. The A&M board, of course, accepted the division unanimously.[48]

The next year, the agreement worked out by the two boards was written into law by the legislature. A&M was to receive $200,000 annually from the Available Fund for three years, and one-third of the Available Fund oil money thereafter. The University in Austin retained two-thirds of the oil revenues plus all of the income from grazing leases and from state bonds derived from the sale of the original fifty leagues. This arrangement remains in force.[49]

As soon as they agreed to share the wealth, the two boards began to cooperate on other matters. They worked together during subsequent legislative sessions to raise each others' nonconstruction appropriations and corresponded about the University's suits against oil companies.[50]

The division of the Available Fund did not mean complete harmony between the two schools, however. The University was still responsible, through its two seats on the board for lease, for controlling the land that produced the oil revenue. Although it was sharing in the benefits from oil lands, A&M participated not at all in their management. Once their right to income from the land was acknowledged, the members of the board of directors began to feel that they should be involved in its operation, also.

In 1937, Francis Law approached his cousin, Regent Jubal R. Parten, about sharing the management of the oil lands. Parten and Harry Y. Benedict, president of the University, had been expecting such a request, and had been trying to devise a strategy to deal with it. As Parten in 1981 recalled the episode:

> I thought about it early one morning, and it flashed on me what to do—if I could get the consent of my colleagues and other Board members—just forthrightly go to my friend Law and say "We doubt very seriously if we can make any sense of two boards being charged with the responsibility for that. We think that it would be logical and fairly feasible if we simply combine these boards: then we will have overall responsibility." ...Combine A&M with the University of Texas...
>
> I sold Benedict and the Board on it. Then I go down to see him [Law]. Well, he said that does make sense, or something like that. You couldn't argue with it. Let's combine the universities; that would solve the problem. Can't have two boards working on

the same thing...and he said he'd think about it. And that was the end of it. As I expected...Because I know that they thought they'd be meeting all the time in Austin.[51]

The University board of regents, therefore, is still entirely responsible for managing the Permanent Fund lands.

Although it retained control of the oil lands, the board of regents in the 1930s made considerable changes in its manner of handling them. Its gradual creation of an institutionalized management process has already been discussed. One major change, however, was more abrupt: the switch from sealed bids to open auction as a method for awarding oil leases.

From the first operation of the board for lease in 1929, it had awarded leases by sealed bid. After the first two of these sales, the benefits to the University had declined precipitously. The ten sales held between 1931 and 1935 garnered an average bonus of only $19.78 an acre, which was below even the land office average of the 1920s. In one sale in 1932, the University received only 50¢ an acre on sixteen tracts.[52] Although they left no records of their discontent with these results, the regents must have suspected that the Permanent Fund was not growing at its maximum possible rate.

In 1935, Major Parten and George D. Morgan were appointed regents by Governor James V. Allred. They were quickly elected to the regents' land committee, joining Hilmer H. Weinert. Both men owned independent oil companies and consequently were familiar with the problems of managing producing land. Both believed that open auctions would be superior to sealed bidding in the leasing of University land.[53]

As these oil men saw it, there were four disadvantages to sealed bidding. First, by allowing companies to bid on tracts without openly showing their interest, some areas were permitted to go for low prices through sheer ignorance on the part of the competition. By making operators publicly display their enthusiasm for certain tracts, the new regents reasoned, an auction system would stimulate interest in those tracts, bringing in extra participants, and thus inevitably driving up bids.[54]

Second, the secrecy of the sealed bids allowed operators to be too rational, and perhaps cautious, in their calculation. An auction might catch them in a competitive frenzy, thereby inducing them to bid more than they intended.[55]

Third, sealed bids were subject, at least in theory, to fraud. Since everyone knew that secret bids could be "sweated open" by insiders the night before the official opening, those people who doubted the integrity of either the regents or the General Land Office would not participate, thinking that the process had been fixed. Parten and Morgan did not believe that there was dishonesty involved in the sealed bids for University property. It was common knowledge within the industry, however, that there had been collusion during the sale of leases on New Mexico public land, and they suspected that the general belief in such practices was enough to drive away some potential bidders. The fewer the bidders, the less the competition, and the lower the bids.[56]

Fourth, they believed that the sealed-bidding system favored the major integrated oil companies over the independents. The majors, as huge corporations with extensive research budgets, could afford to employ scientists and technicians to evaluate University property. Few independents had such resources. Majors therefore worked from relative knowledge, independents from relative ignorance. The sealed-bid system permitted the majors to keep their knowledge to themselves; independents discovered what a major's researchers had concluded about a given property only after it had acquired a lease, when the knowledge was too late to help them. But in an auction, when a major showed interest in a tract, the independents would automatically learn the results of the major's research, *before* the tract was sewn up. By forcing the majors to tip their hands, a public auction would eliminate their advantages in information gathering.[57]

For some years, Major Parten had been familiar with the method used by the US government to award oil leases on the Osage Indian lands of

Oklahoma. Since 1901, tracts on these lands had been leased to oil operators at open auction sales after the appropriate public announcements. In November of 1935 Parten and Morgan, under the auspices of the land committee, prepared a report to the regents in which they discussed the Osage experience, criticized closed bidding, and recommended open auctions. The regents unanimously endorsed these recommendations on November 23.[58]

When word got out about the new system, the major companies were not happy. In March 1936, Hines Baker of Humble's legal department wrote Parten a letter criticizing the proposed change and arguing that auctions would actually bring in less money. Some higher executives of the major companies lobbied with Parten and probably Morgan to change their minds, but to no avail.[59]

The first public auction of leases on University land was held July 20, 1936, in Austin. As there was no legal provision for paying the expenses of such an occasion, Parten and Morgan imported from Oklahoma Colonel Jacob Wolters, the federal government's Osage auctioneer, at their own expense to conduct the proceedings. Fifty-four tracts brought in $300,600 to the Permanent Fund, or $37.36 an acre, nearly double the average of the previous five years. A subsequent auction in October collected a similar high return. Both the regents and the A&M directors were pleased.[60]

There remained only to institutionalize the new order. In 1937, vigorous lobbying in Austin by regents and directors induced the legislature to pass SB 343, which formalized the Parten and Morgan recommendations. This law made open auctions mandatory, provided for paying an auctioneer with public money, and required companies to submit all the information they gathered exploring University lands to the General Land Office, where it would be made publicly available. This is essentially the system in place today.[61]

By the outbreak of World War II, better than 250,000 of the University's acres were under lease for oil and gas. Wells in twenty-three fields were adding approximately a million dollars a year to the Permanent University Fund, which had grown so that it supplied nearly $564,000 to the University's share of the Available Fund during the 1942 fiscal year.[62]

The Permanent Fund did not guarantee a problem-free development for the University of Texas and Texas A&M. By 1980, its $1.3-billion book value was again attracting covetous glances from other state schools, and future legislative sessions promise more battles over the money from the oil lands. But whatever the future of the Permanent Fund, its desirability in the present is at least partly the result of the competent way it was handled in the past.[63]

Carlos Castañeda, a University of Texas at Austin history professor and an offcial of the Fair Employment Practice Committee, which challenged discrimination in the oil industry, speaking at the dedication of the San Jacinto Monument, April 1939. *Courtesy Mexican American Collection, Benson Latin American Collection, University of Texas at Austin.*

JANUARY 1992

The Failed Promise of Wartime Opportunity for Mexicans in the Texas Oil Industry

EMILIO ZAMORA

MEXICANS CAME OUT of the Depression facing an unprecedented opportunity to improve their traditional position as low-wage labor and to alter the generational effects of prior occupational discrimination. The wartime rhetoric of democracy, public policy measures that prohibited discrimination by defense industries, government employers and labor unions, and, above all, dramatic job growth in high wage firms led Mexicans to believe that their time had indeed arrived. The occupational gains made during the war may have raised their hopes further. Obstacles continued, however, to deny Mexican workers equal employment opportunities. Most of them remained working for low-wage employers, and those that secured jobs in high-wage firms assumed the least-skilled and lower-paying ones.[1]

This study examines wartime discrimination as an obstacle to Mexican workers in the oil refining industry of the Texas Gulf Coast, a region bounded by Texas City, Houston, and Beaumont. Oil refineries normally denied Mexicans opportunities. Unionized and nonunionized Anglo workers played an important role in sustaining the resultant inequality primarily by opposing the adoption of a nondiscrimination policy in the oil industry. This opposition was cast in racial terms, though it was fundamentally motivated by economic and political concerns over the issue of job control. Although more work is required before we can properly gauge the effects of persistent discrimination, this study supports the conventional yet rarely substantiated view that Mexican workers continued facing formidable barriers when they entered high-wage firms during the war.[2]

The primary focus here is the role played by the Fair Employment Practice Committee (FEPC), the agency responsible for implementing President Franklin D. Roosevelt's Executive Orders 8802 and 9346 prohibiting various forms of discrimination by defense industries, government employers, and labor unions.[3] The FEPC waged a 2½-year challenge against discrimination in twelve oil refineries.[4] FEPC examiners focused on group complaints submitted by Mexican workers against three of the twelve refineries (Humble, Sinclair, and Shell), a company union at Humble named the Baytown Employees' Federation and two Congress of Industrial Organizations (CIO) unions, Locals 227 and 367. FEPC officials sought favorable settlements in the three refineries as a first step in pushing for a policy of nondiscrimination in the entire regional industry. Anglo worker opposition was so strong, however, that the FEPC was unable to assure Mexicans the wartime promise of full and unobstructed job opportunities. The agency's failure to effectively combat discrimination in three major refineries underscored its powerlessness; it also demonstrated the durable strength of a system of racial inequality.[5]

The experience of Mexican oil workers reflected a pattern of employment discrimination in other war-related industries. As the wartime expansion of the southwestern economy opened up new job opportunities, Mexicans for the first time began to obtain employment in urban-based war industries such as garment, meatpacking, construction, shipping, aircraft repair, and oil. The new-found opportunities, however, soon dried up as high-wage firms filled up their laborer positions, the jobs that were normally available for Mexicans. As a result, war industries only reached an employment level of approximately 25,000 Mexicans during the war, which represented a low utilization rate of 5 percent. The wartime gains, therefore, accompanied persistent inequality. This inconsistency was especially evident in growth industries such as oil.

Employers usually assigned Mexicans unskilled jobs that paid the lowest wages and denied them the opportunity to advance into the better-paying skilled positions. They shared this condition with African American workers. Moreover, when the war ended and industrial production decreased, they were generally denied further access and displaced from the jobs they had recently acquired.[6]

The booming oil industry in the Gulf Coast offered some of the more attractive job opportunities since it claimed one of the highest wage rates for skilled and unskilled workers in the state. The sheer fact that oil refineries offered a large and growing number of jobs also attracted the attention of workers. Also, by the mid-1940s the Oil Workers' International Union (OWIU), which was affiliated with the Congress of Industrial Organizations (CIO), had organized eleven of the twelve major refineries in the Gulf Coast and claimed some of the most favorable contractual agreements won by labor in Texas.[7] Despite the attractiveness of oil, only between 1,041 and 1,388, or less than 5 percent of the 25,000 Mexicans in the state's war industries, were drawn into the refineries by the time of Pearl Harbor. They also represented a small portion—between 6 and 8 percent—of the industry's workforce.[8]

A significant number of the Mexican oil workers may have been born in Mexico. The only known source of information on nativity characteristics, a survey conducted by the FEPC in one of the refineries in 1943, indicated that 59 percent were born in Mexico and 41 percent in the United States. According to one observer, the US-born Mexicans were underrepresented because they were better informed about the discrimination that awaited them in oil and preferred to search for jobs elsewhere.[9] Mexican nationals presumably had fewer options and tended to accept the low-paying jobs. The presence of a large number of Mexican nationals explains why Anglo workers may have been especially sensitive to the possibility of a wage-cutting threat from below. It also reveals why the Mexican Consul from Houston assumed an important role in representing the Mexican complaints before the FEPC.

Mexicans rarely found employment in the pipeline and production branches of the industry. Management usually assigned them common laborer jobs in the refineries, paid them less than Anglos that were similarly classified, and denied them opportunities to advance into better-paying skilled occupations. When Mexican and African-American workers assumed skilled jobs also held by Anglos, their job classification and pay normally remained unchanged. Rarely would management promote them to such jobs as mechanics, truck helpers, truck drivers, and bottle washers.[10]

The practice of placing minorities in the common laborer positions and denying them upgrading opportunities created a hiring ceiling that was often maintained through contractual agreements or informal understandings with labor unions. Organized labor was thus instrumental in defining the occupational hierarchical order, a fact that became clearer when unionists openly pressured the refineries to resist FEPC directives to end discrimination. Popular anti-Mexican-immigrant feelings that resulted from fears of increased job competition had previously influenced labor's defensive posture and the industry's hiring practices regarding both Mexican nationals and US-born Mexican workers. The widespread anti-Mexican agitation by Anglo workers during the tight market days of the depression, for instance, resulted in decisions by Humble, Sinclair, and Shell to temporarily halt the employment of Mexican workers. The result was a gradual depletion of their Mexican workforce. More importantly, these early tensions and protests coincided with union campaigns and contractual negotiations that formally and informally defined the Mexican's bottom position in the industry.[11]

Despite the expressed displeasure of national CIO officers who publicly supported the president's executive orders, the local unions and the leadership of the OWIU rarely challenged the discriminatory practices of the companies or the racially exclusive organizing policies of company unions and American Federation of Labor (AFL) locals. In fact, in at least four refineries CIO locals negotiated collective bargaining agreements that established dual wage systems, segregated work areas, separate occupational categories, and upgrading procedures that effectively barred minority workers from the skilled occupations. These agreements as well as numerous informal understandings established at other refineries were negotiated with the knowledge and support of the OWIU. The OWIU and local union leaders presumably shared the sentiments of their local membership or thought that it was less than worthwhile to disturb widespread and deeply ingrained racial customs.[12]

Although it may be impossible to know to what degree racial thinking motivated the union leadership, it is clear that both the unions and company representatives resisted compliance on the grounds that widespread opposition by Anglo workers threatened to disrupt production. This was a recurring claim that seriously hampered the FEPC throughout the war period. There was ample evidence and good reason to believe this claim. Some FEPC officials, however, suspected that management and union leaders were concealing their own opposition to integration and seeking to encourage dissent by stalling the compliance process. Although company representatives may have shared racial views with the Anglo workforce or even entertained the idea of promoting racial thinking to ingratiate themselves with labor or to encourage divisions among the workers, their stated position was credible to an extent given the economic losses they could incur as a result of a disruption in production. The unions, on the other hand, were responding to more than just fears of possible Anglo workers' reactions. Underneath their claims of possible disruptions lay an interest in protecting the privileged position of their constituency from the FEPC threat.

Although the refineries often publicly complained of FEPC compliance pressures, they usually appeared to be projecting an image of disinterested players rather than actively provoking a reaction. Local unionist leaders, however, at times openly encouraged workers to see the intervention of the federal government as a threat to racial privilege and job control. This was evident when union leaders representing the company union at Humble and the CIO locals at Sinclair and Shell openly defied FEPC directives and defended discrimination, particularly against blacks, as the prevailing custom in the South. Among the ideas entertained by unionists and the rank and file was the notion that if concessions were made to Mexicans, blacks would follow with similar allegations, competition would intensify, and management would decrease wages and release Anglo workers.[13]

Although opposition to FEPC directives significantly undermined compliance, other factors constrained the agency's work. These included the short life span of the FEPC, the lack of enforcement powers, and internal divisions that periodically surfaced on the question of whether to challenge discrimination in the entire industry or on a plant-by-plant basis. These problems, however, did not seem to seriously impair the FEPC in its work in other industries. In fact, what most often appeared to be the case is that opposition to the FEPC in oil magnified internal constraints.[14]

Mexican workers began submitting their complaints in 1941 to the Office of Production Management in San Antonio and the FEPC office in Washington, DC. Problems associated with distance and a lack of personnel kept government officials from servicing these complaints adequately until the president's Executive Order 9346, issued on May 26, 1943, made it possible to establish the Region X office in Dallas. FEPC examiners began their oil investigations almost immediately. Although the Dallas office recorded a continuous stream of settlements in other industries throughout the state, the oil refineries, especially Humble, Sinclair, and Shell, kept it occupied until the agency ceased its operations in 1945.[15]

Dr. Carlos E. Castaneda, the University of Texas history professor who directed the Dallas office, was an especially important figure in FEPC work, in part because of his membership in a national network of Mexican American civil rights leaders that was actively testing the sincerity of the wartime rhetoric of world democracy and pan-Americanism. His battles against the oil refineries, particularly the fight against Shell, thus became focal points of concern in the civil rights movement and drew attention to the importance of discrimination against Mexicans in Mexico-United States relations.[16]

Castaneda processed Mexican complaints against eight of the twelve major refineries between May 1943 and December 1944. He adopted a dual strategy that first focused on complaints against Humble, Sinclair, and Shell, hoping that favorable adjustments in these refineries would compel the entire industry to enforce the president's executive orders. The second part of the strategy involved a decision to challenge the general practice of racial discrimination with complaints by Mexican workers. Since he feared stronger Anglo opposition to African-American complaints, Castaneda decided first to establish the existence of racial discrimination on the basis of Mexican complaints and then direct the refineries to adopt a policy of nondiscrimination that would benefit all minority workers.[17]

W. Don Ellinger became the director of the Dallas office in December 1944, while Castaneda assumed new duties as special assistant to the FEPC director on Latin American Affairs and as director of a new regional office in San Antonio. Although Castaneda was no longer officially involved in the oil cases, he continued to advise the Dallas office. Ellinger handled the cases against the oil companies until the FEPC ceased operations in Texas during 1945.[18]

Castaneda and Ellinger normally coordinated the preparation and submission of complaints with local groups of workers, officials from the Mexican Consulate at Houston, and community leaders associated with the well-known civil rights organization, the League of United

Latin American Citizens (LULAC). Preliminary fact-finding meetings also included workers and civil rights leaders from the African-American community. Meetings with local minority leaders and investigations conducted immediately after the opening of the Dallas office revealed that the most blatant cases of discrimination were occurring at Humble, Sinclair, and Shell. Moreover, there were a sufficient number of Mexican workers in each plant willing to formally challenge their employers.[19] Although the FEPC handled cases against the three refineries simultaneously, Castaneda obtained the first settlement at Humble.

Humble owned four oil refineries in Texas, including the one at Baytown that became the center of early controversy for the FEPC. The Baytown plant employed approximately 3,000 workers during the war, including about 75 Mexicans and 400 blacks. The complaint against Humble occurred while the CIO-led Oil Workers' Organizing Campaign (OWOC) was joining the issue of unionization with the cause of minority workers. The CIO's national leadership initially directed the OWOC and thus injected a more progressive view on minority rights than was normally the case in the area. The OWOC leadership endorsed the claim of discrimination by Mexican complainants in part because it was actively soliciting the support of minority workers for the CIO union, Local 333, in the upcoming union election. This touched off a near-violent and racially inspired reaction by the company union, the Baytown Employees' Federation (BEF).[20]

In the midst of this highly controversial organizing campaign, a group of six Mexican workers charged Humble with six forms of discrimination. According to the complaint, Mexican laborers received seventy-six and one-half cents per hour for performing the same tasks as Anglo laborers who were paid eighty-nine and one-half cents an hour. While Mexican orderlies in the company hospital received a wage of $137 per month, Anglo janitors received $180 per month. Mexican and Anglo workers doing the same work in and around the acid tanks received seventy-nine and one-half cents per hour and ninety-two and one-half cents per hour, respectively. Although Mexicans cut, bent, and tied steel for seventy-six and one-half cents per hour, Anglos working for contractors on refinery property earned $1.34 for doing the same work. Mexicans were usually assigned to the labor department without opportunities for promotion, and Humble had refused to hire Mexicans since at least 1937.[21]

The company superintendent, Gordon L. Farned, responded to the complaint with a lengthy justification of Humble's record with its Mexican workers. He also broached the issue of Anglo worker opposition that was to loom over compliance negotiations in the industry. Farned cautioned the FEPC about disrupting the deep-rooted custom of discrimination against Mexicans in the state and urged a strategy of gradual change to minimize Anglo hostility.[22]

> Unless and until there is a change in public feeling and sentiment, regardless of what we as one employer may do about the matter, it is an undeniable fact that Anglo American workmen and the public generally, exclusive of the Mexicans themselves, do set themselves apart and do consider themselves to be superior mentally, physically and socially to the Mexicans...it probably would be to the best interests of the Mexicans to "make haste slowly;" to make social and economic gains gradually, to educate the populace at large gradually, and to promote their acceptance of the principles aimed at, rather than to take action intended to accomplish the ends you seek, which in actuality, if carried out, would most certainly start serious hostilities and lead to a harmful conflagration.[23]

Farned added a second related reason for resisting compliance that was to plague the FEPC's work in the industry. He suggested that the FEPC seek industry-wide compliance rather than plant-by-plant settlements. Otherwise, each company that complied presumably would be made the focus of the community's wrath with the resulting disruption of production.

Subsequent investigations revealed a glaring inconsistency in the company's claims that Mexican workers were not hired or promoted because they did not meet the company's educational requirements. Company officials admitted that Anglos were frequently hired without meeting the requirements and that Mexicans were denied employment even when they met them. Moreover, the officials failed to demonstrate a lack of ability by the Mexican workers since they often performed the same tasks as Anglos. As a result of the investigation, the complaint was expanded to include charges of discriminatory skill classifications and segregated drinking and toilet facilities.[24]

While Castaneda negotiated with Humble representatives, the company union began to openly declare that Local 333 was threatening the livelihood of Anglo workers by welcoming Mexicans and blacks into the union and by supporting claims of racial discrimination in the refinery. Leaders of the BEF stepped up their race-baiting activities against both Local 333 and the FEPC during the following weeks through a widely distributed organ, *The Bulletin*.[25] The paper consistently warned that compliance would result in granting equal treatment to blacks.[26]

At one point, *The Bulletin* pointed to the association between Local 333 and the FEPC with the following observation: "A vote for the CIO is a vote for absolute equality between the white and colored races on every job in the Baytown Refinery from labor gang to Department head."[27] When the FEPC wired the BEF to cease making inflammatory statements, *The Bulletin* responded that it did not "intend to be swayed from our purpose by any telegraphed reprimands from any of the C.I.O.-owned and operated Fair Labor Practices Committees in Washington, D.C., so this is a notice to them to save stamps and telegraph costs."[28]

Despite the findings of the initial investigation, the FEPC decided to delay action on the joint complaint and an additional complaint in which Local 333 alleged discrimination in the hiring, tenure, and compensation of Mexican and African American workers. This decision to withdraw from the conflict was made pending the outcome of the union election and FEPC deliberations in Washington regarding a proposed hearing to investigate complaints of discrimination against Mexicans in the Southwest. Also contributing to the postponement was the FEPC's indecision on whether to seek compliance on an industry or plant-by-plant basis.[29]

A renewed interest in the oil companies became evident when Castaneda obtained permission for a second investigation at Humble. By this time, the union had failed to secure certification and the FEPC had decided that the proposed hearing be confined to the mining industry in the Arizona-New Mexico-West Texas region and that action against the oil companies be pursued on an individual basis.[30] The second investigation generated complaints by three Mexican workers alleging wage discrimination. By the time Castaneda met with company officials, however, Humble had settled the complaints. A subsequent inquiry confirmed that Humble had granted the complainants a raise. The settlement, however, accompanied a decision by Humble to rid itself of its minority work force by contracting out to the Brown and Root Company all of its laboring work.[31]

One can only conjecture on the almost sudden reversal of opinion by Humble. Officials had been insistent on adhering to the local custom of denying employment opportunities to Mexican workers on the grounds that it would invite trouble. Moreover, company officials had been reluctant to fully admit the existence of discrimination or to correct past abuses, supposedly because of the feared reaction by Anglo workers. Humble officials, however, may have concluded that compliance was inevitable given the FEPC's belated yet determined decision to consider one refinery at a time. The union election, on the other hand, was probably the single most important factor that opened the way for resolving the impasse.

Humble had kept the FEPC at bay while it did battle with the OWOC on its successful march through the rest of the industry. Once the union lost the election the company was free to confront the problem that it faced with the FEPC. By introducing changes in the plant that exceeded the FEPC's directives, the company rid itself of a potentially difficult conflict with the agency. Although Humble may have appeared overly compliant, it had also begun to dispose of its minority work force. With this move, the company also avoided a conflict with its Anglo workforce and nullified one of Local 333's most important organizational and ideological bases of operations.

Local 333 was the only union in the region known to have cooperated fully with the FEPC. This was due largely to the influence of the CIO-run OWOC, which embraced the cause of the Mexican complainants. After a successful campaign that resulted in election victories in approximately six refineries, the CIO organizers in the OWOC boldly confronted racial discrimination. Supporting the cause of the Mexican complainants, however, resulted in the OWOC's only defeat in the early 1940s. The defeat also reinforced local fears of an Anglo workers' reaction to compliance and revealed a serious division between members of the national CIO and local and state leadership around the issue of race.

The OWIU and local CIO leaders had opposed the OWOC's progressive racial policy, including its endorsement of Mexican complaints during the organizing campaign at Humble. Pressure on the national CIO office eventually led to the removal of its organizers and an end to labor's expressed concern for minority workers. Prior to the election, the OWIU renegotiated its organizing agreement with the local and state CIO unionists, which resulted in the replacement of the organizers with personnel selected by the OWIU. The experience at Humble thus demonstrated that the OWIU and local leadership preferred to avoid the race issue for fear of antagonizing Anglo workers, a view that also found expression during the compliance battle at Sinclair.[32]

The Sinclair refinery located in Pasadena employed a workforce of approximately 1,500 that included approximately 100 Mexicans and 250 blacks.[33] At least three joint complaints were submitted on behalf of Mexican workers. J. O. Gray, secretary-treasurer of Local 227, submitted the first complaint in April 1942 to the Office of Production Management in San Antonio. He indicated that a foreman had unfairly issued warnings to the men and that the union's Workmen's Committee had submitted a request to transfer them to another department.[34] There is no evidence that the FEPC acted on the initial complaint, perhaps because around that same time a group of Mexican workers was also seeking the assistance of the FEPC with a more comprehensive complaint that charged the company as well as the union with discrimination.

The forty Mexican complainants secured the assistance of Consul Adolfo G. Dominguez in alleging a historical pattern of discrimination by the company and Local 227.[35] One of their major allegations was that Sinclair had stopped hiring Mexicans since the early 1930s. The workers also claimed that Sinclair routinely hired blacks to replace departing Mexican workers. The complainants further charged that the company, in collaboration with union leaders, maintained a job classification system that placed Mexicans in the laboring positions at an approximate wage of seventy-eight and one-half cents. Many performed the same tasks as skilled Anglo workers, though they were given job classifications as helpers at an hourly wage of ninety-eight and one-half cents. Four of them received eighty-three and one-half cents an hour. They worked as janitors along with nine African-American workers, and they could only transfer to other departments if they kept their classification as common laborers. Moreover, skilled and semiskilled vacancies were never posted, and only Anglo unionists were allowed to bid for these jobs. Only one of the workers had ever been promoted; he was a naturalized citizen who worked as a foreman for a crew of black workers.

The Mexican workers also complained about the company's segregation practices. They were required to punch the time clock in a separate line shared with African- American workers. Also, the company kept separate lockers and bathing facilities for minority workers. During the lunch hour, Mexican workers were given the choice of eating outdoors or joining the African-American workers in a segregated section. Lastly, Mexicans and blacks were transported to work in two crowded buses while the Anglos traveled in a separate, less-crowded bus.

Once Castaneda had confirmed the allegations through on-site investigations, he submitted the joint complaint to Sinclair and Local 227.

When neither responded, Castaneda visited the complainants at the Mexican Consul's office to further substantiate the charges. On the basis of this inquiry, the FEPC once again forwarded a complaint and requested a response to specific wage and upgrading allegations of discrimination against both Mexican and African American workers.[36]

The superintendent of the refinery, D. A. Young, responded with a denial of the charges. He added that despite the fact that few Mexican and African-American workers qualified for the better-paying jobs, Sinclair had upgraded three Mexican workers to semiskilled and skilled positions. Probably because he anticipated a finding in favor of the Mexican complainants, Young resorted to placing the burden of compliance on Local 227. He warned FEPC officials that the union would not "permit the commingling of the different races employed at this plant."[37] To demonstrate that this was not a ploy to evade compliance, Young furnished Cochran with correspondence in which the union expressly opposed the promotion or reclassification of Mexican workers.

During a subsequent meeting with Castaneda, Young expressed a willingness to provide upgrading opportunities to Mexican as well as African American workers if the union could be made to guarantee support for compliance. Local 227 representatives, on the other hand, admitted that the union had opposed upgrading but promised to seek the cooperation of the entire membership for a policy of nondiscrimination. Company and union representatives, however, denied that discrimination existed regarding wages, the posting of vacancy notices, and the use of transportation facilities.[38]

Two months later, Castaneda was reporting that the upgrading case against Sinclair had been adjusted. The company had kept its word, and the union membership had grudgingly decided not to contest what Castaneda admitted were "minor advances given Latin Americans" at Sinclair.[39] A major factor in the settlement was Castaneda's decision to settle the complaint on the basis of the admissions made by the company and union representatives. Castaneda's conciliatory approach was clearly intended to capitalize on the single admission of upgrading discrimination in order to proceed with a directive calling for the adoption of a general policy of nondiscrimination.

Although Castaneda had initially filed the case alleging discrimination against Mexicans at Sinclair, he sought a settlement that favored the entire minority work force. Consequently, when he confirmed the settlement, he made binding an agreement that benefited both Mexican and black workers. In a letter to an officer of the union, he stated:

> I am pleased to note that as the result of the meetings held your union has agreed to permit the company to abandon its discriminatory practices and to give all employees an equal opportunity for promotion in accord with their experience, ability and aptitude, regardless of race, creed, color or national origin.[40]

Although the company and the union may have been cooperative during the final settlement negotiations, they did not satisfy the concerns of the Mexican workers who continued to informally complain of discrimination. One year after Castaneda had secured the settlement, the same Mexican complainants were again formally contesting Sinclair's discriminatory practices. They claimed that Sinclair was refusing to hire qualified Mexican applicants and denying them upgrading opportunities. The company had allegedly refused employment to three Mexican applicants at the same time that it had been hiring African-American and Anglo workers. Moreover, Sinclair had refused to upgrade at least three Mexican workers. On the basis of this complaint, Ellinger informed Sinclair that despite the recent settlement, the FEPC had determined that discrimination against Mexicans was continuing.[41]

The company responded to the complaint by denying the charges, while the union simply chose to disregard it. The FEPC, on the other hand, did not press the issue even though additional complaints continued to arrive. This was probably due to the fact that mounting political opposition to the FEPC in Washington was already signaling the end of the agency and thus discouraging forthright action. Also, the FEPC was then waging its most trying battle at Shell, which may have drawn its resources and attention from the fight at Sinclair.[42]

The case against Sinclair once again demonstrated the FEPC's difficulty in securing permanent settlements. One obvious problem was the discontinuance of the agency's operations at a time when settlements were still pending. Additionally, indecision regarding the compliance strategy that the FEPC wished to pursue contributed to the initial delays. Other more important factors included the opposition of the union and the refusal of the company to comply until it could be guaranteed that Local 227 would not strike in protest. Also, the company failed to live up to its promise to comply with the FEPC directives and continued to challenge allegations of discrimination confirmed by the FEPC. The union was generally indifferent to the second complaint, preferring instead to leave the minority workers to fend for themselves against Sinclair.

Reminiscent of the fight at Humble, the FEPC often appeared to back away as if it was facing an opponent too formidable to confront. Despite the large amount of evidence accumulated in support of the complaints, the FEPC exhibited a conciliatory attitude in the settlement process. It may have been expedient, however, for Castaneda to seek a speedy settlement in light of the trouble that the agency was having at the time with Shell. This willingness to settle allowed Castaneda to correct one case of upgrading discrimination and to justify a directive calling for the adoption of a policy of nondiscrimination. Rushing into a settlement that conceded ground on key charges, however, no doubt left the impression that the FEPC lacked the confidence and enforcement power to challenge employment discrimination, a perception that plagued the agency in its dealings with Shell.

The Shell Oil Company maintained a large refinery at Deer Park with a work force of approximately 1,200 workers that included at least one hundred Mexican and African-American workers.[43] Mexican workers faced the same problems evident in the Humble and Sinclair refineries. Widespread discrimination restricted them, as well as African-American workers, to the lowest-paying unskilled positions. Moreover, both groups of workers were limited to segregated transportation, eating, and restroom facilities. Mexican complaints against Shell resulted in one of the most bitter fights over the issue of discrimination. It involved open defiance by the union and the continuing embarrassing ineffectiveness of the FEPC.

The FEPC initiated its case against Shell in May 1943 with a complaint submitted by Consul Dominguez on behalf of thirty-four Mexican nationals who had tried unsuccessfully to settle their claims with the company during the previous two years. They had also failed to convince Local 367 to intervene on their behalf. As a result, they had quit the union and were now appealing to the Mexican Consul and local LULAC leaders as an act of last resort. The workers made the familiar charges of occupational, wage, and upgrading discrimination, a hiring ceiling, and segregated facilities.[44]

During a meeting at the Mexican Consulate that was attended by company, union, and Mexican workers' representatives, an FEPC investigator confirmed the allegations, though he was not able to settle the complaint. When Consul Dominguez asked that Mexican workers be granted a just wage and the promotional guarantees enjoyed by Anglos, management and union representatives responded that they could not give assurances because of the all too prevalent fear of antagonizing Anglo workers. They claimed that there was a widespread belief among Anglo workers that a concession to the Mexicans would encourage complaints by blacks seeking similar guarantees and that this would result in depressed wages and their eventual replacement by minority workers.[45]

The company and the union maintained that the only way to avoid a disruption was if the FEPC held an industry-wide hearing and ordered all the refineries in the area with CIO union contracts to adopt a policy of nondiscrimination. The union offered to communicate the plan to the other locals. Seeing no other option, Consul Dominguez expressed his support for the plan and recommended that the FEPC initiate such a

Oil workers at a World War II war bond rally held at Shell's Deer Park Refinery, 1943. *Courtesy of Shell Deer Park Historical Society, Deer Park, Texas.*

settlement in a meeting with O. A. Knight, president of the OWIU, and D. W. Hobey, president of the Gulf Coast Refiners Association.[46]

The FEPC may have allowed Shell and the union to independently implement their proposed plan because there is no evidence that Castaneda participated in it. When months passed without any news about the implementation of the plan from Shell, the local, or the OWIU, Castaneda called on the FEPC to grant him the authority to proceed with the case. He was particularly concerned that Consul Dominguez and other Mexican leaders would become more disillusioned with the FEPC. Castaneda also expressed the view that the company and the local had called for an industry-wide hearing for the sole purpose of delaying the compliance process. He felt that the most reasonable and promising measure to take was individual action based on the findings of discrimination that Shell and Local 367 officers openly admitted.[47]

A worsening situation at Shell underscored the need for immediate action. On November 3, the manager suspended seven Mexican workers for insubordination. According to the workers, he had instructed them to do a temporary job for eighty-seven cents an hour in the segregated pipe-fitting department, though the prevailing wage for pipefitters ranged between $.97 and $1.39 an hour. When they refused to do the work at the disputed wage, he fired them. The company subsequently advertised vacancies for these same jobs at ninety-seven cents an hour. The workers once again sought the help of Consul Dominguez. This time, however, the Mexican Consul convinced his superiors to intercede in the matter—an indication of growing concern in Mexican government circles. The Mexican ambassador to the United States, Rafael de la Colina, expressed his government's displeasure to the chairman of the FEPC by stating that continuing defiance at Shell violated the Good Neighbor Alliance and undermined the US government's wartime pledge of international solidarity against racial injustice. The issue of discrimination in oil thus reached international proportions, a development that pressured the FEPC to redouble its efforts.[48]

Meanwhile, to support his contention for a hearing that would address the complaints against Shell, Castaneda called for an additional investigation, which later confirmed the prior findings. He also recommended immediate action, particularly because Shell again admitted practicing discrimination.[49] The subsequent conference that Castaneda held with Shell and Local 367 representatives in December ended on a familiar note. The manager of the refinery and the president of Local 367 admitted discrimination but insisted that they would not agree to any changes until a general hearing was held or a directive was issued by the FEPC ordering the entire industry to implement a policy of nondiscrimination.[50] When FEPC officials requested a formal statement documenting this response, the union officer answered defiantly, "The Union at this time does not propose to change without first having a hearing or order, as we consider ourselves and the company both in violation of the Executive Order."[51] The company representative added, "The position of the Management of the company is that the consequences of any change in this respect are so far-reaching and would have such detrimental results that we do not see any reason for change."[52]

Shell defended its bid for an industry-wide hearing and directive with the argument that a unilateral settlement would place the company in an unfair position with its competitors. With this argument, Shell placed the burden of change on the union, while the union officers openly admitted that the membership would strike if the company complied.[53] The deadlock seemed unbreakable, especially since the FEPC had delayed action while its personnel debated on the proper strategy to pursue. While Castaneda insisted on an individual hearing with Shell, other officials in the Dallas office were urging an industrywide hearing. A decision was finally reached to proceed with Castaneda's recommendation and to schedule a hearing for December 1944.[54] On the day that the public hearing was to take place, Shell officials finally conceded. They requested a private conference and promised to abide by the decision to be rendered by the Trial Examiner and a committee of four FEPC representatives that included Castaneda.[55]

In his opening statement before the committee, an FEPC official accused the company and the union of disregarding the skills and experience of Mexican workers and of restricting them to the menial jobs at wages that were lower than those paid to Anglo workers performing the same tasks. This had been accomplished through a formal contract that defined the discriminatory rates of pay, hours of work, and other terms of employment operating in the plant. Since discrimination at Shell had been directed against both Mexicans and blacks, the FEPC called for an end to all forms of discrimination.[56]

The opening statement included other observations that acknowledged the importance that the Shell case had acquired in the international arena, particularly with the major ally of the United States in the hemisphere, Mexico.[57] In calling for an end to racial and national origin discrimination, the FEPC described the denial of opportunities as a problem that undermined the war effort because it harmed relations with Latin American nations:

The eyes of our neighbors to the south are watching with keen interest. The denial of equal opportunities for full participation in the war effort, and for advancement to workers of Latin-American extraction, negatives [sic] our professions of good neighborliness and reflects upon our moral leadership in the family of nations.[58]

The committee appeared to have settled the issue once and for all when it ordered the company and the union to eliminate all forms of discrimination. The company and the union agreed to expunge from the collective bargaining agreement all basis for discrimination and to stop denying Mexican and African American workers hiring and upgrading opportunities. The committee also gave specific instructions directing Shell to submit a separate wage complaint to the War Labor Board for adjustment and to upgrade two Mexican complainants to carman's helper and truck driver. The FEPC followed by rendering a decision on January 27 that directed the company and the union to comply with the president's executive order within ninety days.[59] The stage was now set to determine if compliance could proceed to its logical conclusion without setting off a reaction by Anglo workers.

The compliance process quickly became burdened with difficulties that tested the FEPC's ability to influence the ensuing course of events. When several Mexican workers, including the complainants who had been assured promotions, signed up for available jobs, a foreman and the personnel manager informed them that Shell did not intend to abide by the FEPC directive until the April 27 deadline. FEPC officials rightfully saw this as a direct challenge against the spirit, if not the letter, of the settlement. Pressure was again brought to bear on Shell.[60]

In response to the FEPC's requests for support, other government agencies reminded the company that it was obligated to honor the president's executive order or risk losing lucrative federal contracts. The FEPC had mixed results, however, in convincing labor leaders to pressure Local 367. While the national CIO office declared support for a policy of nondiscrimination, key state leaders such as O. A. Knight and Timothy Flyn, state CIO director, claimed that the parent organizations did not dictate policy to their locals. Nonetheless, pressure from government agencies finally convinced Shell to cooperate. The first upgrading occurred on March 8, when Shell appointed a Mexican worker to a carman's helper position. A week later, a second Mexican worker was upgraded to a truck driver's job.[61]

Increased pressure by the FEPC eventually forced Shell to upgrade additional minority applicants. This, however, did not occur without Shell first announcing that the FEPC was forcing the company to integrate the workforce against its will. Two vice presidents of the local added to the growing tensions by resigning from their positions as a sign of disapproval of the FEPC directives. On March 22, the company nevertheless upgraded one Mexican and seven blacks to general helpers in each of the eight separate craft departments. An incident followed that raised the developing conflict to a higher level.[62]

A company foreman who obviously sought to disassociate himself from the issue of compliance convened Anglo workers from each department and asked them to publicly state if they would work alongside the upgraded minority workers. Although some of the Anglo workers may have been inclined to accept this proposition, the fear of reprisals from coworkers was probably too great because none agreed to work with them. In opposing the upgrading decision, the Anglo workers were absolving the company from any National Labor Relations Board (NLRB) blame in the compliance conflict and accepting the major responsibility for defending the status quo. Soon after the vote, an undetermined number of Anglo workers and the two union officers that had resigned threatened to stage a strike if the minority workers were placed in their new positions. The company quickly returned the workers to their previous jobs. Emboldened by this immediate response, the protesting Anglo workers then demanded that the previously upgraded Mexican workers also be returned to their former jobs. The company again capitulated.[63]

FEPC officials called a series of conferences with company and union representatives to try to remedy the situation that had clearly gotten out of hand. The company maintained that it was forced to concede to the demands of the Anglo workers. Union representatives, on the other hand, expressed an interest in complying with the FEPC directives but requested time to convince a portion of their membership that was opposed to integration.[64] Matters deteriorated further as Shell officials continued to publicly present the company as a helpless victim and as the union membership began to more forcefully express its opposition to the issue of integration. Although the union did not guarantee support for compliance, continued FEPC pressure led the company to upgrade two Mexican workers on April 27. The results were predictable.[65]

Anglo workers in the automotive department responded by walking off their jobs. Negotiations followed between the union, Shell, and a conciliator from the Department of Labor. When negotiations failed to produce any results, the FEPC brought in the assistant disputes director from the Dallas office of the War Labor Board to help resolve the issue. The result was a six-day hearing that affirmed the FEPC directive and the Smith-Connally Act, which required workers to issue a petition before waging a strike in wartime. As part of the settlement, the workers agreed to remain on the job and not insist on the removal of the upgraded Mexicans without first filing a strike petition with the NLRB. In granting the union the right to hold a vote on what was essentially a compliance matter, however, the War Labor Board undermined the FEPC directives and provided the segregationists the opportunity to legitimately defy the FEPC at a future date.[66]

The tenuous settlement involved important concessions by FEPC officials who by now seemed to be desperately seeking to regain their influence. First of all, they failed to dispute the decision by the War Labor Board that granted the union the right to challenge the compliance directive. In fact, the FEPC granted Shell and the local a thirty-day extension on the compliance order to accommodate the scheduling of the election.

Moreover, a general understanding was reached whereby no more upgrading actions were to be taken until the strike ballot was cast. Although the FEPC was essentially forced to back down, the prospects of losing complete control led Ellinger to declare with a sense of relief, "we have won a tremendous victory by the skin of our teeth in the agreement of the men to work with the Latin-Americans on the job."[67]

Mexican government officials and Mexican civil rights leaders from Texas did not share Ellinger's enthusiasm. They began to more openly view the Shell case as a stark demonstration of deep-rooted racism and ineffective government intervention. Mexico's foreign minister, Ezequiel Padilla, for instance, commented while attending the first United Nations Conference at San Francisco that nothing less than the hemispheric prestige of the United States as a democratic nation was at stake. Also, Castaneda reported that Mexican leaders from throughout the state expressed "strong resentment" against Shell and felt that the FEPC was not sufficiently aggressive.[68]

Minority workers remained steadfast in support of compliance. Mexican workers called for full integration, while African-American workers supported the idea of a segregated workforce on a separate but equal basis. In other words, both Mexican and African-American workers sought guarantees of equal access to all jobs at the same pay while the latter group did not insist on working side-by-side with Anglo workers. Minority workers also agreed that the FEPC should continue to press the company and the union with claims of discrimination by Mexican workers since they had the best chance of succeeding and setting the necessary precedent for the complete integration of the workforce.[69]

Anglo workers refused to concede despite the urgings of the FEPC and the negative publicity that the case brought the oil industry and the labor movement. This became openly evident when a majority of them voted in favor of a strike on June 6, 1945. The NLRB-sanctioned election not only affirmed the segregationist posture of the union; it also demonstrated the union's new-found talent for legitimately defying the president's executive order. As a result of the election, the FEPC scuttled its compliance directive and endorsed a settlement proposed by the union. The union's plan designated a small number of skilled jobs for minority workers to be set aside in still-segregated departments. Shell representatives, on the other hand, washed their hands of the whole matter. They declared a willingness to adopt whatever plan the FEPC and the union favored.[70]

Minority workers expressed deep resentment over the strike vote and were adamant in demanding that the FEPC not relent in its dealings with the company and the union despite efforts by Anglo workers to divide them. Mexicans were told that if African American workers had not been included in the directive, Anglos would have complied. Blacks, on the other hand, were told that the Mexicans ought not be supported because they were pretentious and claimed to be better than blacks. With matters still unresolved, the FEPC first restricted and then closed its operations in Texas when Congress decided to deny the agency the needed appropriations for the postwar period. There is no record that the FEPC was able to negotiate a settlement acceptable to the minority workers. Presumably, they were left to fend for themselves against continued occupational and wage discrimination.[71]

The Shell case once again demonstrated the agency's weakness. The case underwent numerous delays primarily because the company and Local 367 consistently refused to comply with the president's executive order. The Shell local acted much like the BEF and Local 227 in reinforcing racial inequality. Local 367 collaborated with management in restricting minority workers to the laboring occupations and in denying them the opportunity to advance into the higher-paying and skilled jobs in the refinery. Unlike Local 227, the Shell union was steadfast in its refusal to support compliance. This refusal, coupled with the FEPC's setbacks at Humble and Sinclair, underscored the significance of discrimination in denying Mexicans equal employment opportunities in the Texas Gulf Coast oil industry.

The problem of discrimination in the oil industry had special importance when one considers that there may never have been a better time than the period of the Second World War for Mexicans from Texas to have altered their occupational standing relative to Anglos. The wartime demand on the economy had expanded job opportunities to unprecedented levels. Increased job growth, coupled with labor shortages occasioned by conscription, resulted in immediate occupational gains that seemed to presage a new era of equality. Accompanying these promising developments was the rhetoric of world democracy that encouraged even higher expectations of racial justice and equality at the home front. Lastly, with the establishment of FEPC regional offices in Texas, the federal government promised Mexican workers protection against employment discrimination.

Mexican oil workers were part of the relatively small yet important wave of upwardly mobile workers making the transition from low-wage employers to high-wage and well-organized firms during the war. Their disproportionate representation in the lesser-skilled and lower paying jobs, however, defined the limits that discrimination placed on them. The twelve oil refineries located in the Gulf Coast generally maintained low hiring quotas for Mexicans, assigned them laborer occupations, paid them a lower wage than Anglos, denied them upgrading opportunities, and restricted them to segregated work, eating, and restroom areas. A key element in maintaining a racial order in the refineries were the race-conscious Anglo workers, including members of CIO-affiliated unions. Anglo workers and their representatives also assumed an important role in defending the segregated order by pressuring the companies against complying with FEPC directives. Fearing the loss of their hard-won gains during the 1930s, they claimed job prerogatives and reacted defensively toward the FEPC.

Although some improvements for minority workers resulted from the intercession of the FEPC, the agency was not able to challenge discrimination and inequality effectively at Humble, Sinclair, and Shell. Since the FEPC directed most of its attention to these three companies and other refineries do not seem to have been compelled to implement non-discrimination policies, we can conclude that the FEPC did not make an appreciable impact in the oil industry. Its work was a positive yet minor contribution next to the demand for labor that provided Mexican workers the initial limited opportunity for employment. The FEPC's lack of enforcement powers, its short duration in Texas, internal divisions, and management's ambivalence in the face of a threatened Anglo workers' reaction no doubt contributed to the failure of governmental intervention in the oil industry. The most decisive factor in the fight over compliance, however, was the opposition of Anglo workers. The most striking result was yet another delay in the full incorporation of Mexican workers into the Texas occupational structure.

By the later 1930s, oil company camp housing evolved in an upscale direction, and houses stretched along tree-lined streets, as in this Humble Pipe Line camp at Wink. *Courtesy of the Permian Basin Petroleum Museum (Midland, Texas), Humble Oil & Refining Company collection.*

APRIL 2008

Creating Company Culture: Oil Company Camps in the Southwest, 1920–1960

DIANA D. HINTON

During the first half of the twentieth century, thousands of oil company employees and their families in the American Southwest lived in largely self-contained communities constructed by their employers. Oil company camps included both white- and blue-collar personnel and met the immediate need for housing for those who worked in the field. Companies sometimes built camps on the outskirts of booming oil towns as an alternative to the rough living conditions that were usual in boomtowns. They were virtually obliged to build camps in oilfields located in remote, thinly settled areas, where lack of roads made housing in the field essential. When companies built camps, however, they intended to do more than simply meet the need for shelter. They created communities that would foster shared experiences, perspectives, and values, a company way of life that would establish a distinctive company culture. As the Humble Oil Company put it in the first issue of *The Humble Way* magazine, "There is, and always has been, a Humble way of doing things. It is a distinct way."¹ Like other oil companies, Humble aimed to use company culture to retain a loyal, efficient white- and blue-collar workforce that would not trade life with Humble for jobs with other employers or for union membership.

Oil companies were by no means American pioneers in creating company communities to provide housing in remote areas. Western coal, copper, and timber companies commonly bought land, platted a rectangular grid of streets, constructed large numbers of nearly identical wooden houses, and supplied dwellings with water and electricity. Mining and timber towns often had company-owned stores, schools, hospitals, hotels, and recreational facilities. The company might even include a saloon on the premises, though saloons, like houses of prostitution, more usually located just over the town boundaries. Depending on the company, the town might reflect, as historian James B. Allen has suggested, an "enlightened paternalism." Alternatively, in the instance of the Texas

In new fields remote from settled areas, the first workers usually lived in tents. Humble Oil supplied these tents for Yates field workers shortly after the field's discovery in Pecos County in 1926. *Courtesy of the Permian Basin Petroleum Museum (Midland, Texas), Joe Salmon collection.*

and Pacific Coal Company's town of Thurber, a six-foot-high barbed-wire fence surrounding the town demonstrated the company's determination to keep out troublemakers like union organizers. Company-town newspapers and company-organized activities sought to kill worker discontent with a sense of company unity. Community life ran according to company rules.²

Oil company camps differed from the earlier company mining and timber towns in many respects. Most camps—the Big Lake Oil Company's Texon an exception—did not try to be towns. For all the amenities they included, they usually did not include stores, post offices, schools, hotels, movie theaters, or churches. Saloons were conspicuously absent. Camps, moreover, were usually part of a geographically extensive company network within which employees could expect frequent relocations. A Humble employee, for example, might spend several months at the McCamey camp in West Texas, be transferred to Hobbs, New Mexico, return to McCamey, and be sent on to East Texas, depending on the need for his services. Whitecollar personnel like geologists and petroleum engineers experienced more frequent transfers than blue-collar workers. One Humble geologist remarked, "The movers knew my furniture better than I did!" Oil camp population, furthermore, was more ethnically homogeneous than that of mining towns, reflecting the overwhelmingly Anglo composition of the oilfield workforce before 1950. Oil company camps were no melting pots; ethnic homogeneity made it easier for companies to create a sense of company unity.³

Compared to mining and timber towns, oil company camps were latecomers among company-run communities, a timing that reflected conditions peculiar to the petroleum industry. Petroleum presents conditions unusual in mineral exploitation because it moves through rock under the ground. Depending on how a well is produced, a large discovery may mean sustained high levels of production or output that winds down in short order. In the American petroleum industry's first half century, when oil wells came in, operators produced them at top capacity

This view of unpaved Main Street in the brand new oil town of Iraan, seen in the late twenties, suggests that living conditions in town were relatively rugged. Finding any housing in such a new community was difficult. *Courtesy of the Permian Basin Petroleum Museum (Midland, Texas), Orbeck collection.*

until production declined. They then put wells on the pump until meager output warranted shutting them down and abandoning them. Such flush production reflected legal reality. The producer owned what came from his well, and, since oil moved underground, a man who did not produce all he could risked seeing neighbors drain oil from underneath his lease. Producers also knew that any well's production could be a sometime thing, prompting them to get what they could as fast as possible and move on. They shared a mentality of boom and bust.

Though exploitation of hard rock minerals often begins with a "rush" or boom following discovery, once the parameters of an ore deposit are known—far easier to do when the mineral does not move underground—it is reasonable to expect a large discovery to mean sustained production over time. By contrast, in the early oilfields, where discoveries were a matter of happy accident, a magnificent wildcat well might uncover a large field or a small pool. As underground pressure pushing oil to the wellhead diminished, so did well and field production. No one could explain or predict the rate of decline. Given the uncertainties of exploration and production, it was not tempting to invest in oilfield infrastructure beyond the essentials of rigs, tanks, pumping apparatus, and gathering lines. Compared to hard rock mineral extraction, early oilfield production was evanescent. Boom might not be followed by bust, but settled production was often a small fraction of the output of the first heady months of field development.[4]

As oilfield production came and went, so did oilfield workers. Once drilling and production slackened in one field, workers moved on to the next discovery. In any new field, with producers racing to get their oil before their neighbors did, demand for labor was intense. It was easy to find work and easy to leave it; any worker dissatisfied with the boss could readily find a new one, a reality that did not encourage labor organization. The terms of employment, moreover, varied little from employer to employer in the early oilfields. Pay was high relative to that in many blue-collar occupations, hours uniformly long (a twelve-hour "tour" or shift was usual), working conditions more than ordinarily unsafe, and living conditions squalid. On the other hand, as workers followed discov-

By 1930, the Mid-Kansas-Transcontinental Oil Company had this tidy camp in place for its Yates field personnel. The shotgun houses were typical of West Texas oil company camps of the time. *Courtesy of the Permian Basin Petroleum Museum (Midland, Texas), Marathon collection.*

eries, the boomer's life was rough but exciting, and work was anything but monotonous routine.[5]

After 1900, a variety of developments modified the pattern of oilfield exploration and production. Perhaps most important was increased petroleum industry use of geoscience. Oil companies began to hire geologists to help find oil. As geologists knew more about how rock formations trapped oil, they were better able to predict where oil might be found. With increased understanding of prehistoric stages in oil formation, they began to theorize about petroleum's occurrence throughout entire regions. At times, their speculation was way off the mark, as when, prior to 1920, they dismissed western Texas as a place where there was likely to be little oil. But geologists' ideas encouraged leasing and exploration of broad areas, as opposed to hit-or-miss wildcatting. The emergence of petroleum engineering in the late teens was equally as important as geology in changing patterns of petroleum exploitation. Building on the work of the geologists, petroleum engineers came to understand how petroleum moved through rock to the wellhead and how oil and gas reservoirs worked. The engineers developed technology to sustain and prolong production to get many more thousands of barrels of oil out of the ground, thus changing the time-honored "here today, gone tomorrow" pattern of oilfield production. In particular, engineers showed that moving from flush production to controlled output would extend field life.

Applied geoscience made it realistic for oil companies to plan investment in a field or a whole region with an extended presence in mind. So did the opening up of some truly stunning petroleum bonanzas in the Southwest and in California. In Texas alone, the first three decades of the twentieth century saw the Gulf Coast, North Texas, Panhandle, Permian Basin, and East Texas produce millions of barrels of oil. By 1930, for example, the Permian Basin clearly had potential for decades of exploration and production, and it would take many years to find and extract all the oil in a place like Pecos County. Companies leasing in prolific regions would be busy for a long time—at least, that was what the geoscientists told them. And companies would need thousands of workers, people willing to stay on the payroll rather than move on to the next boom. Oil companies would need a settled workforce.

A settled workforce, however, would be more accessible to labor organizers. By the late teens, there were signs that unions might gain ground in the oil industry, not only in refining centers but in the oilfield itself, a phenomenon hitherto held back by the high level of worker mobility. Early in 1917, the Oil and Gas Well Workers' Union emerged in California, and both California and the Texas Gulf Coast oilfields saw labor unrest in 1917-1918.[6] Oil men not only had the usual motives for avoiding confrontation with organized labor, but field operations made it seem especially desirable to head off union activity. According to prevailing industry belief, wells shut down would never be fully restored to production capacity, an idea not without foundation in the infancy of petroleum engineering. A strike or a walkout of organized field workers was thus much more threatening than a factory shutdown, because it might mean permanent loss of production. Thus, company managers sought strategies to kill union organization with kindness. One possibility was to create an attractive way of company life in oil camps.

Creating an appealing way of life could also help retain married workers. In the early oilfields, married workers faced the problem of what to do with wives and children. If families followed breadwinners to the oilfield, they could expect to live in shacks and cope with primitive and unsanitary living conditions. The popular image of boomtown life as rough, dangerous, and generally immoral also made wives reluctant to follow their husbands. As a result, workers often left wives and children in settled communities far from the oilfield. But company camps, with their bungalows, gardens, clubs, and recreational facilities, would be like a little bit of the suburbs transplanted out to the field. Camp housing offered a way to insulate families from the traditional rough and tumble of oilfield life. It kept families together and wives happier about their husbands' work. Contented wives would mean retaining dependable workers. In the words of one company executive, "When you hire a man, you [also] hire his wife."[7] After 1920, as companies began to hire highly educated professionals like geologists and engineers, there was even more incentive to provide an appealing way of company life for the whole family.

The first oil company camps appeared in the California oilfields. As early as 1903, Standard Oil of California built bungalows and bunkhouses at isolated pipeline pumping stations in the central and southern parts of the state. Standard made these oil installations attractive by putting in lawns, trees, and gardens. The same year, British-backed California Oilfields, Ltd. started construction of a model oil community in the booming but isolated Coalinga oilfield. By the time Shell took over the camp ten years later, it had bungalows and bunkhouses, dining rooms, a library, luxurious guest quarters, a water plant, an ice plant, an electric plant, a cooperative store, and a post office. To meet the needs of oilfield operations, the camp also had machine shops, tank works, and a lumberyard. Company managers recognized the value of employee recreation in an isolated location by putting in a swimming pool, golf course, and tennis courts; there also were baseball, soccer, and basketball teams. For the non-athletically minded, there was an amateur theater group, a glee club, and weekly movies. The Shell Coalinga camp proved a trendsetter, and Standard Oil of California developed similar camps at Coalinga, Montebello, and other locations. Remoteness from established communities offered an immediate incentive to build these camps, but the desire to create worker loyalty was also obvious. As Standard's John J. Carter wrote in 1908, "Treat employees well, pay them well, house them well, demand and you will receive the best work possible from the men."[8]

From California, oil company camps soon spread to Texas and Oklahoma. In 1919, for example, W. S. Smullin, production superintendent for Standard Oil of California at Coalinga and other southern California oilfields, went to work for Humble Oil as vice-president in charge of North Texas drilling and production. With the Ranger boom at its

Gulf Oil's McElroy field camp was located east of the new boomtown of Crane in the late 1920s. Because of the danger of poison gas coming from wells, Gulf moved the entire camp to a site nearer Crane in 1936. *Courtesy of the Permian Basin Petroleum Museum (Midland, Texas), Hogan collection.*

height, Humble management believed that this part of northern Texas contained enormous reserves, and small fields already discovered would ultimately be connected in one giant producing region that would take years to develop. Smullin lost no time in launching construction of a California-style camp on a grand scale near the small town of Cisco. Humbletown had over 140 bungalows, as well as bunkhouses, a dining hall, warehouses, offices, a waterworks, an ice plant, and a powerhouse. The bungalows had hardwood floors and bathrooms; the dining hall dished out pint-servings of ice cream. By the time Smullin was done, Humble spent over a million dollars on Humbletown. Unfortunately for the company, the Ranger area did not prove to be part of a gigantic oil pool, but Humble kept the camp running until the 1950s.[9]

After Humbletown, Humble continued to build impressive camps for its field workers, albeit on not so grand a scale. In 1921, it placed a camp in the Hewitt, Oklahoma, field, three miles from the town of Wilson. Four-room bungalows stretched along graveled streets with cement side-

The Big Lake Oil Company's camp at Texon in Reagan County came closer than most oil camps to being a completely self-contained town. Its cafés served beer to thirsty workers and visitors. *Courtesy of the Permian Basin Petroleum Museum (Midland, Texas), Delz collection.*

walks, a change from the usual oil town thoroughfares deep in dust or mud. Hewitt had a range of amenities like Humbletown, but its recreational facilities were especially noteworthy. They included a clubhouse with a Victrola phonograph, a swimming pool, a trap-shooting range, and a would-be zoo. At its start, the zoo had two Alaskan bears, two coyotes, and a possum; but the coyotes died, the bears were sold to a Fort Worth zoo, and someone ate the possum before a year was up. Going beyond housing field workers, Humble began building a large community at Baytown in 1920 for the workers at its new refinery. The refinery sat in marshy rice fields and swampland some thirty miles from Houston, so the company not only built housing but also three school buildings and a grocery store. By 1923, however, Humble moved away from the camp model at Baytown to more conventional development. It not only provided streets, sidewalks, and utilities in the growing community, it also sold employees lots on which they would build their own houses.[10]

By the mid-1920s, oil company camps were common enough for the *Oil and Gas Journal* to tell its readers how much workers' living conditions in the field had improved, in contrast to "the old days" when workers considered themselves lucky if they could board with a nearby farm family. Workers now had "fine camps, with neat boarding houses for the unmarried men or cottages for the families of the married men." These modern camps featured all modern conveniences, including clubhouses with "an innovation of recent date," radios. Not surprisingly, the author concluded that, "In many respects...the oil worker is given better care than his fellow workmen in other industries."[11] If one was lucky enough to live in a company camp, that was true.

In terms of size and amenities, oil company camps varied considerably with the company and the type of installation. During the twenties and thirties, drilling and production employees lived in the larger camps, while pipeline stations and small field refineries and gasoline plants might have only a dozen or so houses attached to them. Major companies like Humble, Gulf, or Magnolia often built camps with fifty or sixty houses, as well as offices, garages, warehouses, machine shops, and a wide range of recreational facilities. Usually, smaller companies provided much more

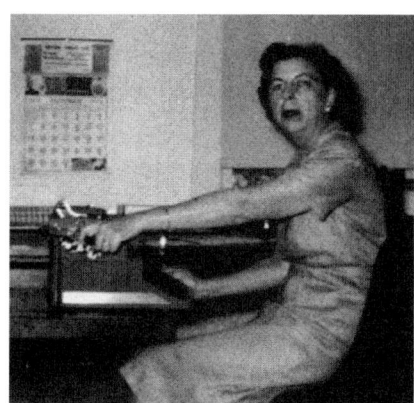

Above left: Few women found work in the oil field before the 1970s, but oil company camps did hire women to be nurses in camp clinics and office workers in camp offices. Golda Rogers is seen at her desk in the Big Lake Oil Company's main office in November 1951. *Courtesy of the Permian Basin Petroleum Museum (Midland, Texas), John David Grissett collection.* Above right: Given prevailing patterns of employment discrimination, the only African Americans living in oil company camps were usually employed in janitorial capacities. These workers, Jim Jones and Earl Holmes, attended a Big Lake Oil Company barbecue. Jones was a retired porter and Holmes a sanitation department employee. *Courtesy of the Permian Basin Petrolium Museum (Midland, Texas), John David Grissett collection.*

modestly for workers, although the Big Lake Oil Company's camp at Texon surpassed all West Texas camps in grandeur. Texon had everything a town would have—grocery stores, drug stores, barbershops, a library, a post office, a hospital, and an elementary school. Nearly twice as large, and far more impressive than the nearby county seat of Big Lake, Texon even had a theater, an airstrip, and a landscape gardener who tended over nine hundred rose bushes. At its peak in the 1930s, Texon had over 240 employee houses.[12]

The Gulf Oil camp in the McElroy field in Crane County, Texas, was more typical of oil company communities. In 1926, Gulf placed a camp three miles east of the new boomtown of Crane. It not only built houses but also moved in houses from camps it was phasing out at Breckenridge, over a hundred miles away. By 1933 the Gulf camp had sixty-five houses, six bunkhouses of thirty rooms each, a boarding house, a guest house for visiting company dignitaries, a small hospital building, and a clubhouse, as well as the usual offices, warehouse, garage, and pipe yard. The houses, uniformly painted white with green-shingled roofs, were of the "shotgun house" plan, with living room, kitchen, and two bedrooms lined up front to back. Houses had electricity, gas, and running water, but because local water was highly mineralized, residents bought drinking water shipped in from the town of Alpine at a dollar a barrel. In 1936, Gulf addressed the problem of poisonous gas in the surrounding oilfield by moving the camp—buildings and all—to a site one mile south of Crane. The move took place so rapidly that an employee asleep in one of the bunkhouses woke up to find the door nailed shut and the building on the move. Water was more abundant and potable at the new location, so the company put in lawns and trees. Instead of grass on the golf course's putting greens and the baseball field, however, Gulf simply used oiled dirt.[13]

Companies usually required employees to pay rent and the cost of utilities, but the amount was very low. One Gulf employee recalled that the house rent at Crane was $8 a month. After World War II, Gulf began to charge employees for utilities at a rate of $7.50 a month; by that time

Thanks to the company, camp children at Big Lake Oil Company's Texon school had a uniformed harmonica band in the late 1930s. *Courtesy of the Permian Basin Petroleum Museum (Midland, Texas), Arthur C. Flores collection.*

rent for a three-bedroom house was $10 a month. For the most part, rent for a three- or four-bedroom house in the thirties and forties averaged $10-$12 a month. Bunkhouse rooms for single men were far cheaper. One worker recalled room rents at Texon of $5 a month; another remembered paying only $1 a month in the late 1920s for a shared bunkhouse room in the Humble production camp at McCamey. Whatever the rent, employees renting houses got all repairs and maintenance free, with services supplied by company carpenters and painters. Rooms could be painted on demand, though in most camps the company chose the colors and required exteriors to be uniform. In some circumstances, companies supplied additional items. In the late 1920s, for example, Humble gave residents in its McCamey camp mosquito netting. During the late 1940s, Shell camp dwellers near Denver City, Texas, received carpeting, window shades, light bulbs, floor wax, and toilet paper from the company. By this time, Shell camp housing routinely included linoleum on floors in kitchens and baths, screened-in porches, and built-in cabinets and ironing boards.[14]

With housing came rules and regulations. In the Cabot camp at Wickett, Texas, the safety department conducted house inspections every month, checking for fire hazards and looking for damage and neglect. Companies maintained lawns and shrubbery in shared areas, but residents usually had to maintain the yards around their homes. A Humble camp resident remembered, "The lawns were very carefully pruned, and everyone had a high sense of pride." Many camps had rules about animals. Some companies forbade owning any animals, including dogs, and most prohibited keeping livestock within the camp. Residents often circumvented the animal ban by locating chicken coops, hog sties, and livestock pens just outside the camp fence. At Gulf's McElroy camp, for example, the camp borders were surrounded by chicken coops and pens for horses, cows, and pigs. Chicken raisers sold birds to a local grocery store, and camp teenagers made money plucking them for the owner.[15]

Housing within company camps reflected employee status within the company. Not every married employee qualified for a company house. Companies assigned larger houses, located in the front rows of residences, to supervisory and white-collar personnel. The lower one's rank in the company, the smaller and farther back from the front row of the camp one's house was likely to be. A newly hired engineer, for example, might be assigned a house on the back row, with tool pushers and drillers as neighbors. Low-ranking blue-collar workers might wait several years before being given a house. In the interim, they occupied that part of camp known as "poorboy camp" or, if this section of camp included tents, "rag town." Poorboy camp dwellers provided their own shelter, which might be shacks, boarded tents, or, after World War II, mobile homes. Once assigned a site, they received water, electricity, and gas from the company but usually had to resort to using privies. Still, they could aspire to move into a regular company house someday—if they were reliable employees and stayed with the company. Housing patterns offered a visible sign of reward to loyal workers who stuck by the firm. However, they also demonstrated one's place in the company hierarchy. A former Humble camp resident pointed out, "There was this definite break of your station in the company, if you were in the first row or the second row or the third row."[16]

Regardless of their positions in the local hierarchy, all residents participated in camp activities and company-organized events. Swimming pools, tennis courts, and golf courses served everyone. After World War II, camps added playground equipment for children. Camp clubhouses were the site of Christmas parties, teen dances, and children's birthday celebrations. Never to be outdone by other companies, Big Lake Oil Company gave children in its Texan camp expensive toys—large toy trucks, baby dolls, toy tea sets with dishes as big as tableware—at its Christmas parties. Wives organized bridge and sewing groups, while children joined scout troops. Baseball was an extremely popular employee recreation in the twenties and thirties, and major companies not only encouraged employee teams but also built camp ballparks and hired semi-professional players for company teams. Gulf, for example, built a ballpark in its McElroy camp in the late thirties and recruited players from major league farm teams for its company team; it hired former Chicago Cubs pitcher Bob Osburn to manage the Gulf team. Ostensibly, men hired as ball players had oilfield jobs, but they were advised not to get tired out before evening practice. These company ball teams provided a way for employees to enjoy games together and fostered pride in their companies, but they also served public relations; one former Gulf employee observed that they advertised Gulf "through their ball playing." Company baseball thrived until the draft of young men during World War II made it difficult to find players.[17]

Several times a year, most companies held camp picnics and barbecues. Conceived on a grand scale, these events often included residents of nearby ranches and communities. At "Humble Day" in Cisco in 1921, over five hundred Humble employees and their families gathered together at nearby Strickland Lake for a barbecue. A day of volleyball, tug of war, sack races, and something billed as a "Fat Men's Race" ended in a dance held at the Humbletown recreation hall. On Labor Day, 1937, Magnolia Oil held a day-long celebration for 1,250 employees' families and friends in Kermit; the event included a golf tournament, three softball games, and a barbecue serving up 1,400 pounds of beef and 250 pies. Such get-togethers drew residents from camps in a wide region, as well as area ranchers and local dignitaries. Dances and parties on a smaller scale were often monthly events and could include residents of other company camps in the immediate area.[18]

While company managers tried to reach employee hearts through their stomachs, they also recognized the value of fostering company culture through company magazines. Humble Oil president Ross Sterling explained in the first issue of what would become *The Humble Magazine* that the publication would circulate company news and promote "a closer feeling of co-operation and friendly interest among ourselves, thereby bringing the 'Humble Family' closer together." Humble had grown so rapidly that employees in one place were unaware of what employees elsewhere were doing. Employees needed to know that all were working together for "Humble interest" and that "the company's interest and that of the em-

The company barbecue was an oil camp institution. This 1926 Big Lake Oil Company barbecue not only included enormous amounts of food served up in one of the company garages, but also a band on a balcony. *Courtesy of the Permian Basin Petroleum Museum (Midland, Texas), M/M Roy Gardner collection.*

Bathing beauty contests were a popular feature of oil camp barbecues in the 1950s. *Courtesy of the Permian Basin Petroleum Museum (Midland, Texas), John David Grissett collection.*

ployees are identical." Employees were encouraged to share all happenings of note, so the magazine carried regional reports, obituaries, retirement notices, vacation stories, and news of company ball teams.[19] Similarly, in its company magazine, Magnolia encouraged employees to send in news of company events; announcements of engagements, weddings, births, and graduations; and children's accomplishments, with pictures whenever possible. During World War II, the *Magnolia News* regularly carried features on company employees and their family members in the armed forces.

Oil company magazines reinforced the sense of company identity and networking among employees. Employees could expect to move from oilfield to oilfield and from camp to camp, but they moved within a network of friends and former neighbors. Former camp resident Charles Stroder commented, "Maybe you would have a neighbor in an oil camp, and they would move, and later on you would move, and you would find yourselves neighbors again in some other town. You never really lost contact, you might say." "It was kind of a family deal," recalled a Humble camp resident. "Everybody knew what everybody was doing."[20] Certainly everybody knew what transpired in a specific camp, but magazines extended local knowledge throughout the company system and allowed employees to maintain bonds with one another as well as with the company.

Living by one another, many camp residents developed close friendships and emotional ties. "It was as if we had a very large family with lots of brothers and sisters," reflected one woman who grew up in a Gulf camp. In the event of a family emergency, residents helped each other. As another camp veteran stated, "If anything happened, they were right there. You never lacked for help. In fact, I think some of the friends would do more in circumstances like [a crisis] than even family would." In some camps, however, many residents actually were kin, not uncommon since family members often followed one another to the oilfield and helped each other get jobs. Gulf's McElroy camp included a large number of persons in extended families who worked for the company—brothers, fathers and sons, and cousins. In 1937, the *Magnolia News* featured the Crocker family; nearly a hundred relatives and descendants of George W. Crocker had gone to work for Magnolia—which had only existed for a little over three decades. The easiest way to be hired by a company was to have a relative already on the payroll. A Gulf veteran noted, "Gulf policy encouraged 'keeping it in the family.'" Hiring kin improved the odds of retaining experienced employees and further cemented identification with the company, in this instance, by extended family.[21]

What might be called a golden age of oil company camps in the Southwest spanned a period from the 1920s to the mid-1950s. Thereafter, companies began phasing out the camps for a variety of reasons. Chief among them was expense. When American oil producers faced competition from imported oil produced at a fraction of their costs, they tried to cut operating expenses wherever possible. That could mean joining the overseas bandwagon and setting up company communities in places like Saudi Arabia, rather than West Texas. It could also mean using technology to cut costs. Improvements in drilling technology, for example, meant faster well completions and less need for drillers on company payrolls; companies could save money by hiring contractors to put down wells. The installation of lease automatic custody transfer (LACT) systems reduced need for daily services of pumpers going from well to well in the field. After World War II, pipeline companies used small planes to fly along lines looking for leaks, replacing those who once walked or rode horseback along the lines. Eventually, computerization would make even plane spotters unnecessary. Overall, there was less need for workers to live out in the field for extended periods. Highway construction launched in the 1930s and skyrocketing after the war, moreover, meant workers could live in town and commute to work in the field, even if that commute might mean several hours' drive. With good roads, a company unit could be radio-dispatched to deal with specific field problems. As for decent housing, improvement in design and availability of mobile homes meant that workers could take their housing with them as they traveled from assignment to assignment, eliminating the tents and shacks once typical of boom-time housing. In short, oil industry economics and technology, combined with improvements in transportation, doomed the oil company camp.

Camp life, for that matter, was not without liabilities. Lack of privacy was the norm, and there was scant opportunity to keep one's personal life from common knowledge. Camp residents seldom locked doors and entered one another's homes at will. Unbridled gossip and the need to conform to camp rules were as much a part of existence as decent housing. Residents did not always get along well with each other. Children's playground differences could escalate into adult disputes. In some camps, residents split into factions, and in some longtimers were not cordial to newcomers.[22] But even in the most congenial of circumstances, life in locations far from the nearest town could be confining rather than comfortable. Whatever the liabilities of an oil town like Midland or Odessa, life in town was more exciting than life in the Crane or Winkler County sandhills, and schools and grocery stores in town were right at hand, rather than a two-hour drive away.

In any event, during the 1950s, oil companies phased out their camps. As early as 1951, Gulf started selling houses in its McElroy camp. By the end of 1955, all of them were sold, often to employees who bought the housing they lived in. Many purchasers of homes moved them elsewhere—to the nearest town if they had been in an isolated location, or to a large town like Odessa or Midland. In some instances, companies gave camp sites to cities or counties as parks. Humble Oil began abandoning its Means camp in Andrews County in 1956, moving its district offices to the city of Andrews in 1957. The 25.5-acre site, with its lawns, trees, and water lines, became a county park. The county purchased some of the camp buildings as well as the water, sewer, and electrical systems. Similarly, Humble gave the site of its Wink camp to the Boy Scouts.[23] Such donations both resolved the question of what to do with unnecessary facilities and enhanced community relations.

Although company camps disappeared from the oilfields of the Southwest, for forty years they were part of the oilfield experience of thousands of workers and their families. Beyond providing necessary shelter, company camps served to retain efficient, valued employees by offering them a comfortable, middle-class environment with an attractive community life. Camps offered a tangible reward for employee loyalty and a visible recognition of company status—that house on the front row. Labor organizers, handicapped in recruiting highly transient workers, made no headway among field workers settled in company camps.

Instead, camps encouraged identification with the company. "We were all led to believe that we were working for a company that encouraged the employee to have an elevated part of pride," recalled a Humble retiree. Company camps and company magazines successfully created a strong sense of company community and a common company culture. Oil camps were much more than just a place to live. Thus, a woman who lived in Gulf's McElroy camp observed: "We depended on one another, the Good Lord, and the Gulf Oil Corporation."[24]

Slim Willet (born Winston Lee Moore) in action, 1953.
From the author's collection.

JANUARY 2010

"I'm a Tool Pusher from Snyder": Slim Willet's Oil Patch Songs

JOE W. SPECHT

FOLKLORIST MODY BOATWRIGHT, writing in 1963, commented on the dearth of folksongs about the petroleum industry: "There was some singing in the oilfields and attempts were made to compose songs about oilfield people and their work, but none of the efforts was of sufficient appeal to attain more than brief and local distribution."[1] Bill Malone, the dean of country music historians, concurred, "almost none [oil songs] emerged from the culture of oil work."[2] And Elmer Kelton, the award-winning Western novelist who grew up outside of Crane, Texas, during the town's oil boom days of the late 1920s, confessed, "When I think of the oil patch, I don't think of music."[3]

Boatright mentioned several factors that help to explain the sparsity of spontaneous songs flowing from the oilfield. First, the transitory nature of the work meant "a sense of community" was absent because crews seldom stayed together for extended periods of time.[4] When compared to the romance of the range with rider on horseback serenading the herd, life on the rig was dirty, difficult, and dangerous, requiring total concentration to prevent serious injury or even death. And then there was the almost constant noise of the drilling operation itself, which did little "to encourage conversation, much less singing."[5]

It is certainly true, then, that a body of *traditional* song passed down aurally did not flourish in the oil patch as it did on the cow trail or in the coal mine.[6] Still, in 1859 when Edwin L. Drake successfully drilled for oil in northwestern Pennsylvania, professional songwriters and sheet music publishers responded with their own brand of oil fever odes.[7] If oilfield workers were tightlipped when it came to singing about themselves, many petroleum-related songs—musical narratives that speak to life in the oilfield as well as the continuing social and economic impact of the industry itself—nevertheless reside comfortably within the realm of commercially recorded music, especially as waxed by performers with roots in the Southwest.[8]

One need look no further than Slim Willet, perhaps best remembered as the composer of the 1952 bestseller "Don't Let the Stars Get in Your Eyes," to find a cache of oilfield songs vividly depicting life in the oil patch. In fact, his first recording in 1950 for Dallas-based Star Talent Records was "I'm a Tool Pusher from Snyder." "Hadacol Corners," the flipside of "Don't Let the Stars Get in Your Eyes," paid homage to a tiny crossroads community in oil-rich Upton County. And with *Texas Oil Patch Songs by Slim Willet*, recorded in 1959, he produced one of the earliest country music concept albums and the first devoted entirely to the petroleum industry.

Willet describes with accuracy, sympathetic understanding, and humor an oilfield in transition, as hard hats and safety shoes become a fact of life on the derrick floor. All of his songs are sung in the first person, usually from the point of view of the ordinary Joe of the oilfields: the roughneck, the driller, the boll weevil, the rig moving man. Each character Slim created was cocky and boastful, full of bluster and swagger, often with tongue planted firmly in cheek. He had a penchant for the nightlife. Never quite content, and always thinking about pulling up stakes and moving on, his credo could well have been, "I'd rather have me a young girl or two and a job on a rig I can quit when I choose."[9] He was realistic, too: "I'll never get rich punchin' holes in the ground."[10] But make no mistake. He was hooked. The oil patch was home.

Born Winston Lee Moore on December 1, 1919, in Victor, Texas, in western Erath County, Willet grew up only a few miles down the road from Desdemona.[11] In 1919, Desdemona, long known as Hogtown because of its location on Hog Creek, was a town literally overflowing with oil as earthen tanks, sumps, and slush pits built to temporarily store the "Texas tea" were not able to keep up with the excess. The first strike had blown in the previous year, but unlike the Ranger boom of 1917, where the Texas and Pacific Coal Company held the majority of the leases, independent wildcatters in Desdemona had ample opportunity to spud in.[12] Author and journalist A. C. Greene noted that "Hogtown, for sheer bad manners, was the worst oil boom in Texas history…From the beginning it was a mean, sinful place."[13] It also proved to be one of the most wasteful. Gas venting was a daily occurrence, and gushers were given their head to entice more investors.[14] A local newspaper reported, "The roar [of the gushers is so great in Desdemona that conversations are shouted and gesticulated. Talking over the telephone is almost impossible. Mothers can't coo to their babies and lovemaking is a problem."[15]

For young Winston Moore growing up nearby, these were exciting times, even as the Desdemona field swiftly declined. He recalled later, "[I] liked the oilfield people from the day [I] was born."[16] And, while he never worked a day in the oilfields, he did not forget the smells and gritty sights of the Hogtown oil patch.

In 1935, the Moore family moved to Clyde, located eighteen miles east of Abilene. Winston briefly attended Clyde High School, then spent the next two years holding down a variety of odd jobs, even riding the rails, before signing on with the Civilian Conservation Corps (CCC) in 1937. During World War II, he and his wife Jimmie (the couple married in 1938) found employment in an aircraft plant on the West Coast.[17] After serving in the US Army during the waning months of the war, in 1946 Moore took advantage of the GI Bill and enrolled in Hardin-Simmons

University, where he began his radio career as student manager of KHSU, the school radio station. Here he adopted his pseudonym Slim, making light of the fact he was far from slender. He took Willet from the Willets, characters in his favorite comic strip "Out Our Way."[18]

Upon graduating from Hardin-Simmons in 1949, Willet went to work full-time for Abilene radio station KRBC. He was also writing songs.[19] As Texas music historian Kevin Coffey observed, "Slim really had a knack for writing lyrics...his lyrics jump off the page...the rhythm is there already, imbedded in the word play."[20] In 1950, for his initial session for Star Talent Records, Willet recorded one of his signature tunes, the brightly paced (*con brio*) "I'm a Tool Pusher from Snyder" (Star Talent 770).[21]

In 1948, Snyder and Scurry County formed the epicenter for a new discovery of oil and natural gas along the Canyon Reef in the Permian Basin.[22] The Snyder bonanza attracted investors from as far away as Hollywood, with Bob Hope and Bing Crosby cashing in.[23] The boom was still in full progress in 1950 when Willet's recording became a popular seller in West Texas. Thinking the song might have more than regional appeal, Jesse Erickson, owner of Star Talent Records, re-released it the same year with a different title, "Tool Pusher on a Rotary Rig" (when Slim recorded the song again in 1959, he also used the alternate title).

"I'm a Tool Pusher from Snyder" offered the first opportunity to sample Willet's insider knowledge of the petroleum industry. He had the lingo down pat.

> That gal's all time complainin' about my talk of a Christmas tree.
> She said a drill stem test or a rotary rig don't mean a thing to me.
> She thinks core drillin's a Navy term, now what else could it be.
> She quit a sailor boy in Houston and threw her rig at me.

A tool pusher is the man in charge of the drilling rig. A Christmas tree is a series of valves and chokes connected to the top of the wellhead to regulate the flow of oil and has the appearance of a small tree with outreaching branches. A drill stem test is used to determine a well's poten-

"I'm a Tool Pusher From Snyder," recorded at Slim Willet's first session for Star Talent Records in 1950. *From the author's collection.*

tial output. Core drilling is the process of taking a sample plug of rock to establish the probable productivity of the formation. By 1950, the rotary rig had largely replaced cable tools.[24]

The song also gives a sense of the mobility and itinerant nature of oilfield life. "I've drilled at Kilgore, Beaumont, Borger/.../I've drilled in Gladewater, Midland, and Tulsa, this is the best I've found." And the singer acknowledges the potential opportunities for romance, a topic Slim will return to often. "I've drilled in California with a Fort Worth yo-yo rig/For Standard Oil on Arabian soil where the gals were dark and big/I've drilled in old Wyoming for a little western squaw/I'd a made my home on the Tea Pot Dome if it hadn't a been for her pa."

Naturally, local Snyder residents took delight in the tune, and grade school students were still being asked to memorize the lyrics twenty years later. Mike Hammack attended Snyder's Stanfield Elementary in the early 1970s: "I do not remember all the words today, but I can still sing the chorus and remember the pride I felt knowing that our oilfields were better than those in 'Gladewater, Midland, and Tulsa.'"[25]

In 1952, Willet began an often stormy association with Bill McCall and 4 Star Records. When McCall first heard Slim's recording of "Don't Let the Stars Get in Your Eyes" (Slim Willet OP 135, 4 Star 1614), he was not impressed, describing the song as "offbeat, off meter, off everything." [26] As a result, Willet initially plugged the flipside, "Hadacol Corners," and folks in the Permian Basin still remember it fondly. Taken at a sprightly clip (*allegro*), the chorus goes like this.

> Hadacol Corners caliche road
> Once it rained once it snowed.
> But most of the time the wind just blowed
> Hadacol Corners caliche road.

Hadacol Corner (not Corners), the town that Willet memorialized, sprang up in 1950 at the intersection of farm-to-market road (FM) 3095 and FM 2401 in northeast Upton County, just south of the Midland County line. Named for the town's first businessman, Donald John (D.J.) "Hadacol" Dardis, the small crossroads community with two cafes, two grocery stores, barber shop, domino parlor, and liquor store served hundreds of oilfield workers who passed through each day on their way to the recently discovered Spraberry Trend field .[27] In 1952, when the United States Post Office Department refused to approve Hadacol Corner's application for a post office because of the association with a commercial product—in this case, the infamous Hadacol patent medicine—the town changed its name to Midkiff.[28]

The flipside of the 1952 bestseller "Don't Let the Stars Get in Your Eyes," "Hadacol Corners," was Slim's tribute to a small crossroads community in Upton County. *From the author's collection.*

In "Hadacol Corners," Willet makes a pointed reference to the new field, "They're callin' me the Spraberry Stray," while continuing to express affection for the peripatetic oilfield lifestyle. "I drilled from Freer to Cheyenne/In Midland twice and back again /I love the life of a drillin' man/ I'll stay in Midland if I can." Willet is aware of Odessa's rough and tumble reputation when boasting, "Odessa is where I chase the girls." He speaks further to the dilemma often facing the oilfield worker who has to commute to work in the fields. "I used to try and live in town/The road is rough and dirty/The car will last ya ninety days/If you don't drive over thirty." And true to the stereotype of the roughneck as hell-raising, footloose, and fancy free, he laments getting married and settling down: "Don't think I'm not the oil patch boy that use to give you trouble/Don't think I wouldn't like to play, but living costs have doubled."

With the success of "Don't Let the Stars Get in Your Eyes" (Perry Como's version on RCA Victor alone sold over 1 million copies), Willet expanded his business activities in Abilene, starting his own record label, first Edmoral, then Winston. In addition to handling the emcee duties for the Big State Jamboree on Saturday evenings, he also hosted a weekly variety show on KRBC-TV. And he continued as radio disc jockey on KRBC before moving over to KNIT in 1957.[29]

Even though Taylor County had minimal oil and natural gas reserves, Abilene benefited significantly from oil and gas production in the region as the city became headquarters for independent oilmen, drilling companies, and oilfield equipment supply houses.[30] In his capacity as radio and television personality, Willet had ample opportunity to rub shoulders with wildcatters and roughnecks alike, often in the lobby of the Windsor Hotel, where oil leases were bought, sold, and traded. This continued interest in the petroleum industry—something that harkened back to his younger days tromping around the patch in Hogtown—eventually provided inspiration for Slim to craft *Texas Oil Patch Songs by Slim Willet* (Winston LP 1040). He began work on the album in early 1959 in his backyard studio.

The song titles alone on *Texas Oil Patch Songs* present a microcosm of the culture: "Rig Moving Man," "Tool Pusher (On a Rotary Rig)," "Oil Patch Girls," "El Paso Gas," "Off Shore Drillin' Rig," "Boom Town Man," "Smell That Sweet Perfume," 'Johnny Don't Drill Here Any More," "Drill Bit Honky Tonk," "Morning Tower," "Haywire Jones," "Roughneck." Slim continued his geographical gadabouts on the album, from Texas to Alaska; offshore in the Gulf of Mexico; Panama; East Texas to Iran and back again; Farmington, New Mexico; Ranger and Burkburnett in north central Texas; Borger and Dalhart in the Panhandle; and especially the

Permian Basin: McCamey, Odessa, Hadacol Corner, Crane, Monahans, Kermit, Andrews, and Hobbs.

Willet had a definite feel for the lay of the land where the wind and the dust and the sand are always present: "The day they struck oil at Hadacol is the day I'll always curse/The sand wasn't deep as McCamey, but the wind didn't blow any worse."[31] In the oilfields to the east, just a sprinkling of rain could turn the roads and drilling sites into muddy quagmires, but in the Permian Basin with its marginal rainfall, sand, not mud, was often the nemesis: "We were drillin' a hole near Monahans when we had to pull the stem/As the bit came out, the sand poured in and filled right up again."[32]

Still, as Slim pointed out in "Offshore Drilling Rig," there is something to be said for the redeeming qualities of terra firma, and one can even get homesick for the parched environs of West Texas when surrounded by water in the Gulf of Mexico. "The heat got high the other day, and the driller fainted down/It took ten pounds of Texas dust to bring that man around." Our singer vows to never again "fuss about sand and dust if I ever get back to Texas soil."

By 1959, when Willet recorded his oil patch album, successful petroleum exploration in the Gulf of Mexico had been underway for more than a decade.[33] In "Offshore Drilling Rig," Slim also depicted the isolation of the job through his own carefree point of view. "But they shipped me off to an oil rig in the Gulf of Mexico/It makes no difference what money you make, there ain't no place to go." Trapped on a platform anchored in the Gulf, a fella is left to daydream: "Offshore drilling rig, sea gulls flying 'round/Nothing but water here to drink, but wait 'til I get to town."

If boisterous hyperbole flourishes in Willet's compositions, it cannot obscure the fact that his songs are solidly grounded in reality, reflecting both the hard work and danger that go with making a living in the patch. The first verse of "Morning Tower" offers an excellent example.

I got to the rig just 'bout midnight with sleepin' on my mind.

> Hoping to smell a little diesel smoke and hear the cable
> turnin' 'round.
> But what did I find but a twisted stem, and ground popped
> through the floor.
> The pump was out, the engine down, and the pusher yellin'
> for coal.

In four simple lines, Willet captures the sights, sounds, and odor of the job. The title also shows that he was singing to those in the know. Drilling operations usually ran nonstop around the clock. A work shift or "tour" lasted either eight or twelve hours; however, in the Southwest, "tour" is frequently pronounced "tower."[34]

"El Paso Gas" provides more of a personal note. Oil and gas were discovered in Lea County, New Mexico, in 1928. The next year, the newly incorporated El Paso Natural Gas Company built a pipeline from Jal, New Mexico, to El Paso (the largest city in Texas without natural gas service at the time). With Jal as production center, the company quickly became a major presence in the area. Geologists and engineers joined roughnecks and drillers, many with families in tow. In the early years, going to work for "Paso Gas" almost certainly meant being assigned to Jal and the hard-scrabble, mesquite-infested country sitting atop the western edge of the Permian Basin (it's worth noting, too, the company later built a plant along with housing for the workers at Midkiff). In the late 1920s and 1930s, Clyde, Texas, had a special connection to El Paso Natural Gas when the company began recruiting young men from the community to come to work.[35]

Willet's "El Paso Gas" is replete with similar references to the company's history. The first pipeline from Jal to El Paso was 204 miles in length: "When I first went with Paso Gas, their lines were short and small."[36] Then there's the Clyde connection, the town Slim's family had moved to in 1935: "Dog my hide we was all from Clyde, we'd grown a tater or two/ Picking taters or pipe in the deep, deep sand was nothing new." With the pipeline to El Paso complete, desolate Jal became a company town much to the chagrin of some: "But what did we do when we got through but build a brand new town/I guess I'll spend the rest of my days with the desert all around." By the 1950s, El Paso Natural Gas had expanded operations to Farmington, New Mexico, and into the Texas Panhandle: "Farmington or Dalhart, Kermit, it's all the same to me/I've cussed 'em all, and everyone says that's how it's meant to be." The company even operated a chain of service stations: "Vacation time I fill my tank with gasoline I find/Wherever I go, El Paso Gas is always on my mind."

Several of Willet's compositions on *Texas Oil Patch Songs* touch on the social order in the field, and the working hierarchy is clearly defined from "weevils, roughnecks, drillers, too."[37] In this case, a boll weevil or weevil is the term used to describe a new hand. A roughneck is a notch above a weevil, while the driller is the supervisor of the rig crew. Others in the supporting cast include the drill rig moving man and his assistant, the "swamper." The tool pusher, or simply "pusher," is in charge of the entire operation; he's the man who "comes by in his Cadillac" to check on things.[38] The songs also captured the rhythm of work on the derrick floor: "Got to pack that pump and fish that stem, get the ground block out of the hole/When the daylight boys get to this rig, it's gotta be drillin' for sure."[39] Not to forget the presence of the "doghouse"—an all-purpose shed adjacent to the rig floor—and the "mouse hole"—an opening in the rig floor that enables rapid connections while drilling.[40] Of course the tableau wouldn't be complete without the wildcatter or independent oil man, who personifies the oilfield's go-for-broke reputation: "I was the first one there at the Ranger boom, and I once ran Burkburnett/But for Cadillac cars and girls and bars, I'd own ol' Borger yet."[41]

Willet also had a feel for the social life of the oil workers away from the rigs. Take, for example, "Drill Bit Honky Tonk." It was the roadhouse "on the edge of town, and the sign is a drill bit a-going 'round and 'round." The oil boom in Texas continued into the 1930s, and with repeal of Prohibition in 1933, honky tonks sprouted at county lines and on the outskirts of many communities to meet the liquid needs of the oilfield workers.⁴² This is where roughnecks met at the end of the day. "You can hear about fortunes won and lost/But when the beer's getting cold who cares about the cost." Whether you are looking for a longneck bottle or the next job assignment, you can find it here. "Drill bit honky tonk never closes/Ain't even a lock on the door/No use lyin' to that bartender/You can't tell one he hasn't heard before." For Slim's protagonist, "Anytime I meet anyone I've known/They know the drill bit honky tonk is still my home."

In "Smell That Sweet Perfume," the locale moves to South Texas "drilling for oil by the Rio Grande" and reveals more of the leisure time of the oilfield workers. Willet evokes the stereotypical gringo paradise, "La Zona de Tolerancia—The Zone of Indulgence," just across the river.⁴³ "When payday come we'd swim that creek and be in Mexico/And listen to the gauchos play guitars and smell that sweet perfume/Make sweet love to the senoritas and smell that sweet perfume." This demonstrates again the impact a roustabout with a pocketful of money could have on a local economy. The calypso syncopation of the composition creates the proper south-of-the-border atmosphere, too, as the singer remembers fondly: "I look back now and it seems to me it's been a hundred years/Since I first swam the Rio Grande and drank that Mexican beer."

And how do the women fare in Willet's world? Life for a woman in the oilfields was never easy, whether she was a wife or an oilfield dove.⁴⁴ Some wives chose not to venture out but rather stayed with relatives or friends and endured the separation. Or as Slim matter-of-factly intones, "that gal of mine is left behind, I see her when I can."⁴⁵ For those who did follow their husbands, the primitive living conditions in a tent or shotgun shack proved daunting.⁴⁶ And while things could be better in an oil company camp, Willet expresses a sentiment common to many when he sings, "listen to the wives complain/Most of 'em say, if they ever get away, they'll never be back again."⁴⁷

Not surprisingly, much of Slim's attention is focused on the single girl, who ends up in one of the oil boomtowns. You might find her working in a drill bit honky tonk, where "the beer is cold and the waitress, too/ If you talk to her sweet, she'll dance with you."[48] For the fella, the trick is not to get tied down, and Willet devotes an entire song, "Oil Patch Girls," to this cat and mouse game. 'There's oil patch girls all over the world, and a few have fell for me/When we strike pay, I never do say where the next well's gonna be." But when the gals want to track you down, not even an offshore rig offers a safe haven: 'The oil patch girls will find the boys even drilling out in the Gulf/They'll hire a boat and come where you are, to lose 'em sure is tough." Poor Slim laments the "marrying kind it always seems are the ones who fall for me." And while he admits to getting hitched sixteen times—"That's why each payday I'm without a dime to call my own"—he readily accepts his fate. "Oil patch girls there'll always be, and I've got to have me one/They've kept me broke for twenty years, and they've really just begun."

Texas Oil Patch Songs went beyond offering slice-of-life portraits and touched on the mythology of the patch, just as Mody Boatright was later to do. Boatright devoted a chapter to tall tales in *Folklore of the Oil Industry*, reviewing the oilfield exploits of Paul Bunyan, Kemp Morgan, and Gib Morgan.[49] Of Bunyan, it was said "he once drilled to China," while other accounts had him teaming up with Kemp Morgan in Texas to sink a well to China that produced not black gold but chow mein and chop suey instead.[50] Willet also created a larger-than-life hero with designs on reaching the other side of the globe in his saga "Haywire Jones."

> I was sittin' around in the Windsor Hotel in a town called
>   Abilene, Texas
> When a fella came along with mud on his boots and a pint of
>   Tennessee brandy.
> He lit up a cee-gar longer than his arm and took a little nip from
>   the brandy
> One whiff and a look and everyone knew he was an oilfield dandy.

Haywire Jones has "drilled a million holes from Texas to Alaska," and his goal is to buy his whiskey "by the barrel" and become a millionaire, even if he has to "drill clear through to China." He hires a crew, and they "spud the rig in the top bend of Texas/With nobody lookin' but a weevil or two and a thousand miles of cactus." A year later, the crew is still drilling, not without mishap: 'We lost three bo' weevils in the mouse hole, and the ground block killed a few." The hole is so deep it took "forty-one nights without sleepin'" just to change the drill bit.

After two years of drilling, they were deep into the Earth's core. "The coyotes wailed, and the buzzards sailed, and the drill bit kept a-grinding/We all knew now if we lost that bit ol' Satan alone could find it." Eventually the ground begins to rumble. The stem and bit are blown out, and oil blackens the sky. But "like a worn out clock it suddenly stopped and flowed on out in China/We cursed the bones of Haywire Jones, he'd drilled clear through to China."

The musical production for the *Texas Oil Patch* album is a mix of hillbilly, honky tonk, and rockabilly beats.[51] Willet combined quirky rhythms and tempos to recreate the cadences of the oilfield. For example, "Rig Moving Man" is taken at breakneck speed and punctuated with bursts of boogie-woogie piano and hot electric lead guitar, a perfect complement to deliver the sense of blacktop highway momentum Slim's lyrics convey.

> A million miles I've moved these rigs so keep that diesel burning
> Can't even make a coffee break gotta keep these wheels a turning.
> These roads all look so flat and smooth with a hundred thousand pounds
> Suddenly the hills are long, the gears keep grinding down.
> I hope that bridge can take this load, the weight load sign is low
> My swamper's snoring fast to sleep, he doesn't even know.
> That gal of mine is left behind, I see her when I can
> I guess I'm stuck with a diesel truck, I'm a drill rig moving man.

For the front cover photo of *Texas Oil Patch Songs,* Willet was outfitted with appropriate roughneck clothing—greasers and hardhat—standing

Slim Willet's 1959 release, *Texas Oil Patch Songs*, was one of the earliest country music concept albums and the first devoted entirely to the petroleum industry. *From the author's collection.*

in front of a derrick. Sometime during the spring of 1959, Slim asked Earl Carmack, a friend who had co-directed the weekly Willet television show on KRBC-TV in addition to serving as staff photographer, to bring his camera along, and the two spent a day "driving all 'round the country looking for a rig that worked for the shot" before eventually finding one near Albany.[52] Because he purchased the wardrobe especially for the occasion, "Slim had to get his clothes and gloves dirty beforehand."[53]

Willet released "Boom Town Man"/"Tool Pusher (On a Rotary Rig)" (Winston 1036-45) in May.[54] *Texas Oil Patch Songs* followed in the fall of 1959.[55] While highly prized by Willet collectors, the album is largely unknown to historians of the petroleum industry due to its limited distribution.[56] Regardless, the songs Slim crafted for the album provide a unique snapshot of the industry, all from his fun-loving, devil-may-care, and often poetic perspective.

Although the compositions on *Texas Oil Patch Songs* languished in relative obscurity, "I'm a Tool Pusher from Snyder" retained a life of its own. In 1953, Ramblin' Jimmie Dolan recorded the song for Capitol Records using the alternate title, "Tool Pusher on a Rotary Rig" (Capitol 2713). Ken Nelson, Capitol's A&R man, was already familiar with Willet the songwriter, having produced Skeets McDonald's version of "Don't Let the Stars Get in Your Eyes."[57] The appearance on a major record label insured national exposure for "Tool Pusher on a Rotary Rig," especially on the West Coast, where Dolan was headquartered. The Library of Congress later selected Dolan's recording for inclusion in its *Music in America* series.[58]

"I'm a Tool Pusher from Snyder" next turned up in 1964 as merely "Tool-Pusher" on *Alex Zanetis Writes and Sings the Story of the Oil Fields* (RIK M 1000). Zanetis, who was raised in the oilfields of Illinois, had a long and successful songwriting career in Nashville. Recorded in Music City with an all-star lineup, the album featured Floyd Cramer, Grady Martin, Charlie McCoy, the Jordanaires, and liner notes written by Winthrop Rockefeller, himself a former oilfield roughneck and soon-to-be governor of Arkansas.[59] The Nashville production crew was apparently oblivious to Willet's *Texas Oil Patch Songs*, however, because the blurb on the front cover of the Zanetis album proclaimed: "Alex Zanetis…sings a dozen songs which tell the story of the oilfields and the people who live and die by oil…This is the only album of its kind ever produced."[60] In 1974, Zanetis penned the liner notes for Sam Thompson's *Songs of the Oil Field* (House of Michael MLP 1001), a song-by-song recreation of *Alex Zanetis Writes and Sings the Story of the Oil Fields*. Also recorded in Nashville, "Tool-Pusher" is carelessly credited to Zanetis, not Willet.[61]

Willet's song came full circle and returned to its West Texas locale in 2008 when Jody Nix, the son of legendary Big Spring fiddler and western swing band leader Hoyle Nix, chose to include "Tool Pusher from Snyder" on his compact disc, *The Fiddle Man* (JNP). The younger Nix's association with Willet dated to 1960, when he played drums on one of the four tunes his father recorded for release on Winston Records.[62] In the summer of 2008, with crude oil prices approaching $150 a barrel and with drilling activity in the Permian Basin at full bore, Jody, still based in Big Spring, decided "to re-cut ['Tool Pusher from Snyder'], a great novelty tune, and with the oil boom going again...who knows?"[63]

After 1960, Willet took less interest in his own recording career, although he continued to issue the occasional single on Winston Records. "Everything Is Shakin' Fine" (Winston 1061-45) even earned a review in *Billboard* in 1962.[64] The flipside, "Big Money," finds Slim's thoughts returning to the oil patch once again: "But I knew dame fortune had smiled on me when my first oil well blew in/That sweet black gold turned to big long green, the kind that I'd craved all those years." In this tale of insatiable desire to get rich and enjoy "a fling or two," the singer already knows the answer to the rhetorical question, "Was one oil well goin' to be enough to dry all the sweat and tears?"

Slim Willet died of an apparent heart attack in 1966. He was only fortysix years old. He is buried in the cemetery at Victor. The epitaph on his headstone reads, "There is just one way to live/Like you were going to live forever."[65] But just as appropriate perhaps are the closing verses from Willet's "Boom Town Man."

> When they call the roll on judgment day They'll call my
>   name alright.
> To climb that rig through eternity And hang out the stars
>   at night.
> I know this rig and a mile of stem Will be the first thing I see.
> For heaven or hell without an oil well Just wouldn't be home
>   for me.

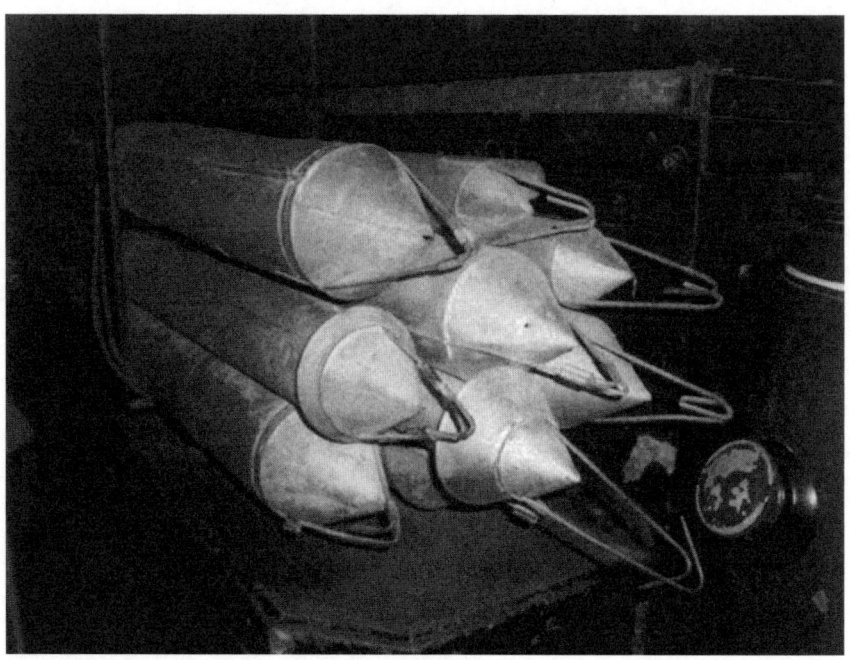

A load of torpedoes, the devices oil well shooters used to stimulate production.
Photo taken by the author at the Petroleum Museum, Midland, Texas.

JULY 2010

Risky Business: Oil Well Shooters in the Southwestern Oilfields

DAVID F. DIXON

EARLY ON MAY 11, 1934, Bill McKinney pulled out of the nitroglycerin factory he and his brother Lee operated in the Permian Basin town of Penwell, Texas. The operation was part of the Eastern Independent Torpedo Company, a business that exploded nitroglycerin-laden devices at the bottom of newly drilled oil wells to stimulate production. He drove a specially designed and equipped REO Speedwagon north with a load of nitroglycerin to replenish the company's explosives storage facility near Amarillo. He had checked his load before he left and knew the cargo was secure. He drove all day fighting a relentless, excoriating west wind that buffeted the side of his truck. Red dust loomed like a fog hundreds of feet in the air; its choking grit swirled in the cab, stinging Bill's eyes and burning his throat. In two days, that same superfine remnant of Texas Panhandle topsoil would foul the air along the Atlantic Seaboard and even coat the decks of ships 300 miles out to sea. The lingering effects of the first Dust Bowl dust storm would mean nothing to Bill McKinney, though, because eight miles south of Tulia, the nitroglycerin he hauled spontaneously exploded, perhaps as a result of a static charge produced by the constant hot dry wind that scoured the Great Plains from Canada to Texas.[1]

From the 1860s until after World War II, oil well shooters represented the leading edge of petroleum production technology. Known professionally as torpedo companies, shooters like Bill McKinney developed their palette of skills largely through on-the-job training and trial-and-error experimentation. Their involvement ranged across the entire spectrum of the dangerous trade, including manufacturing and transporting explosives, developing and manufacturing specialized tools, understanding and incorporating the benefits of tamping to shape and direct explosive charges, and designing and testing detonation devices.

Of the thousands of oil wells completed since William "Uncle Billy" Smith drilled the Drake Well at Titusville, Pennsylvania, in 1859, only a fraction have come in as gushers or free-flowing wells. Even the output from those wells that initially erupt with oil gradually diminishes as natural pressure within the formation subsides. When production falls off, and even when a newly drilled well appears to be dry, productivity can be stimulated by fracturing the oil-bearing stratum (known as the oil sand) at the bottom of the well bore. For over a century after the first well stimulation in 1866, drillers fractured the oil sand by shooting, or detonating explosive charges at the bottom of the well. Creating a controlled explosion at a precise location hundreds and later thousands of feet beneath the earth's surface required a specialized combination of emerging science and technology, practical experience, and great personal risk—a job that few in the oil patch had the background or the nerve to consider.

Oil producers learned the importance of well stimulation, both as a function of well completion and in secondary recovery efforts, early in the history of the industry. Producers applied the rule of capture, a legal concept rooted in medieval English common law that dealt with migratory game, to the recovery of oil. Just as the game belonged to whomever could capture it, oil trapped in subsurface formations belonged to whomever drilled down into the earth and recovered it.[2] The idea was to extract as much oil as possible before someone else got it all. The shot created fissures that formed a web of channels in the rock surrounding the well. Shooting occurred only in fields where the sand was hard or nonporous. In fields such as those in where the oil sand is soft and porous, such as those in East Texas, shooting would be more likely to destroy rather than stimulate production. However, most oilfields in the United States, like those in West and North Texas, produce from sandstone, limestone, or socalled granite wash: formations that respond to shooting. Gravity moved the oil freed by the shot toward the well bore where it gushed to the well head or pumps delivered it to the surface.[3]

The first oil well shooter was E.A.L. Roberts, a Civil War lieutenant colonel cashiered for drunkenness on duty shortly after his 28th New Jersey Volunteer Infantry Regiment's participation in the Battle of Fredericksburg. Seven years after Col. Edwin L. Drake brought in his well on Oil Creek near Titusville, Pennsylvania, Roberts detonated eight pounds of black powder 453 feet down the Ladies Well on Walton Flats, just south of Titusville. He designed an explosive device that when set off at the bottom of an oil well would create a phenomenon he called superincumbent fluid tamping. He had formulated his theory after watching artillery explosions in a millrace below Marye's Heights, on the outskirts of Fredericksburg, where his regiment languished for two days in December 1862 under constant Confederate rifle and cannon fire. He speculated that just as an artillery shell explosion produced a momentary hole in the water, a confined explosion at the bottom of an oil well would permanently affect the plasticity of rock to form a reservoir of oil at the bottom of a well. Initially, producers dismissed Roberts's theory as counterintuitive; a powerful, confined explosion seemed more likely to tighten the cork than free the genie from the bottle. After his success with the Ladies, however, Roberts's procedure became standard oilfield practice.[4]

Roberts realized early that black powder lacked the power to effectively fracture the hard rock formations that confined oil deposits. His experiments with alternative explosives led to the development and patent of a nitroglycerin torpedo specifically for oil well stimulation. Nitroglycerin, a lightly viscous, slightly yellowish, highly unstable liquid created when concentrated nitric and sulfuric acids reacted with glycerol, quickly became the shooter's stock in trade. Ascani Sobrero, the Italian chemist who discovered the extremely sensitive and highly explosive compound in 1846, called it "pyroglycerin." Other early labels included "glonoil oil" and "trinitrate of glycerin" before scientists finally settled on nitroglycerin. Among other more earthy colloquialisms, shooters called it "soup," "stock," or simply "nitro."[5] At first, nitroglycerin had limited value as a technical explosive despite its power. Extremely sensitive and highly unstable, nitroglycerin would not detonate predictably. This inherent instability restricted its use. However, chemists found that adding nitroglycerin to black powder and gun cotton (raw cotton mixed with nitric and sulfuric acid) significantly increased their explosive potential and improved the stability of nitroglycerin as well.[6]

Although nitroglycerin retained its inherent instability, it nonetheless became a widely used explosive in mining, quarrying, and the burgeoning petroleum industry. Alfred Nobel, an engineer and later a renowned philanthropist, began experimenting with Sobrero's volatile concoction in Sweden in 1859. Nobel developed an ignition device based on mercury fulminate, a detonating agent discovered in 1799 and used in percussion caps since 1815. The device, which evolved into the modern blasting cap, could predictably detonate nitroglycerin. Nobel also refined the process for manufacturing nitroglycerin, which he called blasting oil, and began exporting it, particularly to the United States for use in the California goldfields. By 1866, after several explosions claimed dozens of lives and reduced nitro-laden vessels to kindling, steamship companies refused to transport Nobel's product. He subsequently organized the U.S. Blasting Oil Company in New York, patented the formula, and granted licenses to manufacture nitroglycerin for industrial use in the United States.[7]

P. Davidson, another oil patch colonel, established the first nitroglycerin factory exclusively for oil well stimulation. Unfortunately, Davidson's factory blew up not long after he began production, killing him and all his employees. George M. Mowbray opened two nitroglycerin factories in 1868, one in North Adams, Massachusetts, and the other in Titusville. He had operated a refinery near Titusville until highly unstable oil prices driven by rampant speculation convinced him that explosives might be a less volatile line of business. However, he shut down the Titusville operation not long after beginning production, probably due to patent conflicts with Col. Roberts, who set up a factory of his own to produce nitroglycerin for his Roberts Torpedoes. Roberts's facility exploded too, but the colonel survived. He continued to make torpedoes and shoot wells, but apparently decided to outsource his nitro.[8]

Torpedoes or shells—shooters used both terms interchangeably—were long thin tubes manufactured of tin made for delivering the nitroglycerin down a well. They had either a conical false end at the bottom or a loop for attaching another shell, an anchor, or a weight. The top had a funnel soldered into it for pouring in the liquid nitroglycerin. They could be either double- or single-walled. The top also had a heavy wire bail to accommodate additional shells. Torpedoes varied in length from just over two feet to nearly thirty feet, with diameters ranging from two to nine inches. Each shell could hold approximately twenty quarts of nitro. The shooter strung together as many shells as necessary to reach the ordered load and cover the length of the pay zone (the strata containing recoverable hydrocarbons) the operator wanted shot. If the shot was to occur above the bottom of the well or if the order called for several shots in different rock strata, he used anchors to hang the shells at the proper location in the bore. Anchors were one-and-a-quarter inch tin tubes up to twenty feet long equipped with metal fingers that the shooter manipulated to fasten the unit to the well wall. Like the shells, shooters could load anchors with liquid nitroglycerin.[9]

Nitroglycerin manufactured under laboratory conditions and stored properly was not likely to decompose; decomposition almost invariably led to spontaneous explosion. However, oilfield nitro seldom measured up to laboratory standards. Manufactured under primitive conditions in rustic factories built near oilfields, nitro rarely went through an efficient washing and neutralizing process, which meant it retained residual amounts of acid that made it even more unstable. Impurities gave nitroglycerin an amber hue, but other than noting a variance in color, shooters seemed indifferent to—or more likely were just ignorant of—the meaning of its lack of clarity.[10] Not all shooters made their own nitro, but many did.

The factory, when set up properly, consisted of a series of small, interconnected buildings that snaked down sloping ground to allow gravity to move the batch through the various stages of production. The uppermost building housed the nitrator, a lead-lined wooden (or later, steel) tank equipped with agitators and sometimes fitted with lead pipes that circulated cool water. The operator mixed sulfuric and nitric acid with water in the nitrator tank, then with mechanical agitators constantly stirring the mixture, he slowly added glycerin, a packinghouse or soap factory byproduct. If agitation stopped during the mixing cycle, the compound, called the charge, could begin to decompose, and all hell would break loose. The mechanical agitators had a manual backup crank, just in case.

After the nitration step, the run moved into a drowning tank, where it mixed with cold water to start killing the acid and separate out the heavier nitroglycerin. This was another dangerous procedure because the compound could heat up dramatically as the water drained. Workers measured the temperature assiduously during drowning and added water to the mix if the temperature suddenly spiked. The soup then moved to washing tanks, where it was agitated again to render out a fatty substance they called "slime." From there, the nitro came to the neutralizing tank, where it underwent treatment with sodium bicarbonate to neutralize any remaining acid. Some factories omitted this last step and simply sent the batch through one or two more washing cycles. This omission often left latent acid in the finished nitroglycerin, giving it the telltale straw color that could be a harbinger of disaster. Like Grandma's recipe for apple pie, the formula for nitroglycerin rarely existed in written form. Manufacturers learned to make nitroglycerin as apprentices, assisting experienced manufactures who themselves learned as apprentices.[11]

Torpedo companies stored nitro in bunkers they referred to as magazines or dumps located a safe distance from the factory and populated areas. Magazines could hold hundreds of quarts of liquid nitroglycerin, along with boxes of dynamite and cases of blasting caps. Rather than advertise the magazines with danger signs, many torpedo companies camouflaged them. Some kept cows fenced in around them, both to disguise the dump as some sort of farm building and to keep grass and weeds from growing up and presenting a fire hazard. Some had double-wall construction, with earth and rocks between the walls, and some were augmented with interior steel plating. Others were no more than tarpaper shacks. While more elaborate magazines featured ventilators that pulled warm air out to maintain an ambient temperature below ninety-six degrees, some manufacturers felt heat buildup in a magazine presented little risk

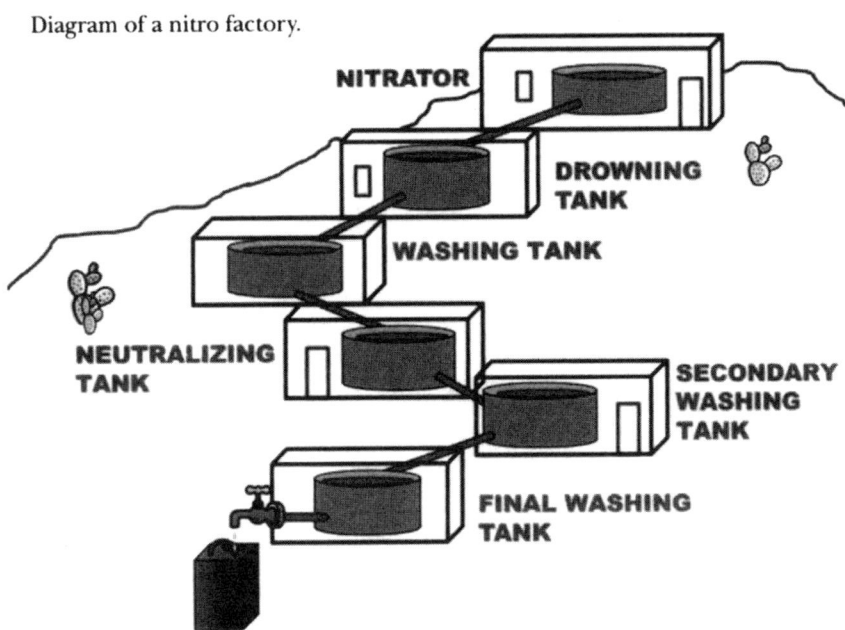

Diagram of a nitro factory.

of causing spontaneous ignition. Shooters often posted signs inside the magazine, such as "Do Not Open Cans or Boxes Inside the Dump!" These signs were not for visitors, whose entrance without a shooter was prohibited, but functioned as reminders to themselves not to act carelessly.[12]

Torpedo companies put nitroglycerin into ten-quart canisters for storage and hauling to the well sites for shots. Local metal shops made nitro canisters from sheet metal coated with tin. The metalworker soldered the seams and plugged the opening in the top with a wooden stopper rather than making a screw-on lid that might compress and detonate nitroglycerin hiding in the threads. The cans had to be watertight because leakage could be lethal. Shooters reused cans despite the fact that empty cans could be more dangerous than full ones. In 1938, a shooter discovered a leak in a can he was pouring into a torpedo prior to a shot. After emptying the canister, he rinsed it out and took it to a nearby machine shop. Although the welder at the shop considered the canister worthless, he agreed to weld the split seam. The shooter assured him he washed it thoroughly. The welder said, "All right, then. If you didn't, it'll be your funeral, too, because you're going to hold it while I weld it." As soon as he touched the flame to the canister, it exploded, amputating the shooter's right arm and driving the torch completely through the welder's body.[13]

After World War I, twenty-two-year-old C. L. "Lee" McKinney, of Gordon, Texas, went to work in a nitro factory in nearby Mingus, close to Ranger in the North Texas oilfields. He was an uneducated farm boy who worked odd jobs until he came to the nitro factory. He began by firing the boiler and later helped the owner with production. He learned the recipe for nitroglycerin, like nearly everyone else in the business, by making it. After a couple of years, the proprietor stopped coming to work. McKinney ran the factory alone, brewing twelve to fifteen hundred quart runs by himself. He accrued his expertise from on-the-job training, diligence, and liberal doses of common sense. Since the huge North Texas boom created extraordinary demand for McKinney's product, he hauled nitroglycerin to Ranger, Hog Town, Breckinridge, and other active oilfields, where he began to learn about shooting wells. Eventually McKinney moved to the Permian Basin, where became owner and operator of Independent Eastern Shooting Company.[14]

Transporting nitro, or hauling stock as shooters called it, was risky business. In the early days of oil well shooting, teamsters hauled nitroglycerin in horse-drawn buckboard wagons. Nitroglycerin canisters hung in rope nets padded with straw that doubled as sponge material to catch leaks. By the time shooters like Lee McKinney and Amarillo shooter and nitroglycerin manufacturer Tex Thornton transported nitro in the late 1940s and early 1950s, they drove trucks specially outfitted with oversized tires, rubber floor mats and seat covers, and bristling with the tools and paraphernalia of the shooting trade. "DANGER-EXPLOSIVES," written in reflective paint, emblazoned all sides of the vehicle, warning other drivers to give the nitro truck a wide berth. The nitro canisters rode in a network of rubber boots inside the "soup box" of the truck. The boots separated the canisters and acted like shock absorbers to deaden the jostling as the vehicle bounced over unpaved washboard roads. If a canister developed a leak, the box, lined with asbestos, copper plating, and thick felt, insured it would stay confined.[15]

Many premature explosions occurred during transport. When a vehicle blew up, it left little behind to indicate what happened, the example given at the start of this article being an illustrative case in point. McKinney's brother Bill died when the REO Speedwagon he was driving blew up south of Tulia. The explosion dug a crater six feet deep and twenty feet across, and lifted a car that had just passed into the air, hurtling it forward several feet. Authorities recovered only scraps of flesh and bone for burial.[16] McKinney recalled another catastrophic nitro truck explosion. A truck driven by a friend named Wes Judy blew up between Wink and Monahans. McKinney remembered that people claimed the truck hit a bump in the road that set off the explosion, but he argued that leakage caused the blast. No evidence survived to prove what triggered the explosion, but McKinney knew that nitro canisters sometimes leaked.

A soup box with two nitro cans visible in the upper right-hand side. These items were used by oil well shooters to transport nitro, which was a dangerous and occasionally deadly task. *Photo taken by the author at the Petroleum Museum, Midland, Texas.*

If just a drop managed to leak out and contact the brakes or a hot muffler, it could ignite the entire load. Leaks did not usually happen through carelessness or faulty soldering; instead, over time the latent acid left in the nitro when the factory skipped the final neutralization step attacked weak spots in the canister's protective tin coating, eating tiny pinholes where nitroglycerin sweated out.[17]

When the shooter arrived at the well, everyone else left. He worked alone or with a helper employed by the torpedo company. The operator gave him verified well measurements and critical information that could affect the shot, including total depth of the well, depth to the bottom of the last string of casing, depth to the bottom of the formation, depth from the surface to the top of the fluid in the hole, and any imperfections that might cause a torpedo to hang up, such as cavings, crooks, or reductions in the diameter of the borehole. Before the shooter arrived, the operator bailed out all the drilling mud and "frog," oil and cuttings left in the well bore, which could damage the casing during shooting. The drilling crew made sure no tools used in the drilling operation remained near the control head and leaned the drill stem over on the derrick floor, with the drill bit securely chocked to prevent movement during the shot. When

Fully equipped shooter's truck originally owned by Lee McKinney (top), and interior of shooter's truck (above). Notice the heavy rubber floor mat, seat, and door cover to protect against static electricity discharge. *Photo taken by the author at the Petroleum Museum, Midland, Texas.*

the drilling crew finished preparing the well, the shooter got to work. He backed his truck up to the control head, the fitting on top of the casing to close off the well in the event of an emergency, and he or his helper began unloading torpedo shells and the gear for the shot. The truck had a winch driven by a power takeoff from the engine that he used to lower the torpedoes down the well. The winch had two spools of shooting line that worked independent of each other. One contained steel wire and the other quarter-inch manila rope. He used the manila rope only on shallow wells. He rigged a heavy pulley about five feet above the derrick floor and fed either a steel wire or a quarter-inch manila shooting line through it, to suspend the torpedo shells in the hole.[18]

Before the introduction of the truck-mounted winch, a reel attached to the flywheel of the drilling rig's engine provided the power to lower the torpedo string down the well. The unit afforded a limited amount of control over the manipulation of the string after it entered the well. With the winch and a less powerful engine, the shooter could "feel" subtle changes in the shooting line as the string descended and thus avoid some of the problems the earlier rig posed. The truck allowed the shooter to position the winch to gain the most control over his charge. Gauges indicated the brake load and weight on the shooting line, providing tangible evidence of what he felt through tension of the shooting line and the strain on the truck's power takeoff. The experienced shooter first lowered a dummy shell filled with water to the bottom, both to insure the torpedo passed down the casing without hanging up, and to determine the length of the shooting line. As the dummy came out of the well, the shooter tied flags to the line to mark critical points. As the loaded torpedo string went down, the flags helped him adjust the speed of the descent as it passed through bottlenecks and approached the bottom of the well.[19]

After assuring that the well would accept the torpedo, the shooter brought the first shell over to the control head and lowered it into the well, hooking it onto the shooting line, and thus suspending it over the shaft. He or his helper would bring two canisters of nitroglycerin from the soup box over to the derrick. He carefully pried off the wooden cork from the first can and placed it in a bucket of cold water. The corks absorbed nitroglycerin and tiny droplets clung to the bottom from the sloshing of the liquid inside the canister, making them potential bombs. Isolating the corks prevented accidental kicks or contact with tools on the derrick floor. As the shell dangled on the shooting line knee-high above the control head, he slowly and carefully poured the lightly viscous soup into the shell. He recorked the empty can and repeated the process with the second canister of nitro. He or his helper carried the two empties back to the soup box. With the first shell chocked in the control head, the shooter slacked the line, hooked on a fresh shell, put the first shell's bail into the eye of the new one, picked up the weight with the winch and then gently eased the first shell down into the shaft until the empty shell came to pouring height. The operation continued on to successive shells until the entire string of nitro-laden shells hung over the abyss. He cleaned up any spills or drips of nitroglycerin with solvent and warm water kept near the control head during the filling process.[20]

View of torpedoes on a shooter's truck.
Photo taken by the author at the Petroleum Museum, Midland, Texas.

The torpedoes hung on the shooting line by a brass hook designed to release a loaded shell when it reached the bottom. Lee McKinney pointed out that while being lowered, a string of shells might encounter a bridge or hit rising fluid caused by gas or water pressure. When that happened, the shooting line would go slack, causing the hook to release the string. Both scenarios portended disaster. Either the string would lay stranded on the impediment somewhere down the hole, forcing the shooter to puncture the torpedoes to bleed the nitro out, or the fast rising fluid would push the string of torpedoes up the shaft and launch them onto the derrick. The string could also float momentarily somewhere down the bore and then fall abruptly as the pressure slackened, sending it rocketing down the well to ignite by friction with the well casing or explode on impact with the bottom.[21] Instead of the standard hook, McKinney favored an alternate type designed by a shooter named Ord Mayes. Mayes came up with the concept of a double hook in 1934 while in the hospital recovering from a well explosion in Kermit, Texas. The double hook, also made of brass to prevent sparks, worked as a built-in backup. If the bail came out of the first hook, it slipped into the second hook and retained its burden. Mayes also invented a shot anchor with steel fingers that dug into the wall of the bore to suspend strings of shells for multiple strata shots. Mayes's inventiveness came to an untimely end when he blew himself up in a shot that went bad.[22]

With the string of shells loaded and all the empty canisters in the truck's soup box, the shooter lowered the string to the ordered depth and unhooked it from the line. It was time for the detonator to make the trip to the bottom. Col. Roberts ignited his torpedoes with a firing device called a "go-devil," a cylindrical weight that he dropped down the well to strike a blasting cap attached to the top of the last torpedo. The go-devil worked in shallow formations, but even a minor cave-in could be enough to insulate the blasting cap and prevent detonation. Torpedo companies later used a squib to detonate shots. This cylindrical tin shell, usually attached to a weight to carry it down the well, contained liquid nitro or dynamite. The top of the squib contained a firing head with a firing pin wedged into one or two blasting caps. The shooter lowered the squib down the well using a copper wire, hooking it onto the uppermost shell. He then pulled the wire snug and slid a hollow go-devil or a steel nipple down the wire to strike the firing head and detonate the explosion. Variations on the squib came and went, but most required the shooter to remain at the control head until virtually the last minute, leaving him precious little time to vacate the area.[23] In order to detonate the string of torpedoes, squibs required an unobstructed path all the way down the well shaft.

At the start of the 1920s, torpedo companies began to use time bombs as detonation devices. Although unreliable and dangerous at first, competing explosives companies eventually developed dependable products that displaced all other detonators. Time bombs allowed the shooter to prepare a shot up to twelve hours before detonation, leaving time to pull the casing, place tamping material, and perform other pre-shot tasks. Above all, they gave everyone time to move a safe distance away from the well before the shot. Time bombs carried ominous names such as Bolshevik and Zero Hour. Not much more than pipe bombs, they consisted of dynamite surrounding several blasting caps, dry cell batteries, and an alarm clock connected to a firing mechanism. Their elegance lay in their simplicity. They were durable, safe against high pressure, and impervious to liquids. Nevertheless, their tough steel casing often produced bridging that interfered with cleanout after the shot. The King Mechanical Time Bomb, however, with its components housed in a thick glass tube, disintegrated in the explosion. Manufacturers ultimately replaced the steel pipe with tubes made from Bakelite (a synthetic resin used broadly in industry before plastics) that vaporized in the explosion.[24]

With the nitroglycerin and the time bomb safely down the well, the shooter could breathe a little easier. Only the tamping remained. Tamping was the equivalent of plugging a gun barrel—it contained the force of the explosion within a confined area below the torpedo string. He low-

Timing mechanism and housing for Bolshevik time bomb.
Photo taken by the author at the Petroleum Museum, Midland, Texas.

ered and set a bridge, either hand-made of rubble or one manufactured with steel ribs and burlap covering, approximately two feet above the time bomb. The bridge was a plug that prevented tamping material fed down the shaft from striking the detonator or the shells. After dropping some twenty feet of stones or brick fragments on the bridge, he ran a cage (an open-ribbed tool that could be adjusted to fit the size of the hole and used to make measurements in the well hole) down to make sure that no rubble bridged the shaft. He then slowly and methodically dumped shovels full of sand or gravel down the hole until he had a column roughly three times the length of the shooting string covering the stone or brick rubble. With the tamping in place, the well stood ready to shoot.[25]

When the alarm on the time bomb went off and the caps detonated the dynamite, some three hundred feet of virtually immovable sand or gravel forced the dynamite blast downward into the one hundred-foot column of nitroglycerin. The detonation did not ignite the volume at once. Instead, the blast moved through the column of nitroglycerin at 23,000 feet per second, forcing a wave of energy downward with increasing pressure as it rushed toward the bottom of the erupting string. As the incredible initial force of the primary explosion pushed down and out simultaneously, it immediately increased the size of the hole and caused local radial fracturing along the column. When that explosive force encountered the bottom of the well bore, it triggered another explosive reaction. Unable to defeat the perpendicular inertia of the blast, the secondary explosion ricocheted off the bottom of the well, rushing out at the same 23,000 feet per second at a forty-five degree angle, like a puff of smoke bouncing off a flat surface. As this colossal secondary shock moved through the overburden, it lost some of its original energy, but it retained enough force to fracture the pay zone in a radius proportional to its density and the amount of explosive per foot of bore within the zone. It was all over in 1/230 of a second.[26] So Colonel Roberts's theory of incumbent fluid tamping had merit after all. Sort of. The blast enlarged the hole only a small amount. The greatest extent of the force of the explosion went upward, seeking the path of least resistance, microscopically lifting and separating the strata to introduce the web of fractures that formed a network of channels to drain the oil trapped in the pay zone into the fractionally larger reservoir formed by the borehole.[27]

The shooter knew the shot went well if he felt a "bump on the ground." The bump was the effect of a secondary explosion moving up through the ground. Due to the angular trajectory of the shock wave through the ground, spectators who stood further away felt the effect more than the shooter, watching from a location nearer to the shot. If the tamping did not succeed in holding back the force of the explosion, the shot would come back up the casing, spewing oil, mud, rocks and debris with it and producing the dramatic eruption reminiscent of nineteenth-century shots that some thought of as "humdingers."[28]

The shooter made three types of shots, depending on the well and the requirements of the man in charge of the drilling operation, called the driller or operator. The first type of shot was a production shot, which was done on a new well after it reached the prescribed depth. To achieve what he perceived would be maximum effect, the operator might order a shot with hundreds of quarts of nitroglycerin. He ordered the shooter to use the largest diameter torpedo shell that could pass down the casing. The wider the shell, the more nitroglycerin concentrated in a given area, and thus, the harder the shot delivered per foot. Typically, the shooter used a shell with a diameter one inch less than the casing in order to maintain a clearance of a half inch around its circumference. The second shot in his repertoire was a utility shot, which was used to break frozen casing, free a string of pipe for removal, sidetrack lost tools, straighten a crooked hole, or other similar service requirements. Shooters used narrow torpedoes of various lengths in these shots to deliver a shallow pulverizing explosion to sever pipe or scour away a narrow layer along a length of the bore. Sometimes pipe-pulling contractors hired what shooters called bootleggers to break casing. These non-professionals, usually oilfield hands with little or no experience handling explosives, worked cheap and were readily available. The shot was small and accomplished with more stable solidified nitro, or jelly, because torpedo companies refused to sell liquid nitroglycerin to anyone other than experienced shooters. If the bootlegger miscalculated the placement of the jelly or used too much, he could "blow the hell out of the pipe and like as not kill some of the crew." The third type of shot, a recovery shot, increased production in wells in older, settled fields. In some cases, a recovery shot included two or three shots, with greater amounts of nitroglycerin used in each successive shot, sometimes reaching two thousand or more quarts. In these shots, he often used dump bailers to increase the amount of explosive per foot. These specialty shells emptied liquid nitroglycerin directly into the bottom of the well when the plunger at the lower end opened on contact with a solid surface.[29]

Shooters continued to play a vital role in the oil patch even as significant changes developed in the oil industry throughout the 1930s. When the East Texas oil boom hit in the early years of the Great Depression, oil prices dropped to as low as two cents a barrel. The Texas Railroad Commission (TRC) initiated a program of proration, or the assignment

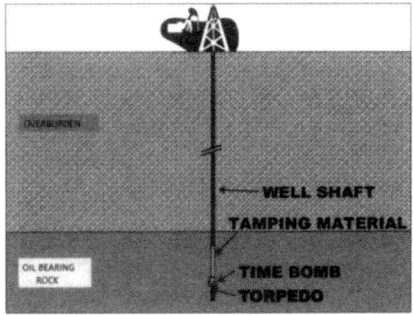
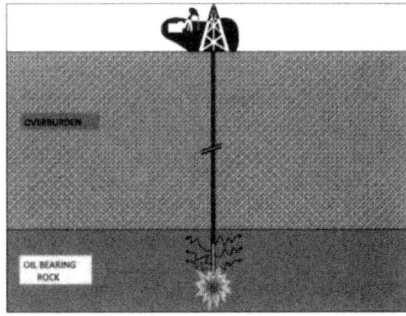
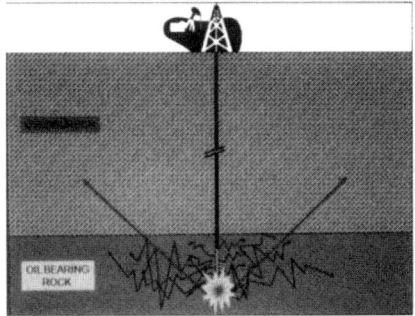
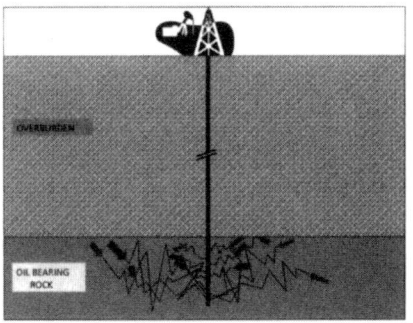

A well shot and its effects. The first diagram shows a cross section of a well indicating location of torpedo, time bomb, and tamping material; the second shows how the initial force of the nitroglycerine explosion immediately increased the size of the hole and caused local radial fracturing of the pay zone; the third shows how the secondary shock of the confined explosion created additional fractures as energy ricocheted off the bottom of the well bore and moved through the formation; and the fourth shows oil gathering in fissures created by the explosion. If formation pressure was high enough, oil moved through the fissures and then gushed toward the surface. Otherwise, gravity moved oil through the fissures where it collected at the bottom of the well and pumps brought it to the surface.

of quotas on production, to stem the glut of oil. The program set limits on the amount of oil each well in a given field could produce. At first, the TRC lacked the power to enforce the new regulations, but after federal authorities moved in, producers began to see the logic behind proration and acquiesced to regulation. However, they still took advantage of every opportunity available to extract as much oil as possible. Regulations allowed a specific number of barrels per well but conceded a percentage of production over the limit based on the potential of individual wells at the time of completion. Operators ordered a production shot as soon as the well came in to try to increase its potential above the prescribed limit and raise its "allowables."[30]

Wildcatting slowed considerably during the 1930s, in large part because of the effects of proration on exploration, and consequently so did the number of new fields opened. Shooters gladly gave up their itinerant lifestyle and worked a select few settled fields. They gained experience in particular fields that made many of them as knowledgeable about subsurface structures as some of the drillers and geologists who ordered the shots. Lee McKinney, for example, knew that a shot placed in the black lime (limestone) above the pay zone in Mentone on the western edge of the Permian Basin transferred better than if it were placed directly in the oil sand itself. Nonetheless, shooters generally kept their opinions to themselves and followed instructions in order to deflect blame if something went wrong.[31]

When an operator called for a shot, the shooter, or sometimes his wife, would negotiate the price based on the operator's specifications and then schedule the shot. Torpedo companies handed out wallet-sized cards printed with a table of rates, which varied little between companies, and a telephone number to call to order shots. Many wives gained so much experience that they could figure shots as closely as their husbands. McKinney spoke of his wife getting a call from an operator ordering a shot one day when he was out of town. After they discussed the requirements, she impressed the operator enough that he suggested she come out and make the shot herself. Although women did not participate in shooting wells, on at least one occasion they did transport nitroglycerin. Tex Thornton's wife and the wife of his assistant took two days to haul a load of nitro from Amarillo to Corpus Christi. Lee McKinney said his wife sometimes accompanied him to a site to watch a shot, but she never went on the job with him.[32]

Until the late 1930s, shooters were no more than mechanics who rendered a service based on the operator's demands. They gladly poured as much nitro down the hole as the operator called for because their pay was in direct proportion to the amount of soup in the shot. For big producers, the shot often meant the difference between profit and loss. For the poor boy operator, it could decide success or failure. They all wanted the most bang for their buck. To ensure that they achieved their goal, they usually ordered the shot to cover the entire pay zone from top to bottom, concentrating as much explosive as possible per foot of hole as soon as possible after the last bailer of mud and cuttings came out of the hole. Until around the Great Depression, the tamping, or covering, over the string of torpedoes that contained and shaped the explosion usually consisted of nothing more than a few feet of water. The operator considered the shot a good one if it spewed oil and debris out of the well like a Roman candle, whether production increased or not.[33]

Tamping added to the shooter's work and increased the lead time before a shot, but the results outweighed the extra cost in time and labor. Explosives engineers began to exert a strong influence on the art of oil well shooting during the 1930s, and tamping was an area where their research made a big impact. Experiments on rock formations in quarries helped engineers understand the value of effective tamping and concentrated shots in increasing the potential fracturing effects of explosions. They demonstrated that the more completely confined the explosion and the greater its density, the greater the lateral effect it would have on the formation. Their work indicated that, in addition to providing greater deflection of the force of the explosion, tamping with material such as sand or pea gravel dampened the upward pressure of the explosion, which resulted in less damage to pipe and the stratum lying above the pay zone. By 1937, 85 percent of all production shots involved tamping with sand, chert (a sand-like mineral found in limestone), gravel, crushed stone, or cement.[34]

Operators and shooters alike had a limited conception of what happened when nitroglycerin exploded at the bottom of a well. To their way of thinking, harder rock required a bigger shot. Drillers determined hardness by the effect of the drill bit on rock; however, hardness not only reflected drilling speed, but also the frangibility (ease of breaking) and elasticity of rock. The effect of the drill bit on rock contrasted with how rock reacted to the explosive power of nitroglycerin. Paul F. Lewis, an explosives engineer during the 1930s, explained that the frangibility of different types of oil-bearing rock determined the amount of explosives actually needed to produce the desired effect on the pay zone. Dolomites and sandstone are more elastic and less brittle than limestone. Consequently, the former would actually require harder shooting than the latter to achieve maximum oil production. As an analogy, Lewis offered the difference between an unfired clay vessel such as a terra cotta flowerpot and a vitrified vessel like a china teacup. A light blow with a hammer to the terracotta flowerpot would crack it and cause it to crumble near where it received the blow, but it would otherwise remain intact. A china cup hit with a similar blow would shatter completely. Similarly, by ordering a hard shot in comparatively elastic rock, the shot often resulted in caving or bridging, partial blocking of a section of the wellbore with boulders, possibly damaging or ruining the well.[35]

Oil well shooters performed a service that few had the courage to attempt. That service both helped and harmed the oil industry. Stimulation improved the productivity of a well, but too often that stimulus succeeded only in adding to the glut of oil, wasting even more of that vital resource. Shooters were not exactly responsible for such wasteful behavior, however, because they took their orders from the operator, who neither solicited nor valued their advice. The operator told them where to put the nitroglycerin, how he wanted it detonated, and how much to use the more the better. He wanted to get as much oil out of the ground as he could before someone beat him to it.

The shooters are all gone now. After World War II, the petroleum industry started experimenting with safer and more effective acid-fracturing and hydrofracking technology. By the 1960s, it was clear that nitroglycerin-based well stimulation was a dying art. But in their day, oil well shooters reflected the unique character of the oil patch: tough as a boot, rough as a cob, and ready to give it hell. Shooters learned their craft by serving an apprenticeship under the shooters who came before them, gaining expertise through experience. They performed an important service for the oil industry and helped make a few operators rich. They earned a decent wage, better than most in the oil patch, but they paid dearly for even the smallest mistakes. Many lived a solitary itinerant lifestyle, working long hours in miserable conditions and driving long distances over bad roads. They often traveled in the company of a load of nitro they had manufactured themselves, knowing that it could explode without warning, blowing them to kingdom come and leaving little more than a smoking black hole in the road. The shooter's job combined the science of a laboratory technician, the technological skills of a journeyman mechanic, the backbreaking work of a common laborer, and the audacity of a rodeo cowboy.

As well stimulation technology continued to advance during the 1960s and 1970s, a burgeoning service industry developed that replaced these individual entrepreneurs. Now, rather than relying on a knowledgeable and experienced local small businessman whose product had both created and satisfied an important niche in the industry, producers depend on multinational corporations such as Halliburton and Schlumberger that offer myriad services to provide what is now called oilwell completion. Instead of a one- or two-man operation working out of a home-built, multipurpose truck, these huge enterprises employ an army of hired hands with limited, specialized skills working from a fleet of high-tech, task-specific vehicles. But back when shooting wells brought drama and spectacle to the oil patch, they commanded respect from those who knew them and knew of their work. And few of their contemporaries would have faulted them if they had walked with a bit of a John Wayne swagger.

Authors

EUGENE C. BARKER earned his doctoral degree at the University of Texas at Austin, where he taught history for almost sixty years. He served as the director of the Texas State Historical Association (TSHA) for twenty-six of those years, and he published several significant books, most notably a biography of Stephen F. Austin, as well as articles in the *Southwestern Historical Quarterly*. He became a Fellow of the TSHA in 1902.

ROBERT D. BOYLE served on the history faculty at Arlington State College. He may also have been a lieutenant colonel in the Air Force Reserves.

H. BAILEY CARROLL taught at seven Texas institutions of higher education before joining the history faculty at the University of Texas at Austin, where he had earned his doctoral degree. He was the director of the TSHA for twenty years, during which time he edited many publications, including the first edition of the *Handbook of Texas*, and published fourteen articles. He became a Fellow of the TSHA in 1947.

ABBY W. COOPER was an award-winning journalist who wrote for at least seven newspapers and served as a local correspondent for the Associated Press. A longtime resident of Electra, where she worked for the Electra *News*, she was proud of the fact that she was the only woman anyone knew who served as the "oil editor" for her local newspaper.

DAVID F. DIXON earned his bachelor's and master's degrees in history at the University of Texas Permian Basin, where the faculty included Diana

D. Hinton, then studied for a doctoral degree in history at Texas Tech University.

JAMES P. HART, an honor graduate of both the University of Texas at Austin and Harvard Law School, was serving as an assistant attorney general, focusing on oil and gas cases, in 1941. He later served as an associate justice of the Texas Supreme Court, from which he resigned to be the first chancellor of the University of Texas system.

GEORGE A. HILL JR. was an attorney and University of Texas at Austin alumnus who served as the president of both the Houston Pipeline Company and Houston Oil Company. The author of six books on Texas history, he was active in several historical organizations, including the TSHA.

DIANA D. HINTON received a doctoral degree in British History from Yale University, then joined the faculty at the University of Texas-Permian Basin, where she became an endowed chair as a professor of regional and business history. She published a handful of landmark books on Texas oil history with her first husband, Roger M. Olien, then continued to publish scholarly work after marrying Harwood P. Hinton, who retired as a History professor from the University of Arizona. Diana is a Fellow of the TSHA and former president of the West Texas Historical Association.

BOYCE HOUSE came to Texas in 1920 and worked on newspapers in five different towns. He later became a prolific author of books and articles, popular for his humor and insights as a writer and radio personality. His piece on Spindletop contributed to his employment as a technical advisor for *Boomtown*, a movie that featured Clark Gable, Spencer Tracy, Claudette Colbert, and Hedy Lamarr.

CHARLIE [CLARENCE] JEFFRIES lived near Winkler, in Freestone County, but served as the president of the Navarro County Historical Society. He also wrote for the Texas Folklore Society and worked on a novel about the Republic of Texas that he apparently never published.

RICHARD B. McCASLIN, a doctoral graduate of the University of Texas at Austin, is the Director of Publications for the Texas State Historical Association (TSHA). Retired as the TSHA Professor of Texas History at the University of North Texas, he has written or edited twenty books. Eight have won awards, while his biography of Robert E. Lee was nominated for a Pulitzer. A TSHA Fellow and Admiral in the Texas Navy, McCaslin has commendations from the Civil War Round Tables in Dallas, Fort Worth, and Shreveport for his academic work.

DAVID F. PRINDLE is an award-winning author of twenty-one books and a professor of government at the University of Texas at Austin. His first book, *Petroleum Politics and the Texas Railroad Commission*, won the V.O. Key Jr. Award from the Southern Political Science Association. He earned his doctoral degree from the Massachusetts Institute of Technology.

WALTER RUNDELL JR. was a prolific author who wrote five books, including two photographic histories of the oil industry in Texas. A Texas native, he earned his doctoral degree at American University, then taught History at five institutions of higher education. He chaired the History departments at two of them, Iowa State University and the University of Maryland.

JOE W. SPECHT is a music historian with multiple degrees from the University of North Texas. He has worked for three university libraries in Texas, including an appointment as library director at McMurry University. He retired from the latter and became collection manager of the Grady McWhiney Research Foundation. His published work focuses on Texas music.

JASON P. THERIOT is an author, historian, and consultant. He earned a doctorate in history from the University of Houston and a degree in journalism from Louisiana State University. Additionally, he is a former Energy Policy Fellow at Harvard University's Kennedy School of Government. As a professional historian, he has numerous publications related to energy, environment, and business along the Gulf Coast. He specializes in family memoirs, biographies, and company histories.

CHARLES A. WARNER graduated from Cornell University and went to work as a geologist for oil companies in Oklahoma and Kansas. Employed by Houston Oil Company in 1921, he eventually became its vice president. He also served as director of the Houston Pipe Line Company. Warner wrote many articles on the oil and gas business, and his book on the history of that enterprise in Texas, published in 1939, remains an often-cited standard work.

EMILIO ZAMORA earned his doctoral degree at the University of Texas at Austin and teaches history there as an endowed professor. He is an author or editor of ten books, for which he has won seven awards. He is also a Fellow and former president of the TSHA, and he co-directed its production of the online *Handbook of Tejano History*.

Notes

McCASLIN

1. Larry S. Milner, "The History of Texas Business: A Selected Bibliography," *Southwestern Historical Quarterly* 99 (Oct. 1995): 217-244 [quote on 240; hereafter cited as *SWHQ*]; Larry S. Milner, "The History of Texas Business: A Selected Bibliography, Part II," *SWHQ* 99 (Jan. 1996): 371-392.

THERIOT

1. Charles A. Warner, Texas Oil & Gas Since 1543 (Houston: Gulf Publishing Co., 1939).
2. Martin W. Schwettmann, *Santa Rita: The Story of an Oil Well* (Austin: University of Texas Press, 1943).
3. James A. Clark and Michel T. Halbouty, *Spindletop: The True Story of the Oil Discovery That Changed the World* (New York: Random House, 1952). James A. Clark also published *The Chronological History of the Petroleum and Natural Gas Industries* (Houston: James A. Clark, 1963).
4. Clark and Halbouty, *Spindletop*, xi, 79.
5. For an early history of Sun Oil in Texas, see John G. Pew, *Sun Production Department, 1901–1974* (Dallas: Sun Oil Company, 1974). For a personal account of Sun Oil's Gulf Coast Division, see Jason P. Theriot, *From Beaumont to Deepwater, the Legacy of Sun Oil's Gulf Coast Division: An Explorationist Memoir* (forthcoming 2026).
6. For a thorough historical treatment on this topic, see Joseph A. Pratt, *The Growth of a Refining Region* (Greenwich, CT: JAI Press, 1980).
7. James A. Clark and Michel T. Halbouty, *The Last Boom: The Exciting Saga of the Discovery, Development, and Decline of the Great East Texas Oil Field* (New York: Random House, 1972).
8. Paul N. Spellman, *Spindletop Boom Days* (College Station: Texas A&M University Press, 2001).
9. Clarence C. Pope, *An Oil Scout in the Permian Basin* (Austin: University of Texas Press, 1972).
10. Ibid., 89.
11. John O. King, *Joseph Stephen Cullinan: A Study of Leadership in the Texas Petroleum Industry, 1897–1937* (Nashville: Vanderbilt University Press, 1970).

12. Marquis James, *The Texaco Story: The First Fifty Years, 1902-1952* (Houston: The Texas Company, 1953), and Henrietta M. Larson and Kenneth W. Porter, *History of Humble Oil & Refining Company: A Study in Industrial Growth* (New York: Harper & Brothers, 1959). See also James Presley, *Never in Doubt: A History of Delta Drilling Company* (Houston: Gulf Publishing Co., 1981).
13. Larson and Porter, *Humble Oil*, 6.
14. Samuel D. Myres, *The Permian Basin: Petroleum Empire of the Southwest—Era of Discovery* (El Paso: Permian Press, 1973); Samuel D. Myres, *The Permian Basin: Petroleum Empire of the Southwest—Era of Advancement: From the Depression to the Present* (El Paso: Permian Press, 1977).
15. Walter Rundell Jr., *Early Texas Oil: A Photographic History, 1866–1936* (College Station: Texas A&M University Press, 1977).
16. James Presley, *A Saga of Wealth: The Rise of the Texas Oilmen* (New York: Putnam, 1978).
17. For a good study of oil regulation in Texas, see David F. Prindle, *Petroleum Politics and the Texas Railroad Commission* (Austin: University of Texas Press, 1981).
18. Diana D. Olien [Hinton] and Roger M. Olien, *Oil in Texas: The Gusher Age, 1895–1945* (Austin: University of Texas Press, 2002). When Hinton and Olien began publishing together, they were married to each other. She later married Harwood P. Hinton.
19. Diana D. Olien [Hinton] and Roger M. Olien, *Oil Booms: Social Change in Five Texas Towns* (College Station: Texas A&M University Press, 1982).
20. Roger M. Olien, *Easy Money: Oil Promoters and Investors in the Jazz Age* 1982
21. Diana D. Olien [Hinton] and Roger M. Olien, *Wildcatters: Independent Oilmen as Producers and as a Cultural Phenomenon* (College Station: Texas A&M University Press, 1986).
22. Bobby D. Weaver, *Oilfield Trash: Life and Labor in the Oil Patch* (College Station: Texas A&M University Press, 2013).
23. Bobby D. Weaver, *Reinventing Texas: The Legacy of Santa Rita No. 1* (Austin: Texas State Historical Association, 2025).
24. Sheena B. Stief, Kristen L. Figgins, and Rebecca Day Babcock, eds. *Boom or Bust: Narrative, Life, and Culture from the West Texas Oil Patch* (Austin: University of Texas Press, 2021).
25. Jo Ann Stiles, Judith W. Linsley, and Ellen W. Rienstra, *Giant Under the Hill: A History of the Spindletop Oil Discovery at Beaumont, Texas, in 1901* (Austin: Texas State Historical Association, 2002).
26. Gregory Zuckerman, *The Frackers: The Outrageous Inside Story of the New Billionaire Wildcatters* (New York: Portfolio/Penguin, 2013).
27. Ibid., 6.
28. Loren C. Steffy, *George P. Mitchell: Fracking, Sustainability, and an Unorthodox Quest to Save the Planet* (College Station: Texas A&M University Press, 2019).
29. Bryan Burrough, *The Big Rich: The Rise and Fall of the Greatest Texas Oil Fortunes* (New York: Penguin Books, 2009); Harry Hurt III, *Texas Rich: The Hunt Dynasty, from the Early Oil Days Through the Silver Crash* (New York: W. W. Norton & Company, 1981); Jerome Tuccille, *Kingdom: The Story of the Hunt Family of Texas* (Lanham, MD: Beard Books, 2004).

HART

1. H. P. N. Gammel, comp., *The Laws of Texas, 1822-1897,* 10 vols. (Austin: Gammel Book Company, 1898-1902), 1: 1,291; George W. Paschal, comp., *A Digest of the Laws of Texas,* 5th ed., 2 vols. (Houston: E. H. Cushing, 1878), Article 4,402; Oliver C. Hartley, *A Digest of the Laws of Texas* (Philadelphia: Thomas, Cowperthwait, & Co., 1850), Art. 1,811.
2. Gammel, *Laws of Texas,* 2: 178; *Paschal's Digest,* 5th ed., Art. 804.
3. *Cox v. Robison,* 105 Tex. 426, p. 431, 150 S.W. 1,149.
4. *Texas Constitution of 1866,* Art. 7, Section 39.
5. *Cox v. Robison,* 105 Tex. 426, p. 431, 150 S.W. 1,149, 1,151.
6. *Cox v. Robison,* 105 Tex. 426, 431, 150 S.W. 1,149, 1,152.
7. Gammel, *Laws of Texas,* 3: 766; *Special Laws, Third Legislature,* 96.
8. Gammel, *Laws of Texas,* 5: 505; *General Laws of the Ninth Legislature of Texas* (Houston: E. H. Cushing, 1862), 61.
9. *Revised Civil Statutes,* 1879, Art. 3,800.
10. *Revised Civil Statutes,* 1895, Art. 4,041.
11. *Cox v. Robison,* 105 Tex. 426, 150 S.W. 1,149.
12. *Revised Civil Statutes,* 1925, Title 85, Chapters 4 and 5.
13. *Brown v. Humble Oil & Refining Co.*, 126 Tex. 296, 305; 83 S.W. (2d) 935, 940.
14. At Oil Spring in Nacogdoches County. See Charles A. Warner, *Texas Oil and Gas Since 1543* (Houston: Gulf Publishing Co., 1939), 5.
15. *Acts of the Twenty-sixth Legislature,* Regular Session, Chap. 49, p. 68.
16. *Acts of the Thirty-fifth Legislature,* Reg. Sess., Chap. 30, p. 48. For excellent summaries of the background of these statutes and the subsequent litigation relating to oil and gas in Texas, see Robert E. Hardwicke's "Legal History of Conservation of Gas in Texas," and Maurice Cheek's "Legal History of Conservation of Gas in Texas" in American Bar Association, *Legal History of Conservation of Oil and Gas: A Symposium* (Chicago: American Bar Association, 1938).
17. *Texas Constitution of 1876,* Article XVI, Sect. 59a.
18. *Gulf Land Co. v. Atlantic Refining Co.*, 134 Tex. 59, 131 S.W. (2d) 73.
19. See "A Decade of East Texas: Colossus of Oil," *The Oil Weekly,* Oct. 7, 1940, p. 19.
20. See *MacMillan v. Railroad Commission,* 51 F. (2d) 400.
21. *Danciger Oil & Refining Co. v. Railroad Commission,* 49 S.W. (2d) 837.
22. *Champlin Refining Co. v. Corporation Commission,* 286 U.S. 210, 52 S. Ct. 559, 76 L. Ed. 1,062.
23. *People's Petroleum Producers, Inc., v. Sterling,* 60 F. (2d) 1,041; *People's Petroleum Producers, Inc., v. Smith,* 1 F. Supp. 361.
24. *Amazon Petroleum Corporation v. Railroad Commission,* 5 F. Supp. 633. Compare *Boxrollium Oil Co. v. Smith,* 4 F. Supp. 624; *Danciger Oil & Refining Co. v. Smith,* 4 F. Supp. 236.
25. *Rowan & Nichols Oil Co. v. Railroad Commission,* 28 F. Supp. 131.
26. *Railroad Commission v. Rowan & Nichols Oil Co.,* 107 F. (2d) 70.
27. *Railroad Commission v. Rowan & Nichols Oil Co.,* 310 U.S. 573, 60 S. Ct. 1,021, 84 L. Ed. 983.

28. See *Railroad Commission v. Rowan & Nichols Oil Co.*, 310 U.S. 573, 583, 60 S. Ct. 1,021, 1,025, 84 L. Ed. 1,368, 1,374.
29. Ibid.
30. Ibid.

HILL

1. *Journal of the House of Representatives of the Republic of Texas, Regular Session of Third Congress, Nov.5, 1838* (Houston: Intelligencer Office, 1839), 168-170, gives the date as December 20, 1838; Charles A. Gulick Jr. and Katherine Elliott, eds. *The Papers of Mirabeau Buonaparte Lamar, Volume 2* (Austin: A. C. Baldwin & Sons, 1922), 348-349, gives the date as December 21, 1838.

HOUSE

1. The largest well in the United States until that time had been rated at 6,000 barrels daily.

BOYLE

1. Lucille Glasscock, *A Texas Wildcatter* (San Antonio: Naylor Company, 1952), 52-53.
2. Dallas *Morning News*, Oct. 5, 1930, p. 13, c. 3.
3. Mrs. Sam L. Scothorn, Dallas, to R. D. B., interview, Jan. 12, 1962.
4. Paul Bramlett, Longview, to R. D. B., interview, Dec. 2, 1961.
5. Recollection of Lawrence Birdsong, former mayor of Longview, Texas.
6. Bob Bozeman, Gladewater, to R. D. B., interview, Dec. 2, 1961.
7. Jack Cannon, Longview, to R. D. B., interview, December 2, 1961.
8. Ibid., Dec. 9, 1961.
9. E. A. Brown, Longview, to R. D. B., interview, Dec. 2, 1961.
10. Most of the information on litigation and specific cases at law was imparted by E. A. Brown, Longview, to R. D. B., in interviews during the weeks of November 27 and December 3, 1961.
11. Ibid.
12. Ibid.
13. Ibid.
14. Ibid.
15. Ibid.
16. Ibid.
17. Ibid.
18. Ibid.
19. "Booster" Whitelock, Longview, to R. D. B., interview, Dec. 9, 1961.

PRINDLE 1

1. Erich W. Zimmermann, *Conservation in the Production of Petroleum: A Study in Industrial Control* (New Haven: Yale University Press, 1957), 142-159; John M. Blair, *The Control of Oil* (New York: Vintage Books, 1976), 159-169; James P. Hart, "Oil, the Courts, and the Railroad Commission," *SWHQ* XLIV (Jan. 1941), 314-315; Morris A. Adelman, "Efficiency of Resource Use in Crude Petroleum,"

Southern Economic Journal, XXXI (Oct. 1964), 103-109; J. C. Rothwell Jr., "The Conservation Program of the Railroad Commission and the Structure of Crude Oil Prices in Texas" (Ph.D. Diss., University of Texas, 1958)
2. John R. Stockton, Richard C. Henshaw, Jr., and Richard W. Graves, *Economics of Natural Gas in Texas*, University of Texas, Bureau of Business Research, Monograph no. 15 (Austin, 1952), 152-189, 228-246; Zimmermann, *Conservation*, 237-238.
3. *Texas Almanac and State Industrial Guide, 1978-1979* (Dallas: Dallas Morning News, 1977), 410; Zimmermann, *Conservation*, 238.
4. Ernest O. Thompson, "Flare Gas Wastage in Texas: Steps Taken to Utilize," speech to American Gas Association, May 1, 1947, pp. 1-2, Railroad Commission Collection (Texas State Library and Archives, Austin).
5. Interviews. (Some of the information on which this article is based came from interviews conducted by the author. Because it proved impossible to secure informants unless complete anonymity was promised, these interviews cannot be further identified.)
6. Interviews; Stockton, Henshaw, and Graves, *Gas in Texas*, 17, 27-35, 72-75; Kendall Beaton, *Enterprise in Oil: A History of Shell in the United States* (New York: Appleton Century Crofts, 1957), 502.
7. Efforts have been made to quantify the amount of gas used as a proportion of that produced, but unreliable records make all such results extremely imprecise. See Stockton, *Gas in Texas*, 24, 58, 99, 107; for a discussion of the technology and economics of natural gas liquids, see ibid., 55-88.
8. Interviews; Maurice Cheek, "Legal History of Conservation of Gas in Texas," American Bar Association, *Legal History of Conservation of Oil and Gas: A Symposium* (Chicago: American Bar Association, 1938), 269-285.
9. Stockton, *Gas in Texas*, 5.
10. Zimmermann, *Conservation*, 56-57.
11. Ibid., 244; Stockton, *Gas in Texas*, 231-236.
12. Gerald Forbes, *Flush Production: The Epic of Oil in the Gulf-Southwest* (Norman: University of Oklahoma Press, 1942), 140-148; Beaton, *Shell*, 131; Stockton, *Gas in Texas*, 233-235.
13. Interviews.
14. Cheek, "Conservation of Gas," 279; Ernest 0. Thompson, "Natural Gas in the State of Texas," in Miscellaneous Political File, 1942, Railroad Commission Collection; *Energy Information Digest*, Subcommittee Print, 95th Congress, 1st Session, Committee Print 95-17, Stock #052-070-04305-9 (Washington, DC, 1977), 33.
15. Interviews.
16. Ibid.
17. Ibid.
18. Ibid.
19. Ibid. For the principal statutes empowering the Railroad Commission to conserve the state's petroleum resources, see Tex. Rev. Civ. Stat. Ann. art. 6,008-6,008b, 6,014-6,014a, 6,015, 6,016, 6,017, 6,018, 6,029-6,029a, 6,049-6,049e (Vernon).
20. Interviews; Ernest O. Thompson, "Texas Resources," speech to State Convention, Texas Real Estate Boards, Oct. 7, 1937, Railroad Commission Collection.

21. 1899 Tex. Gen. Laws ch. 49, § 3; Tex. Rev. Civ. Stat. 6,008, 6,014 (1925); 1933 Tex. Gen. Laws ch. 100, § 1; Barth P. Walker, "What Is an Oil Well? What Is a Gas Well? What Difference Does It Make?" Southwestern Legal Foundation, *Proceedings of the Fourteenth Annual Institute on Oil and Gas Law and Taxation* (Albany, 1963), 175-232; interviews.
22. Interviews; Tex. Rev. Civ. Stat. Ann. art. 6,008, § d, e (Vernon).
23. Interviews.
24. Ibid.
25. *Clymore Production Co. v. Thompson*, 11 F. Supp. 791 (W. D. Tex. 1935); *Clymore Production Co. v. Thompson*, 13 F. Supp. 469 (W.D. Tex. 1936).
26. Interviews.
27. *History of Petroleum Engineering* (Dallas: American Petroleum Institute, 1961), 862; Texas Railroad Commission, *Annual Report of the Oil and Gas Division, 1942* (Austin: Railroad Commission of Texas, 1942), 49.
28. Cheek, "Conservation of Gas," 269-273, 276-278; Zimmermann, *Conservation*, 252; James A. Clark and Michel Halbouty, *The Last Boom: The Exciting Saga of the Discovery of the Greatest Oil Field in America* (New York: Random House, 1972), 144-237.
29. Interviews; *Canadian River Gas Co. v. Terrell*, 4 F. Supp. 222 (W.D. Tex. 1933); 1933 Tex. Gen. Laws ch. 100, § 1; Cheek, "Conservation of Gas," 278.
30. 1935 Tex. Gen. Laws ch. 120; Cheek, "'Conservation of Gas," 281-284.
31. Interviews.
32. George H. Fancher, Robert L. Whiting, and James H. Cretsinger, *The Oil Resources of Texas: A Reconnaissance Survey of Primary and Secondary Reserves of Oil*, Texas Petroleum Research Committee (Austin, 1954), 70, 112, 210, 289, 310.
33. Jack K. Baumel, "'The Feasibility and Possibility of a Statewide Plan of Gas Proration and Ratable Take," paper presented at meeting of Interstate Compact Commission, Dec. 9-11, 1946, p. 8 (copy in possession of the author).
34. lnterviews.
35. Ibid.; Baumel, "Feasibility,'" 9.
36. *TIPRO Reporter* (Feb.-Mar. 1963), 9-10; interviews.
37. Interviews; Austin *American*, Dec. 7, 1946.
38. Oil *Weekly* (Apr. 16, 1945), 25. A discussion of the national political struggle over the jurisdiction of the Federal Power Commission is beyond the scope of this article, but see Joseph P. Harris, "The Senatorial Rejection of Leland Olds: A Case Study," *American Political Science Review*, XLV (Sept. 1951), 674-692; Anne H. Morgan, *Robert S. Kerr: The Senate Years* (Norman: University of Oklahoma Press, 1977), 56-102.
39. Interviews.
40. Ibid.; Texas Railroad Commission, *Annual Report of the Oil and Gas Division, 1943-44* (n.p., n.d.), 41; Fort Worth *Star-Telegram*, Dec. 22, 1944; George 0. Ives, "Many Phases of Gas Conservation Discussed by Texans at Austin Meet," *Oil Weekly* (Dec. 25, 1944), 30; Dallas *Morning News*, Dec. 21, 1944.
41. Fort Worth *Star-Telegram*, Dec. 22, 1944.
42. Interviews (quotation); *Oil and Gas Journal* (Nov. 10, 1945), 56.

43. Internal Railroad Commission memorandum (no date; copy in possession of the author); Austin *American,* Dec. 19, 1945; Corpus Christi *Caller,* Dec. 19, 1945; *Oil Weekly* (Dec. 24, 1945), 32.
44. Interviews; *Oil Weekly* (Mar. 5, 1945), 30; *Oil Weekly* (Apr. 16, 1945), 25; Charles J. Deegan, "Proper Price Incentive Would Do Much to Further Gas Conservation," *Oil and Gas Journal* (Feb. 9, 1946), 56-58.
45. Interviews; *Oil and Gas Journal* (Nov. 10, 1945), 56.
46. Robert E. Hardwicke, "Texas, 1938-1948," Blakely M. Murphy (ed.), *Conservation of Oil and Gas: A Legal History, 1948* (Chicago: American Bar Association, 1949), 457-458; *Oil and Gas Journal* (Aug. 18, 1945), 109; *Oil and Gas Journal* (Jan. 5, 1946), 45-46; *Oil and Gas Journal* (Feb. 2, 1946), 99; R. B. Tuttle, "Natural Gas and Cycling Industry Operating at 91 Per Cent of Capacity," *Oil and Gas Journal* (Apr. 26, 1947), 140-148; C. O. Willson, "5,000,000-Bbl. Production Rate Needed, Economists Report," *Oil and Gas Journal* (May 3, 1947), 36-37, 145; *Oil and Gas Journal* (Aug. 4, 1945), 117.
47. *Texas Almanac, 1978-1979,* p. 410.
48. *Oil and Gas Journal* (June 16, 1945), 76; *Oil and Gas Journal* (Feb. 16, 1946), 76; *Oil Weekly* (Apr. 16, 1945), 25; testimony by Ernest O. Thompson, "Progress in Oil and Gas Conservation by the Texas Railroad Commission," Federal Power Commission Docket no. G-580, In the Matter of Natural Gas Investigation, Proceedings at Houston, Texas, Feb. 1946 (copy in possession of the author).
49. Austin *American,* Dec. 7, 1946.
50. Austin *Statesman,* Dec. 8, 1946.
51. Interviews.
52. Ibid.
53. Ibid.; Railroad Commission Oil and Gas Docket #129, Order #4-10,351, Mar. 17, 1947 (Records Department of the Railroad Commission, Austin); *History of Petroleum Engineering,* 914; *Oil and Gas Journal* (June 28, 1947), 91.
54. *Railroad Commission v. Shell Oil Co.,* 206 S.W. 2d 235 (1947).
55. These orders are in Oil and Gas Docket #129 (Records Department of Railroad Commission, Austin). See, for example, for Flour Bluff field, Order #4-13,551, Nov. 22, 1948; for Tijerina-Canales field, Order #4-13,554, Nov. 22, 1948; for La Gloria field, Order #4-13-555, Nov. 22, 1948.
56. For historical summaries of the accumulating authority of the Railroad Commission over conservation, see Cheek, "Conservation of Gas," 271-286, and Robert E. Hardwicke, "Legal History of Conservation of Oil in Texas," American Bar Association, *Legal History,* 214-269.
57. *Railroad Commission v. Flour Bluff Oil Co.,* 219 S.W. 2d 506 (Tex. Civ. App. 1949) error ref'd p. 508.
58. The major controversy after 1949 was over the Spraberry field. See *Railroad Commission v. Rowan Oil Co.,* 259 S.W. 2d 173 (1953), and Nelson Jones, "The Spraberry Decision," *Oil and Gas Law: With Articles Pertaining to Sulphur, Taxation, Tidelands and Other Related Subjects,* 2 vols. (Austin: Texas Law Review, 1954), II, 2,093.

PRINDLE 2

1. *Newsweek,* Sept. 17, 1979, p. 39; Thomas Lloyd Miller, *The Public Lands of Texas, 1519-1970* (Norman: University of Oklahoma Press, 1972), xi, xii.
2. Ibid., 120, 121.
3. Ibid., 121, 124; Ed Clark, "The Permanent University Fund: A Foundation for Greatness," *The Addendum* VII (Nov. 1976), 2; Samuel D. Myres, *The Permian Basin, Petroleum Empire of the Southwest: Era of Discovery, From the Beginning to the Depression* (El Paso: Permian Press, 1973), 269; *Texas Almanac, 1978-1979* (Dallas: Dallas Morning News, 1979), 577.
4. Harry Y. Benedict, press release, Nov. 10, 1935, Harry Y. Benedict Collection (Dolph Briscoe Center for American History, University of Texas at Austin; cited hereafter as DBCAH); Miller, *Public Lands,* 124; Tom Smith, University Land Office, to David F. Prindle (DFP), May 20, 1982, telephone interview.
5. Miller, *Public Lands,* 124; San Angelo *Standard-Times,* May 28, 1933, copy in scrapbook titled "Oil Lands—UT, 1938-1961," Clippings File (DBCAH); Berte R. Haigh to DFP, Feb. 1, 1982 (original interview tapes between David F. Prindle and Samuel D. Myres, Clayton W. Williams, Sr., and Berte R. Haigh are in the archives of the Permian Basin Petroleum Museum in Midland, TX).
6. H[arry] Y. Benedict (comp.), *A Source Book Relating to the History of the University of Texas: Legislative, Legal, Bibliographical, and Statistical,* University of Texas Bulletin no. 1757 (Austin, 1917), 233-234.
7. Clark, "The Permanent University Fund," 3; William J. Battle, "A Concise History of the University of Texas, 1883-1950," *SWHQ* LIV (Apr. 1951), 397; Houston *Press,* Nov. 26, 1927.
8. W. Kene Ferguson, *History of the Bureau of Economic Geology* (Austin: University of Texas Bureau of Economic Geology, 1977), 33, 150-151.
9. Campbell Osborn, "Pioneering for Deep Oil in Southwest Texas," *Petroleum Investor* (Dec. 1938), copy in "Oil Lands—UT, 1938-1961;" Ruth Sheldon Knowles, *The Greatest Gamblers: The Epic of American Oil Exploration,* 2nd ed. (Norman: University of Oklahoma Press, 1978), 220.
10. Texas Legislature, *General Laws of the State of Texas Passed by the Thirty-fifth Legislature at its Regular Session Convened January 9, 1927, and Adjourned March 21, 1927* (Austin, n.d.), 158-167; Haigh to DFP, Feb. 1, 1982; Martin W. Schwettmann, *Santa Rita: The University of Texas Oil Discovery* (Austin: Texas State Historical Association, 1943), 2, 4, 5.
11. Myres, *Permian Basin,* 197-200; Haigh to DFP, Feb. 1, 1982 (quotation). Schwettmann, *Santa Rita,* 4, claims erroneously that the price was $500.
12. Carl Coke Rister, *Oil! Titan of the Southwest* (Norman: University of Oklahoma Press, 1949), 287; Haigh to DFP, Feb. 1, 1982.
13. Schwettmann, *Santa Rita,* 5; Knowles, *Greatest Gamblers,* 222.
14. Rister, *Oil!,* 287-288; Knowles, *Greatest Gamblers,* 222-225.
15. Berte R. Haigh, *Land, Oil, and Education* (El Paso: Texas Western Press, 1986).

16. W[alter] M. W. Splawn, "The University of Texas: Its Origin and Growth to 1928," II, 333, W.M.W. Splawn Papers (DBCAH); S. N. McLaren, "Report on Investigation of University Oil Leases and Royalties" (1930) (DBCAH), 14-16, 27; University of Texas Board of Regents Minutes, Vol. F, July 10, 1923, p. 143, Feb. 23, 1925, p. 319, Mar. 16, 1929, p. 417 (online at https://www.utsystem.edu/board-of-regents/meetings/meetings-archive [accessed Aug. 2, 2025]).
17. Regents Minutes, Vol. F, July 29, 1924, p. 287, Sept. 15, 1924, p. 302, Aug. 30, 1926, p. 490.
18. Regents Minutes, Vol. F, Oct. 27, 1924, p. 3o6, May 19, 1925, p. 341, July 16, 1925, pp. 378-379, Sept. 17, 1925, p. 392, Mar. 16, 1926, p. 417, Vol. J, July 21, 1934, p. 181; Myres, *Permian Basin*, 271; Haigh, *Land, Oil, and Education*.
19. Scott Gaines to Board of Regents, May 15, 1941, p. 3, reprinted in Regents Minutes, Vol. N, May 24, 1941, pp. 429-431; Regents Minutes, Vol. F, Apr. 20, 1926, p. 459; Vol. H, July 11, 1931, p. 401; Legislature, *General Laws of the Thirty-fifth Legislature*, 158-167; Texas Legislature, *General and Special Laws of the State of Texas Passed by the Fortyfirst Legislature at the Regular Session Convened at the City of Austin, January 8, 1929, and Adjourned March 14, 1929* (n.p., n.d.), 616-621; Texas Legislature, *General Laws of the State of Texas Passed by the Forty-second Legislature at the Regular Session Convened at the City of Austin, January 13, 1931, and Adjourned May 23, 19JI* (n.p., n.d.), 130-131; Myres, *Permian Basin*, 271.
20. Haigh, *Land, Oil, and Education*.
21. Ibid.; Jubal R. Parten to DFP, Apr. 11, 1981, interview; Gaines to Board of Regents, May 15, 1941, in Regents Minutes, Vol. N, May 24, 1941.
22. San Angelo *Standard-Times*, May 28, 1933, copy in "Oil Lands-UT, 1938-1961;" C. D. Simmons, "A Report on University Permanent Fund Investments: The University of Texas, as of December 31, 1932" (1933), General Administrative Files, "Available Fund: Investment Office, 1931-1944," University of Texas President's Office Records (DBCAH; cited hereafter as UTPOR).
23. Regents Minutes, Vol. F, Sept. 15, 1924, p. 302, Mar. 11, 1925, p. 323 (quotation); Splawn, "University of Texas," II, 338-340; Texas Legislature, *General Laws of the State of Texas Passed by Thirty-ninth Legislature at Its Regular Session, Which Convened January 13, 1925, and Adjourned March 19, 1925* (n.p., n.d.), 415-417.
24. Message of Governor Miriam A. Ferguson upon signing HB 246, Splawn Collection; *Daily Texan* (Austin), Apr. 16, May 2, 1925.
25. Splawn, "University of Texas," II, 356, 361.
26. Haigh, *Land, Oil, and Education*.
27. Ibid., 22-24; Regents Minutes, Vol. F, Aug. 30, 1926, pp. 490, 492; San Angelo *Standard-Times*, May 28, 1933; *Daily Texan* (Austin), Sept. 23, 1926.
28. Ibid.
29. Haigh, *Land, Oil, Education*, 31-34.
30. Regents Minutes, Vol. H, Sept. 30, 1929, p. 18, Vol. K, Apr. 27, 1936, p. 195 (quotation).
31. Frank F. Friend, "The Re-Survey of University of Texas Lands," General Administrative Files, "Available Fund: University Lands, Legal and Surveying, 1931-1944," UTPOR; Texas Legislature, *General Laws, Forty-first Legislature*, 616-617.

32. Ralph W. Yarborough to Attorney General [James V.] Allred: Re: Landreth Case—University, Oct. 9, 1931, private files of Berte R. Haigh (Midland, TX); Splawn, "University of Texas," II, 335; Regents Minutes, Vol. H, Sept. 30, 1929, pp. 18, 19, Dec. 14, 1929, p. 44, Nov. 26, 1930, pp. 255, 256, Vol. K, Oct. 26, 1935, p. 78.
33. Regents Minutes, Vol. K, Oct. 26, 1935, p. 78 (quotation), Vol. H, Sept. 30, 1929, p. 18; Yarborough to Allred, Oct. 9, 1931.
34. Regents Minutes, Vol. H, Dec. 14, 1929, p. 44, Vol. N, Mar. 19, 1940, pp. 6-7.
35. Haigh, *Land, Oil, and Education*; Charles A. Warner, *Texas Oil and Gas Since 1543* (Houston: Gulf Publishing Co., 1939), 321-323; Haigh to DFP, Nov. 16, 1981, telephone interview; Houston *Press*, Nov. 26, 1927.
36. Ibid.; Battle, "University of Texas," 397 (quotation).
37. Texas Legislature, *General Laws, Forty-first Legislature*, 716-718; Texas Legislature, *General Laws, Forty-second Legislature*, 914-915; Benedict, speech to Association of Governing Boards of State Universities, n.d., 3, Benedict Collection; Battle, "University of Texas," 397.
38. Benedict, *A Source Book*, 233-234; Henry C. Dethloff, *A Centennial History of Texas A&M University, 1876- 1976*, 2 vols. (College Station: Texas A&M University Press, 1975), I, 8-12.
39. Extract from the Report of the Agricultural and Mechanical College of Texas, Dec. 15, 1888, Dean of the College Collection (Cushing Memorial Library and Archives, Texas A&M University, College Station; cited hereafter as CMLA); Dethloff, *A Centennial History*, II, 416.
40. Charles Puryear to W. B. Bizzell, Oct. 22, 1923, Dean of the College Collection.
41. Agricultural and Mechanical College of Texas Board of Directors Minutes, Vol. 4, Nov. 26, 1924, p. 27 (Directors Office, Texas A&M University, College Station).
42. Directors Minutes, Vol. 4, Jan. 7, 1925, p. 29, Feb. 20, 1925, p. 32, July 14, 1925, p. 41, Sept. 21, 1925, p. 52, Feb. 23, 1926, p. 66, May 12, 1926, p. 71, Jan. 21, 1930, pp. 135-136; Puryear to Bizzell, Oct. 22, 1923, Dean of the College Collection.
43. *Daily Texan* (Austin), Dec. 15, 1926.
44. Robert L. Holliday to Tom Pollard, Nov. 10, 1928; Benedict to A. J. Wirtz, Nov. 28, 1928; and Holliday to William C. Hogg, Nov. 20, 1928, Benedict Collection; Puryear to W. B. Walton, Oct. 21, 1925, Dean of the College Collection.
45. Directors Minutes, Vol. 4, Sept. 21, 1925, p. 52, May 12, 1926, p. 71, Apr. 22, 1929, p. 118 (quotation); Francis Law to H. J. Lutcher Stark, Apr. 27, 1929, Regents Correspondence (UTPOR).
46. W. M. Odell to R. L. Batts, Mar. 13, 1930, Robert Lynn Batts Collection (DBCAH); Holliday to Myron Blalock, Nov. 21, 1928; Sidney E. Mezes to Benedict, May 10, 1930, Benedict Collection.
47. George S. Perry, *The Story of Texas A and M* (New York: McGraw-Hill, 1951), 97-99.
48. Regents Minutes, Vol. H, Mar. 7, 8, 1930, pp. 77-80, 83, 84, Apr. 21, 1930, pp. 93-95; Holliday to Thomas Watt Gregory, Jan. 16, 1931, Thomas Watt Gregory Papers (LC Stationary Board for Lease of University Lands, General Land Office, Austin); Directors Minutes, Vol. 4, Mar. 8, 1930, pp. 138, 140, Apr. 21, 1930, pp. 143-145, 149.
49. Regents Minutes, Vol. H, Jan. 5, 1931, pp. 268-270; Directors Minutes, Vol. 4, Nov. 26, 1930, p. 157, Jan. 5, 1931, pp. 160, 163; Dethloff, *Texas A&M*, II, 419- 420.

50. Directors Minutes, Vol. 4, June 2-3, 1933, pp. 235-236, June 7, 1933, p. 241; T. O. Walton to Byrd E. White, June 22, 1931, and Holliday to Walton, June 18, 1931, Historical Files, Chancellor's Records (CMLA).
51. Parten to DFP, Apr. 11, 1981, interview.
52. Haigh, *Land, Oil, and Education*.
53. Parten to DFP, Apr. 11, 1981, interview.
54. Haigh to DFP, Nov. 16, 1981, interview; Report of Land Committee to Board of Regents of the University of Texas Recommending Changes in Method of Sales of Leases on University Lands, Nov. 23, 1935, private files of Jubal R. Parten (Madisonville, TX).
55. Ibid.
56. Ibid.
57. Ibid.
58. Ibid.; Regents Minutes, Vol. K, Nov. 23, 1935, p. 90.
59. Hines H. Baker to Parten, Mar. 20, 1936, Parten private files.
60. Berte R. Haigh, "The University of Texas System Public Auction Sales of Oil and Gas Leases," May 27, 1981, Haigh private files; Parten to DFP, Apr. 11, 1981, interview; Haigh, *Land, Oil, and Education*; Regents Minutes, Vol. K, July 27, 1936, p. 325; Directors Minutes, Vol. 5, May 29, 1937, pp. 91-93.
61. Ibid.; Texas Legislature, *General and Special Laws of the State of Texas Passed by the Forty-fifth Legislature at the Regular Session Convened at the City of Austin, January 12, 1937, and Adjourned May 22, 1937* (Austin, n.d.), 280-283.
62. Midland *Reporter-Telegram*, Feb. 16, 1941, copy in clippings scrapbook, "Oil Lands—UT, 1938-1961" (DBCAH); George A. Hill Jr., "The Spirit of Santa Rita," *SWHQ* XLVIII (July 1944), 83; Miller, *Public Lands,* 278; George H. Sheppard, *Annual Report of the Comptroller of Public Accounts of the State of Texas 1942, Part I* (Austin: Von Boeckmann-Jones, 1942), 86.
63. Comptroller's Office, University of Texas, to DFP, Dec., 1981, telephone interview; Amy Johnson, "The Haves and the Have-nots," *Texas Observer*, July 10, 1981, pp. 4-8.

ZAMORA

1. Carlos E. Castaneda, "Statement on Discrimination Against Mexicans in Employment," in Alonso S. Perales, *Are We Good Neighbors* (San Antonio: Artes Graficas, 1948), 59-63; Castaneda, "Testimony," *U.S. Senate Subcommittee of the Committee on Education and Labor Hearings, 79th Cong., 1st Sess., Mar. 12-14, 1945* (Washington, DC: Government Printing Office, 1945), 131-135 (Y4.Ed8/3:Em7/3); Pauline R. Kibbe, *Latin Americans in Texas* (Albuquerque: University of New Mexico Press, 1946), 157-166. Readings on Mexicans during the war include Mario Garcia, "Americans All: The Mexican American Generation and the Politics of Wartime Los Angeles, 1941-1945," *Social Science Quarterly* LXV (June 1984), 279-289; Raul Morin, *Among the Valiant: Mexican-Americans in WW II and Korea* (Los Angeles: Borden Publishing Co., 1966); Gerald Nash, "Spanish-Speaking Americans in Wartime," in Gerald D. Nash, *The American West Transformed: The Impact of the Second World War* (Bloomington: Indiana University

Press, 1985), 107-127; and Robin F. Scott, "Wartime Labor Problems and Mexican Americans in the War," in Manuel P. Servin (ed.), *An Awakened Minority: The Mexican-American* (Beverley Hills: Glencoe Press, 1974), 134-142. The term Mexican refers to both Mexican nationals and US-born Mexicans for two reasons. Incomplete nativity and citizenship data made it impossible in most cases to make such a distinction. Also, the use of the term Mexican seems appropriate since they shared the experiences of occupational, wage, and upgrading discrimination.

2. Publications that treat the subject of the Mexican worker and the FEPC are rare. These include the previously cited works by Garcia and Nash as well as two studies, one by a CIO organizer involved in the OWOC of 1942-1943 and the other by a former head of the FEPC: Clyde Johnson, 'The Battle for Baytown" (MS, June 1984, Clyde Johnson Papers, Southern Historical Collection, Louis R. Wilson Library, University of North Carolina, Chapel Hill), and Malcolm Ross, "Those Gringos," in Malcolm H. Ross, *All Manner of Men* (New York: Greenwood Press, 1948), 265-278. A study by Ray Marshall examines racial discrimination against black workers in the Texas Gulf Coast oil industry and the successful 1955 challenge against it by the government and the NAACP: "Some Factors Influencing the Upgrading of Negroes in the Southern Petroleum Refining Industry," *Social Forces* XLII (Dec. 1963), 186-195.

3. President Roosevelt established the FEPC on June 25, 1941, with Executive Order 8802, a measure intended to end discrimination by unions, defense industries, and government employers. On May 26, 1943, Roosevelt issued Executive Order 9346, which reorganized the agency and strengthened its effectiveness with an improved budget and regional offices in such places as Dallas and San Antonio. Book-length studies of the FEPC include: Herbert Garfinkel, *When Negroes March: The March on Washington Movement in the Organizational Policies for FEPC* (Glencoe, IL: Free Press, 1959); Louis C. Kesselman, *The Social Politics of FEPC: A Study in Reform Pressure Movements* (Chapel Hill: University of North Carolina Press, 1948); and Louis Ruchames, *Race, Jobs, and Politics: The Story of FEPC* (Westport, CT: Negro Universities Press, 1953).

4. The twelve refineries were Sinclair (Houston), Shell (Houston), Texas Company (Houston), Texas Company (Port Neches), Pure Oil (Port Neches), Republic (Texas City), Southport (Texas City), Pan American (Texas City), Texas Company (Port Arthur), Gulf (Port Arthur), Humble (Baytown), and Magnolia (Beaumont). Fair Employment Practice Committee, *Final Report* (Washington, DC: US Government Printing Office, 1947), 23; W. Don Ellinger. "Complete Report on Shell Situation, May 1, 1945," 1-5, Division of Field Operations, Records of the Fair Employment Practice Committee (National Archives, Washington, DC, cited hereafter as FEPC Records).

5. The FEPC conducted preliminary investigations in the Southwest in 1942 that resulted in the discovery of widespread discrimination against Mexican workers in the oil companies of the Texas Gulf Coast. The cases against the refineries and the workers' organizations lasted until the closing of the Dallas office in 1945. Report of Clay Cochran to Castaneda, Oct. 25, 1943, Castaneda to Will Maslow, Jan. 26, 1944, Administrative Division, FEPC Records; John Morton Blum, *V Was For Victory: Politics*

    and American Culture During World War II (New York: Harcourt Brace Jovanovich, 1976), 198: Lawrence W. Cramer to M. C. Gonzales, Nov. 26, 1941, Will Alexander to W. G. Carnahan, Dec. 26, 1941, Division of Field Operations, FEPC Records.
6. Castaneda, "Statement on Discrimination Against Mexicans in Employment," 59-63: Castaneda, "Testimony," 131-135; Castaneda, "The Second Rate Citizen and Democracy," in Perales, *Are We Good Neighbors,* 17-20; C. L. Golightly, "Wartime Employment of Mexican Americans, 1943," Division of Review and Analysis, FEPC Records. The Mexican population, both US- and Mexico-born, was at least one million, or 11.5 percent of the total population in Texas. Approximately 500,000 Mexicans were gainfully employed. The 25,000 figure was calculated on the basis of a 5 percent utilization rate reported by Castaneda.
7. For readings on the oil industry, see Carl C. Rister, *Oil: Titan of the Southwest* (Norman: University of Oklahoma Press, 1949); Joseph A. Pratt, *The Growth of a Refining Region* (Greenwich, CT: JAI Press, 1980); and Charles A. Warner, "Texas and the Oil Industry," *SWHQ* L (July 1946), 7-24. For an account by a participant in the 1941-1943 Oil Workers' Organizing Campaign, see Johnson, "Battle for Baytown." Other studies that treat the subject of labor organizing in Texas include Harvey O'Conner, *History of the Oil Workers' International Union* (Denver: Oil Workers' International Union, 1950); F. Ray Marshall. *Labor in the South* (Cambridge: Harvard University Press, 1967), 194-199, 230-233; Herbert Werner, "Labor Organizations in the American Petroleum Industry," in Harold F. Williamson, Ralph L. Andreano, Arnold R. Daum, and Gilbert C. Klose (eds.), *The American Petroleum Industry: The Age of Energy, 1899-1959* (Evanston, IL: Northwestern University Press, 1963), 827-845.
8. The figure for the Mexican work force was estimated based on a total of 17,350 workers in the twelve refineries reported by the FEPC. Kibbe suggests a lower figure of less than 3 percent. Kibbe, *Latin Americans in Texas,* 159-161.
9. Golightly, "Wartime Employment of Mexican-Americans," 2; G. L. Farned to Cramer, Jan. 26, 1943; pp. 4-5 (Johnson Papers). The nativity figures suggested by the survey have to be taken with caution. They differ substantially from the overall ratio of one Mexico-born to six USborn Mexicans in the state.
10. One important FEPC finding in the Texas Gulf Coast oil industry involved the use of a dual classification system. According to one FEPC report, all refineries in the area, with the exception of the Texas Company, maintained a wage differential that segregated two types of common laborers. The first group was composed of Anglos who received the higher rate of pay, which was approximately eighty-nine cents an hour. The second group was made up of Mexican and African-American workers who received around seventy-nine and one-half cents an hour. Ernest G. Trimble to Francis J. Haas, July 9, 1943, Region X Files, FEPC Records.
11. This summary of conditions has been gleaned from numerous FEPC documents cited throughout the paper.

12. See Johnson, "Battle for Baytown," for criticism of the union leadership. A CIO organizer assigned to the oil industry in the Gulf Coast, Johnson was especially critical of the inconsistent support that the OWIU gave the CIO-backed OWOC, 1941-1943, of which he was a part. Much of the conflict that occurred between the staff of the OWOC and the OWIU hinged on the general reluctance of the latter organization to support the OWOC's strong civil rights planks that called for an end to discrimination in the refineries. Johnson to Emilio Zamora (EZ), Feb. 9. 1988, interview; Johnson, "CIO Oil Workers' Organizing Campaign in Texas, 1942-1943," in Gary M. Fink and Merl E. Reed (eds.), *Essays in Southern Labor History: Selected Papers, Southern Labor History Conference, 1976* (Westport, CT: Greenwood Press, 1977), 173-187. See the following for copies of these contracts or references to them: Castaneda to Maslow, Sept. 17, 1943, Leonard M. Brin to Maslow, May 24, 1944, "Application of Seniority for Selecting Men for Jobs in New Operating Units Not Replacing Other Units," July 23, 1943, and "Mechanical Seniority," Oct. 1, 1936, Region X Files, FEPC Records; and President's Committee on Fair Employment Practice, Stipulation, In the Matter of Shell Oil Company, Inc., and Oil Workers' International Union, Local 367, CIO, Dec. 30, 1945, pp. 3-4, Legal Division, FEPC Records.

13. The leadership of the OWIU freely admitted widespread discrimination by its locals in the Gulf Coast. though they claimed that it was for the most part "company inspired and, to an extent, reflective of local prejudices." OWIU, Report of the Oil Workers' International Union Concerning Experiences in the Field of Racial and Religious Discrimination, 1944, Division of Review and Analysis, FEPC Records. There were exceptions to the general rule of discrimination by the unions. CIO Local 449 from the Southport refinery in Texas City is a case in point. When the refinery refused to end its practice of wage discrimination, the union successfully challenged the company in 1943 before the War Labor Board, which ordered the company to end its dual classification system and pay African-American workers equal wages. Another example occurred at the Gulf refinery of Port Arthur in 1945. When 250 members of the Black CIO Union, Local 254, went on a wage strike, the president of the white CIO union announced the support of his members. See National War Labor Board, In the Matter of Southport Petroleum Company of Delaware and Oil Workers ' International Union Local 449, Case No. 2898-CS-D, June 5, 1943, Johnson Papers; Castaneda to Maslow, June 16-31, 1945, Region X Files, FEPC Records.

14. International divisions regarding the proper strategy to pursue when challenging the oil industry was an especially debilitating problem that reflected wider political concerns within the FEPC. Such differences, which contributed to important delays, usually appeared when management and union leaders proposed industry-wide hearings on the grounds that it was unfair to single out individual refineries. Differences of opinion also coincided with a related ambivalence in Washington. For instance, the FEPC entertained the idea of a general hearing that would investigate the issue of discrimination against Mexicans in the Southwest as early as 1942 but dropped its plans at the insistence of Secretary of State Sumner Welles, who was concerned that revelations of discrimination against Mexicans would damage

relations with Latin America. Lawrence W. Cramer, the executive secretary of the FEPC in 1943, on the other hand, considered a general hearing involving the oil industry but remained noncommittal because he feared that it could provoke a racial reaction much like one that occurred after the FEPC hearings in Alabama. Preparations were made once again in 1944 to hold general hearings at El Paso to investigate discrimination against Mexicans in the mining industry of Arizona. New Mexico, and West Texas. These plans were also rescinded as a result of objections raised by the State Department. Blum, *V Was for Victory,* 199; Kesselman, *Social Politics of FEPC,* 17- 18; Edwin Smith to Johnson, Nov. 6, 1942, Johnson Papers; Castaneda to Maslow, Sept. 1, 1944, Legal Division, FEPC Records.

The FEPC delayed its investigation of the oil industry on two occasions. The first delay coincided with the aborted 1943 plans for a general hearing. The second one occurred during the latter part of 1944, while Castaneda was heading an investigation of the mining industry. Although there is no evidence that these decisions against holding general hearings contributed to similar decisions in oil, the FEPC personnel in Texas, however, did express similar reservations on which strategy to pursue. Castaneda to Maslow, Jan. 26, 1944; Brin to Maslow, June 24, 1944, Stanley D. Metzger to Clarence M. Mitchell, July 11, 1944, Division of Field Operations, FEPC Records.

15. Manuel Gonzales to Sidney Hillman, Nov. 17, 1941, Cramer to Gonzales, Nov. 26, 1941, W. G. Carnahan to Will W. Alexander, Dec. 9, 1941, Division of Field Operations. FEPC Records; Carnahan to Alexander, Dec. 1, 1941, Legal Division, FEPC Records; Gonzales to Trimble, July 29, 1942, Administrative Division. FEPC Records. See Region X Weekly Reports in the FEPC Records beginning in August 1943 for complaint summaries.

16. See articles by Felix D. Almaraz Jr., on Castaneda's highly successful career as a historian and archivist: "Carlos Eduardo Castaneda, Mexican-American Historian: The Formative Years, 1896-1927," *Pacific Historical Review* XLII (Aug. 1973), 319-344; "The Making of a Boltonian: Carlos E. Castaneda of Texas—The Early Years," *Red River Valley Historical Review* I (Winter 1974), 329-350; and "Carlos E. Castaneda and *Our Catholic Heritage:* The Initial Volumes (1933-1943)," *Social Science Journal* XIII (Apr. 1976), 27-37. A recent publication by Mario T. Garcia devotes a chapter to the life of Castaneda: *Mexican Americans; Leadership, Ideology and Identity, 1930-1960* (New Haven: Yale University Press, 1989). See the following for insightful views on Mexican civil rights and labor politics, and its international ramifications, during the 1940s: Juan Gomez-Quinones, *Chicano Politics; Reality and Promise, 1940-1990* (Albuquerque: University of New Mexico Press, 1990). Almaraz and Garcia generally ignore the work that Castaneda did with the FEPC and his active associations with other civil rights leaders of the period, preferring instead to focus on his career as a historian despite the voluminous amount of information that records his civil rights work. See, for example, Carlos E. Castaneda Papers and Eleuterio Escobar Papers (Mexican American Archival Collection, Nettie Lee Benson Latin American Collection, University of Texas at Austin); Perales, *Are We Good Neighbors;* and Castaneda's various testimonies in congressional hearings cited elsewhere in this article.

17. Ross, *All Manner of Men*, 273-274. Castaneda's strategy can be gleaned from his Weekly Reports on the meetings. See Castaneda's Weekly Reports, FEPC Records. The decision by Castaneda to focus on complaints by Mexican workers was based on consultations with Mexican and black complainants as well as with the Mexican Consul and black and Mexican civil rights leaders from Houston.
18. Fair Employment Practice Committee, *First Report* (Washington, DC: Government Printing Office, 1945), 107.
19. Although Mexican workers from various refineries submitted complaints, the workers from Humble, Sinclair, and Shell registered the most and best documented ones. Also, these Mexican workers were consistent in resubmitting complaints through the Mexican Consul's office when the FEPC periodically requested additional evidence in support of the complaints.
20. "Humble Oil and Refining Company, Baytown, Texas" (typed summary of FEPC case against Humble, Nov. 1943), Division of Review and Analysis, FEPC Records. For information on early discriminatory practices, see Henrietta M. Larson and Kenneth W. Porter, *History of Humble Oil and Refining Company: A Study in Industrial Growth* (New York: Harper & Brothers, 1959), 200-201.
21. Statement on Discrimination Against Mexican Workers at the Baytown Refinery, Humble Oil and Refining Company, Baytown, Texas, Signed by Andres Contreras, C. Beltran, J. San tana, Onofre Gonzalez, L. Herrera, and G. N. Ponce, Nov. 25, 1942, Johnson Papers.
22. Farned to Cramer, Jan. 26, 1943, Johnson to Trimble, Mar. 15, 1943, Johnson Papers.
23. Ibid. The summary of Farned's response is drawn from his letter to Cramer, Jan. 26, 1943. and from the FEPC report titled "Humble Oil and Refining Company, Baytown, Texas."
24. Ibid.
25. Ibid.," 4; Victor Rothen, Memorandum for the Solicitor General, pp. 1 - 2. Region X Files, FEPC Records.
26. See issues of the *C/O Campaigner*, the OWOC's organ in the Gulf Coast, for critiques of discrimination in the industry. Also, see copies of *The Bulletin* for examples of the Federation's criticisms of the union. Both are in the Johnson Papers.
27. *The Bulletin*, May 6, 1943.
28. *The Bulletin*, Apr. 27, 1843.
29. Castaneda, Final Disposition Report, Humble, Feb. 9 and 10, 1944, Administrative Division, FEPC Records; Rothen, Memorandum for the Solicitor General, pp. 1-2; "Humble Oil and Refining Company, Baytown, Texas," 2-3.
30. Castaneda to Maslow, Oct. 16, 23, 1943, Region X Files, FEPC Records.
31. Castaneda, Final Disposition Report, Humble, Feb. 9 and 10, 1944, Castaneda to Maslow, Jan. 26, 1944, p. 2, Administrative Division, FEPC Records.
32. See Johnson, "Battle for Baytown," for a description of the OWOC and the conflict with the OWIU leadership.
33. Brin, Final Disposition Report, Sinclair, Feb. 11, 1944, FEPC Records.

34. J. O. Gray to Carnahan, Apr. 15, 1942, Affidavit, A. S. Sanchez, Feb. 15, 1945, Region X Files, FEPC Records.
35. The discussion on the complaint is based on the following documents: Minutes of the Conference Held with Management and Labor of Sinclair Refinery, Houston, Texas, Dec. 28, 1943. pp. 2-6, Region X Files, FEPC Records; Adolfo G. Dominguez, Memorandum on Discrimination of Mexican Workers at the Refinery of the Sinclair Refining Company in Houston, Texas, June 8, 1943, Affidavits of J. R. Flores and Teodosio Gutierrez, Nov. 20, 1943, and Cochran to Sinclair Refining Company, Nov. 26, 1943, Division of Review and Analysis, FEPC Records.
36. Castaneda to Maslow, Dec. 25, 1943, Minutes of the Conference, Dec. 28, 1943, pp. 3-4, Region X Files, FEPC Records.
37. Young to Cochran, Dec. 7, 1943, pp. 1-2, FEPC Records.
38. Minutes of the Conference, Dec. 28, 1943, pp. 1-6; Region X Files, FEPC Records.
39. Castaneda, Final Disposition Report, Sinclair, Feb. 11, 1944, FEPC Records.
40. Castaneda to Clyde Ingram, Mar. 1, 1944, Region X Files, FEPC Records.
41. Ellinger to Sinclair Refining Company, Mar. 15, 1945, Affidavits dated February 1945 and signed by A. S. Sanchez, A. V. Salinas, Juan Robledo, S. Rodriguez, Jesse Lozano Caballero, Henry S. Mendez, and M. de la Garza, Region X Files, FEPC Records.
42. Ellinger to Sinclair Refining Company, Mar. 15, 1945; Affidavits, Feb. 1945, signed by A. S. Sanchez, A. V. Salinas, Juan Robledo, S. Rodriguez, Jesse Lozano Caballero, Henry S. Mendez, and M. de la Garza, Region X Files, FEPC Records.
43. Summary of Shell Oil Case, May 5, 1945, p. 1, Legal Division, FEPC Records. A precise figure for the number of Mexican workers at Shell is not available.
44. Dominguez, Memorandum on Racial Discrimination at the Shell Refining Co.. Houston, Texas, Apr. 26, 1941, and Memorandum on Conference Held Friday, May 14, 1943, at Mexican Consulate in Houston, Texas, Relative to Discrimination of Mexican Workers at Shell Oil and Refining Company, May 15, 1943, Division of Review and Analysis, FEPC Records. The discussion that follows on the complaint is based on the Dominguez documents.
45. Dominguez, Memorandum on Conference, May 14, 1943, pp. 1-4, Division of Review and Analysis, FEPC Records.
46. Ibid.; Trimble to Haas, July 9, 1943, pp. 1- 2, Region X Files, FEPC Records.
47. Castaneda to Maslow, Sept. 18, 1943, Region X Files, FEPC Records.
48. Castaneda to Maslow, Dec. 4, 1944, Castaneda to Dominguez, Sept. 16, Oct. 7, 1943, Castaneda to John J. Herrera, Oct. 7, 1943, Region X Files, FEPC Records.
49. Castaneda to Maslow, Oct. 16, 23, 1943, Region X Files, FEPC Records.
50. Castaneda to O. A. Knight, Jan. 1, 1944, Region X Files, FEPC Records.
51. Castaneda to Maslow, Dec. 31, 1943, Region X Files, FEPC Records.
52. Ibid.
53. Castaneda to Maslow, Dec. 31, 1943, Jan. 1, 1944, Region X Files, FEPC Records.
54. Castaneda to Maslow, Jan. 26, 1944, Castaneda to Brin, May 17, 1944, Region X Files, FEPC Records.
55. Opening Statement, Dec. 28, 1944, Legal Division, FEPC Records; Ellinger to Maslow, Dec. 30, 1944, Region X Files, FEPC Records.

56. Ibid. Also see Statement of Charges and Order for Hearing in the Matter of Shell Oil Company, Inc., and Oil Workers' International Union, Local 367, CIO, Dec. 11, 1945, Statement of the Case, Jan. 27, 1945, FEPC Records; Stipulation, Dec. 30, 1945, Legal Division, FEPC Records.
57. Opening Statement, Dec. 28, 1944, pp. 1, 9, Legal Division, FEPC Records.
58. Ibid.
59. Statement of the Case, Jan. 27, 1945, FEPC Records; Stipulation, Dec. 30, 1945, Legal Division, FEPC Records.
60. Castaneda to Maslow, Mar. 24, 1945, p. 5, Mitchell to Ellinger, Apr. 11, 1945, Region X Files, FEPC Records.
61. Summary of Shell Oil Case, May 5, 1945, p. 1, Legal Division, FEPC Records.
62. Summary of Shell Oil Case, May 5, 1945, pp. 1-2, Legal Division, FEPC Records.
63. Ibid.; Ellinger to Ross, May 1, 1945, pp. 1- 5, Region X Files, FEPC Records. The following description of events is based on information from these two reports.
64. Also see Mitchell to Emanuel Bloch, Apr. 12, 1945, Legal Division, FEPC Records.
65. Ellinger to Ross Re: Attached Memorandum, May 1, 1945, pp. 1-3, Region X Files, FEPC Records; Ellinger to Ross Re: Complete Report on Shell Situation, May 1, 1945, pp. 1-5, Division of Field Operations, FEPC Records.
66. Ibid.
67. Ellinger to Ross Re: Attached Memorandum, May 1, 1945, p. 2, Region X Files, FEPC Records.
68. Castaneda to Maslow, May 16, 1945, p. 4, Region X Files, FEPC Records.
69. Ellinger to Knight, May 24, 1945, Knight to Ellinger, June 2, 1945, Region X Files, FEPC Records. See Ellinger to Ross, May 20, 1945, Legal Division, FEPC Records, for proposal by union on segregated workforce.
70. George Weaver to Ellinger, June 19, 1945, Ellinger to Mitchell, July 14, 1945, Castaneda to Maslow, June 1-15, 1945, pp. 4-5, Region X Files, FEPC Records; J. J. Hickman to Ellinger, July 24, 1945, Division of Review and Analysis, FEPC Records.
71. Castaneda to Maslow, June 16-30, 1945, p. 4, Region X Files, FEPC Records.

HINTON

1. *The Humble Way* (May-June 1945), 1.
2. James B. Allen, *The Company Town in the American West* (Norman: University of Oklahoma Press, 1966), 3-5; John S. Spratt Sr., *Thurber, Texas: The Life and Death of a Company Coal Town*, ed. Harwood P. Hinton (Abilene: State House Press, 2005), 6-9; Marilyn D. Rhinehart, *A Way of Work and a Way of Life: Coal Mining in Thurber, Texas, 1888-1926* (College Station: Texas A&M University Press, 1992), 41-43, 64-65; Don Woodard, *Black Diamonds! Black Gold!* (Lubbock: Texas Tech University Press, 1998), 36-46. Among other scholars, Stuart D. Brandes discusses company towns in the context of "welfare capitalism;" see his *American Welfare Capitalism, 1880-1940* (Chicago: University of Chicago Press, 1976). Oil company camps certainly fit within the parameters of welfare capitalism, as do company magazines.

3. Arvin D. Eady to Roger M. Olien, interview, Oct. 27, 1979, Midland, TX; Roger M. Olien and Diana D. Olien [Hinton], *Oil Booms: Social Change in Five Texas Towns* (Lincoln: University of Nebraska Press, 1982), 30-32, 47; Roger M. Olien and Diana D. Olien [Hinton], *Life in the Oil Fields* (Austin: Texas Monthly Press, 1986), 109-124. Prevailing patterns of discrimination barred African Americans and Latinos from most oilfield jobs; see Olien and Hinton, *Oil Booms*, Chapter 5. Tapes of interviews by Olien are in the possession of the author.
4. For a brief introduction to production realities in early oilfields, see Diana D. Olien [Hinton] and Roger M. Olien, *Oil in Texas: The Gusher Age, 1895-1945* (Austin: University of Texas Press, 2002), 19-20.
5. Olien and Hinton, *Oil Booms*, 22-28.
6. Gerald T. White, *Formative Years in the Far West: A History of Standard Oil Company of California and Predecessors through 1919* (New York: Appleton-Century Crofts, 1962), 584; Henrietta M. Larson and Kenneth W. Porter, *History of Humble Oil and Refining Company: A Study of Industrial Growth* (New York: Harper & Brothers, 1959), 68-69.
7. Albert R. Parker, "Life and Labor in the Mid-Continent Oil Fields. 1859-1945" (Ph.D. Diss., University of Oklahoma, 1951), 167 (quotation). See also Olien and Hinton, *Oil Booms*, 49-51; Diana D. Olien [Hinton], "Domesticity and the Texas Oil Fields: Dimensions of Women's Experience, 1920-1950," in *Women and Texas History: Selected Essays*, ed. Fane Downs and Nancy Baker Jones (Austin: Texas State Historical Association, 1993), 116-126.
8. White, *Formative Years*, 414-415 (quotation); Kendall Beaton, *Enterprise in Oil: A History of Shell in the United States* (New York: Appleton-Century Crofts, 1957), 73-75.
9. White, *Formative Years*, 414-415; Larson and Porter, *History of Humble*, 126; Clell Reed to Olien, interview, Apr. 6, 1984, San Angelo, TX.
10. E. E. Magill, "Where Humble Folk Live at Hewitt," *Humble Magazine* (Mar. 1922), 14-15; T. H. Hamilton, "Baytown," *Humble Magazine* (Aug. 1921), 26; A. T. Newkirk, "Baytown as an Industrial Community," *Humble Magazine* (Nov. 1921), 15-17; Larson and Porter, *History of Humble*, 212-213.
11. Ralph T. Baker, "Oil Field Workers Display Keen Humor," *Oil and Gas Journal* (July 24, 1924), 2l.
12. Olien and Hinton, *Oil Booms*, 47; Samuel D. Myres, *The Permian Basin: Petroleum Empire of the Southwest, Era of Discovery* (El Paso: Permian Press, 1973), 259.
13. Bill D. Ingram, *There Once Was a Spot: People, Perceptions, and Memories of Gulf Oil Corporation Camps in Crane County, Texas, 1926-1955* (n.p., 1998), 3-5, 9-12, 14, 20; William H. Measures to Olien, interview, Feb. 16, 1979, Midland, TX; Hood V. May to Olien and J. Conrad Dunagan, interview, Apr. 19, 1978, Monahans, TX.
14. Ingram, *There Once Was a Spot*, 41; F. B. Taylor, "Management Problems of Company Camps," *Petroleum Engineer* (Oct. 1935), 94-97; Bessie Leonard to Diana Davids Olien [Hinton], interview, May 19, 1978, Midland, TX; Mr. and Mrs. Joe Koesel to Hinton, interview, Mar. 27, 1982, Texan, TX; Bill Collyns to Olien, interview, May 9, 1979, Midland, TX; Lois A. Collins, "The Significance of Company Oil Camps in the Development of the Permian Basin," *Permian Historical Annual* (1988), 90. Tapes of interviews by Hinton are in the possession of the author.

15. Mr. and Mrs. C. E. Cullum to Olien, interview, Aug. 12, 1980, Wickett, TX; Collyns to Olien, interview, May 9, 1979, Midland, TX; Anne Swendig to Hinton, interview, May 31, 1979, Midland, Tex.; Reed to Olien, interview, Apr. 6, 1984, San Angelo, TX; Ingram, *There Once Was a Spot*, 17, 20.
16. Reed to Olien, interview, Apr. 6, 1984, San Angelo, TX; Mrs. Clell Reed to Hinton, interview, Apr. 6, 1984, San Angelo, TX; Patience Blakeney Zellmer to Hinton, interview, Sept. 9, 1983, Midland, TX; Mrs. G. C. McAuley to Hinton, interview, Mar. 24, 1984, Monahans, TX; Alice Keene to Hinton, interview, Mar. 21, 1978, Wink, TX; Ruth Godwin to Olien, interview, Mar. 16, 1978, Kermit, TX.
17. Ingram, *There Once Was a Spot*, 21; Collyns to Olien, interview, May 9, 1979, Midland, TX; Koesel to Hinton, interview, Mar. 27, 1982, Texon, TX; Dave Brazel to Olien, interview, July 28, 1980, Big Spring, TX. For a similar perspective on company athletic teams outside oil, see Brandes, *American Welfare Capitalism*, 77-78.
18. G. E. Bales, "North Texas Celebrates," *Humble Magazine* (Aug. 1921), 22-23; "Kermit Area Celebrates," *Magnolia News* (Oct. 1937), 27.
19. R. S. Sterling, "Understanding and Co-operation: The Keystone of Successful Intra-Company Relations," *Humble Magazine* (May 1921), 5-6. As Stuart Brandes points out, many American companies of the 1920s used company magazines with similar content for similar purposes. See *American Welfare Capitalism*, 62-63.
20. Charles Stroder to Olien and Hinton, interview, Aug. 21, 1980, Crane, TX; Collyns to Olien, interview, May 9, 1979, Midland, TX.
21. Ingram, *There Once Was a Spot*, 43, 12-13; Mr. and Mrs. E.W. Purdy to Hinton, interview, Apr. 10, 1984, Midland, TX; "Reunion," *Magnolia News* (Oct. 1937), 24.
22. Zellmer to Hinton, interview, Sept. 9, 1983, Midland, TX; Swendig to Hinton, interview, May 31, 1979, Midland, TX; Mrs. Joe Starkey to Hinton, interview, Aug. 14, 1980, Monahans, TX.
23. Ingram, *There Once Was a Spot*, 45-46; "Means Camp Site to Become a Public Park," *Humble Way* (Aug. 1958), 23; "Parks from Company Camps," *Humble Way* (Summer 1963), 26-28.
24. Mrs. Reed to Hinton, interview, Apr. 6, 1984, San Angelo, TX; Ingram, *There Once Was a Spot*, 1, 42.

SPECHT

1. Mody C. Boatright, *Folklore of the Oil Industry* (Dallas: Southern Methodist University Press, 1963), 155.
2. Bill C. Malone, *Country Music U.S.A.*, 2nd rev. ed. (Austin: University of Texas Press, 2002), 502.
3. Elmer Kelton, conversation with the author, Dec. 1, 2007. Except for a short-term summer job on a tanking crew, Kelton never worked in the oilfields, but he has provided compelling descriptions of how the discovery of oil in the late 1920s affected daily life in Crane, Texas. See his foreword in Estha B. Stowe, *Oil Field Child* (Fort Worth: TCU Press, 1989); the prologue and author's notes in Elmer Kelton, *Honor at Daybreak* (Fort Worth: TCU Press, 2002); the chapter "Oil Boom

Days in West Texas" in Elmer Kelton, *My Kind of Heroes* (Abilene: State House Press, 2004); and Chapter Five in Elmer Kelton, *Sandhills Bay: The Winding Trail of a Texas Writer* (New York: Forge, 2007).

4. Boatright, *Folklore of the Oil Industry*, 155. Boatright included a chapter, "Song and Verse," in *Folklore of the Oil Industry* to support his point that "in the oil industry the conditions that favor the creation of folksongs were absent," and he provided lyrics for two additional songs in Mody C. Boatright and William A. Owens, *Tales from the Derrick Floor: A People's History of the Oil Industry* (Garden City, NY: Doubleday, 1970), 162, 167-168.
5. Boatright, *Folk/me of the Oil Industry*, 156.
6. Richard M. Dorson, *America in Legend: Folklore from the Colonial Period to the Present* (New York: Pantheon Books, 1973), 214-215.
7. Margaret Anne Mong, comp., *Oil Fever Songbook: A Collection of Popular Songs from the 1860s* (Oil City, PA: M.A. Mong, 1995) gathers nineteen examples of sheet music published in the mid-1860s. Mong further suggests that "the earliest ditties about oil probably appeared [in Pennsylvania] in the 1840s...as advertising verses sung to popular tunes of the day by the teamster-salesmen-entertainer wagon drivers employed by Samuel Martin Kier" (p. ii).
8. In addition to country music, petroleum-related songs can be found in the recorded repertoire of blues, rhythm & blues, Cajun, and rock 'n' roll performers. The author plans to explore this topic further in the manuscript "Smell That Sweet Perfume: Oil Patch Songs on Record."
9. Slim Willet, "Johnny Don't Drill Anymore," *Texas Oil Patch Songs by Slim Willet*, Winston LP 1040 (1959).
10. Ibid.
11. Joe W. Specht, "Slim Willet," in Roy R. Barkley et al. (eds.), *The Handbook of Texas Music* (Austin: Texas State Historical Association, 2003), 354.
12. Walter Rundell Jr., *Early Texas Oil: A Photographic History, 1866-1936* (College Station: Texas A&M University Press, 1977), 164-171; Carl C. Rister, *Oil! Titan of the Southwest* (Norman: University of Oklahoma Press, 1949), 158-163; Boyce House, *Were You in Ranger?* (Dallas: Tardy Publishing Company, 1935), 60-87; John D. Palmer, "A History of the Desdemona Oil Boom" (M.A. Thesis, Hardin-Simmons University, 1938).
13. A. C. Greene, *A Personal Country* (New York: Knopf, 1969), 60 61.
14. Mary Ficklen, "The Midas-Rich Town That Might Have Been," *Dallas Morning News*, May 23, 1976; Rundell, *Early Texas Oil*, 166.
15. Quoted in Anne Dingus, "Diamonds and Galoshes," *Texas Monthly* 14 (Jan. 1986): 66.
16. Slim Willet, liner notes, *Texas Oil Patch Songs by Slim Willet*, Winston LP 1040 (1959).
17. Jimmie Moore to author, Dec. 23, 2008, interview (notes in possession of the author).
18. Specht, "Slim Willet," 354.
19. "Pinball Millionaire" was among the first songs Willet wrote; Hank Locklin (4 Star 1466) and Gene O'Quin (Capitol 1148) each recorded versions in 1950.
20. Kevin Coffey to author, Dec. 17, 2008, e-mail (copy in possession of the author).

21. Specht, "Slim Willet," 354.
22. Walter Rundell Jr., *Oil in West Texas and New Mexico: A Pictorial History of the Permian Basin* (College Station: Texas A&M University Press, 1982), 129-136; Samuel D. Myres, *The Permian Basin, Petroleum Empire of the Southwest, Volume 2: Era of Advancement from the Depression to the Present* (El Paso: Permian Press, 1977), 268-295; Scurry County Historical Commission, *Snyder, Texas: The Boom Year* (Snyder, TX: Scurry County Historical Commission, 2008).
23. "Hope, Crosby Cashed in on Scurry County Oil," *Abilene Reporter-News*, Mar. 22, 1981. Fort Worth oil man W. A. "Monty" Moncrief brought Hope and Crosby in on the deal, but even though the partnership proved very lucrative for Bob and Bing over the long run, the initial well was a dry hole, and the two stars "wanted nothing to do with [Moncrief] after that first loss." See Sally Helgesen, *Wildcatters: A Story of Texans, Oil, and Money* (Garden City, NY: Doubleday, 1981), 88-90.
24. Richard K. Spottswood and Richard A. Reuss, booklet notes, *Music in America, Volume 8: Songs of Labor & Livelihood*, Recording Laboratory LBC 8 (1978), 8. Useful glossaries for petroleum industry terminology and slang can be found in Gerald Lynch, *Roughnecks, Drillers, and Tool Pushers: Thirty-Three Years in the Oil Fields* (Austin: University of Texas Press, 1987), 249-252; Diana D. Olien [Hinton] and Roger M. Olien, *Oil in Texas: The Gusher Age, 1895-1945* (Austin: University of Texas Press, 2002), 277-283; Boatright and Owens, *Tales from the Derrick Floor*, 152-170; and Rister, *Oil!*, 416-423. For "the evolution of equipment and methods used in drilling [with] every major tool and method described in detail," see John E. Brantly, *History of Oil Well Drilling* (Houston: Gulf Publishing Company, 1971).
25. Mike Hammack to the author, Mar. 11, 2008, e-mail (copy in possession of the author).
26. Slim Willet, "Shooting Star," *Cowboy Songs* 25 (March 1953): 10. For more on the "Stars" saga, see Joe W. Specht, "'Don't Let the Stars Get in Your Eyes': Slim Willet's Idiosyncratic Chart-Topper Lives On," *Journal of Texas Music History* 9 (2009), 36-47.
27. Dave Coslett and Jim Carll, "Oil-Created Hadacol Corner Offers Holiday Enchantment," *San Angelo Standard-Times*, May 24, 1951; "Midkiff-Hadacol Corner," Upton County Historical Commission, *Pictorial History of Upton County* (Austin: Nortex Press, 1994), 199; Rundell, *Oil in West Texas and New Mexico*, 130.
28. Teresa M. Latzel, "Midkiff, Texas" (historical narrative submitted to the Texas State Historical Commission, 2007), 4; Julia C. Smith, "Midkiff, Texas," *The Handbook of Texas Online*, http://www.tshaonline.org/handbook [accessed July 7, 2007].
29. Specht, "Slim Willet," 354.
30. Katharyn Duff, *Abilene on Catclaw Creek: A Profile of a West Texas Town* (Abilene: Reporter Publishing Co., 1969), 210-211; Naomi H. Kincaid, "Oil Development in the Abilene Area," *West Texas Historical Association Yearbook* 20 (Oct. 1945): 20-28.
31. Slim Willet, "Roughneck," *Texas Oil Patch Songs by Slim Willet*, Winston LP 1040 (1959).

32. Ibid. Clarence C. Pope, who worked as an oil scout for the Sun Oil Company, characterized the deep sand in the northern part of Crane County as "crawly sneaky sand," and the veteran reconnoiterer always kept a short-handled shovel in his vehicle to dig new ruts in the "sandy thoroughfare" when required. See Clarence C. Pope, *An Oil Scout in the Permian Basin, 1924-1960* (El Paso: Permian Press, 1972), 14.
33. F. Jay Schempf, *Pioneering Offshore: The Early Years* (Houston: Offshore Energy Center, 2007); Robert Gramling, *Oil on the Edge: Offshore Development, Conflict, Gridlock* (Albany: State University of New York, 1996); Joseph A. Pratt, Tyler Priest, and Christopher J. Castaneda, *Offshore Pioneers: Brown & Root and the History of Offshore Oil and Gas* (Houston: Gulf Publishing Company, 1997); Kenny A. Franks and Paul F. Lambert, *Early Louisiana and Arkansas Oil: A Photographic History, 1901-1946* (College Station: Texas A&M University Press, 1982).
34. James W. Winfrey, "Oil Patch Talk," in *From Hell to Breakfast,* eds. Mody C. Boatright and Donald Day (Austin: Texas Folklore Society, 1944), 142.
35. Frank Mangan, *The Pipeliners* (El Paso: Guynes Press, 1977) is the place to begin for the history of El Paso Natural Gas Company; see also John H. McFall, "El Paso Natural Gas Company," *The Handbook of Texas Online,* http://www.tshaonline.org/handbook [accessed Mar. 18, 2008].
36. Mangan, *Pipeliners,* 47.
37. Slim Willet, "Drill Bit Honky Tonk," *Texas Oil Patch Songs by Slim Willet,* Winston LP 1040 (1959). To get a sense of the pecking order on the rig, see Paul F. Lambert and Kenny A. Franks, eds., *Voices from the Oil Fields* (Norman: University of Oklahoma Press, 1984), an insightful collection of interviews with rig builders, drillers, roughnecks, pipeliners and the like who worked primarily in the Oklahoma fields in the early twentieth century.
38. Willet, "Roughneck."
39. Slim Willet, "Morning Tower," *Texas Oil Patch Songs by Slim Willet,* Winston LP 1040 (1959).
40. Slim Willet, "Haywire Jones," *Texas Oil Patch Songs by Slim Willet,* Winston LP 1040 (1959).
41. Slim Willet, "Boom Town Man," *Texas Oil Patch Songs by Slim Willet,* Winston LP 1040 (1959).
42. Malone, *Country Music U.S.A.,* 153.
43. Bill Wittliff, "Afterward," *Boystown: La Zona De Tolerancia* (New York: Aperture, 2000), 107. Willet's "Villa Cuna" (4 Star 1642) is an instrumental tribute of sorts to Villa Acuna (now Ciudad Acuna), located just across the Rio Grande River from Del Rio, Texas, and is further indication of a familiarity with the South Texas border region.
44. For a discussion of the variety of roles available to women who followed the boom, see Roger M. Olien and Diana D. Olien [Hinton], *Oil Booms: Social Change in Five Texas Towns* (Lincoln: University of Nebraska Press, 1982) and Roger M. Olien and Diana D. Olien [Hinton], *Life in the Oil Fields* (Austin: Texas Monthly Press, 1986). Several of the stories in Winifred M. Sanford, *Windfall and Other Stories* (Fort Worth: TCU Press, 1988) capture a sense of life for boomtown women in Texas during the 1920s.

45. Slim Willet, "Rig Moving Man," *Texas Oil Patch Songs by Slim Willet*, Winston LP 1040 (1959).
46. The "rigors and pleasures" of living in "rag town" are described in Diana D. Olien [Hinton], "Keeping House in a Tent," *Permian Historical Annual* 22 (1982): 3-14.
47. Slim Willet, "El Paso Gas," *Texas Oil Patch Songs by Slim Willet*, Winston LP 1040 (1959). For a sampling of firsthand accounts of what life was like for wives in the oilfield, see Stowe, *Oil Field Child*, and Bill Porterfield, *Diddy Waw Diddy: Passage of an American Son* (New York: HarperCollins, 1994).
48. Willet, "Drill Bit Honky Tonk."
49. Boatright, *Folklore of the Oil Industry*, 165-194.
50. Ibid., 166, 171-172. Newspaperman and author Boyce House, who published a series of rousing exposes on life in the Texas oilfields of the 1920s-1930s, repeats a yarn describing Gib Morgan's attempt to "sink the deepest well in the history of the world" when one of the workers fell into the hole and dropped "clear through to China." See Boyce House, *I Give You Texas! 500 Jokes of the Lone Star State* (San Antonio: Naylor Publishing, 1943), 59.
51. The liner notes to *Texas Oil Patch Songs* do not identify the musicians, although it seems clear that Dean Beard handles the piano chores on several tracks. See Dick Grant, "Slim Willet: Smell That Sweet Perfume," *Rockin' Fifties* 68 (June 1998): 17, and Clay Glover, "The Legend of Dean Beard," *Rockin' Fifties* 52 (June 1994): 22.
52. Earl Carmack to the author, Sep. 7, 2007, interview (notes in possession of the author).
53. Ibid.
54. A promotional copy of Winston 1036-45 with date stamped on the label, "May 15, 1959," is in the author's possession.
55. Clay Glover indicates the album was released in November 1959. See Glover, "The Legend of Dean Beard," 22.
56. Ten of the twelve tracks on *Texas Oil Patch Songs* are available on compact disc as *Slim Willet*, Collector Records CLCD 2857 (n.d.).
57. Kevin Coffey, Notes, Jimmie Dolan, *Juke Box Boogie*, Bear Family BCD 16192 (2000).
58. *Music in America, Volume 8: Songs of Labor & Livelihood*, Recording Laboratory, LBC 8 (1978).
59. Zanetis made sure to specifically mention Winthrop Rockefeller in "Arkansas," the last song on the album: "All the big [oil] men ain't in Texas...Rockefeller is a giant that makes most Texas men look pretty small."
60. *Alex Zanetis Writes and Sings the Story of the Oil Fields*, RIK M 1000 (1964), has been further cited as an example of commercially recorded songs that "capture the occupational jargon and nature of work in the Southwestern oil fields." See Patrick Huber, "Oilworkers," in *American Folklore: An Encyclopedia*, ed. Jan Harold Brunvand (New York: Garland Publishing, 1996), 528. Other albums with a focus on the petroleum industry include Wayne Nutt, *Oil Field Man*, Epic [UK] EPC 69232 (1975); Buddy Parman, *Oil Field Trash*, Dayton Records LP 1004 ART (1981); Wes St. Jon, *Oilfield Cowboy*, Star Key (2004) and *Patch Pride*, Star Key (2006).

61. Sheb Wooley's "Roughneck," the other non-Zanetis original on Thompson's album, is also credited to Zanetis; in addition, titles for two songs were changed: "Wildcats from San Antonio" to "Wildcats from Way Back" and "Tom Kelly" inexplicably to "Ballad of Ed Thomas."
62. Joe W. Specht, "An Interview with Hoyle Nix, the West Texas Cowboy," *Old Time Music* 36 (Summer 1981): 11. Jody Nix also recorded another Willet composition, "My Love Song to You," for his 1995 album, *When It's All Said and Done* (JNP).
63. Jody Nix to author, Aug. 13, 2008, e-mail (copy in possession of the author).
64. *Billboard*, Feb. 24, 1962, p. 39. The magazine's ratings department assigned "Everything Is Shakin' Fine"/"Big Money" to the "moderate sales potential" category.
65. Jimmie Moore found this quote on her husband's nightstand, and she thought it just right for the headstone. Moore to author, Dec. 23, 2008 (interview).

DIXON

1. "Dust Bowl Timeline," U.S. Department of Agriculture, Natural Resources Conservation Services, http://www.id.nrcs.usda. gov/about/history.html [accessed Dec. 26, 2007].
2. Daniel Yergin, *The Prize: The Epic Quest for Oil, Money, and Power* (New York: Free Press, 1992), 220-221.
3. C. O. Rison, "Manufacture of Nitroglycerin and Use of High Explosives in Oil and Gas Wells," in *Petroleum Development and Technology, 1928-1929* (New York: AIME, 1929). 209.
4. New Jersey State Library, "New Jersey Civil War Records," http://www. njstatelib. org/NJInformation/ Searchable_Publications/dvil%2owar/NJCWn881.html [accessed June 19, 2009]; Darius N. Couch, "Sumner's Right Grand Division," in *Battles and Leaders of the Civil War*, ed. Ned Bradford (New York: Appleton-Century-Crofts, Inc., 1956), 310; "Shooters," *The Petroleum Age* 4 (Sept. 2007): 8-9; Wilber F. Cloud, *Petroleum Production* (Norman: University of Oklahoma Press, 1937): 401.
5. Shelby Foote, *The Civil War: A Narrative* (New York: Random House, 1963), 33-34; Rison, "Manufacture of Nitroglycerin and Use of High Explosives in Oil and Gas Wells," 239.
6. Ibid., 245.
7. Ibid., 246.
8. Ibid., 247.
9. Cloud, *Petroleum Production*, 405-406.
10. Roger M. Olien, "The Oil Field Shooters," http://www.texancultures.utsa.edu/ hiddenhistory/Pages1/ OlienOilShooter.htm [accessed Oct. 12, 2007].
11. Rison, "Manufacture of Nitroglycerin and Use of High Explosives in Oil and Gas Wells," 248-51.
12. Unidentified oil well shooter to Ned DeWitt [n.d.], in "The Shooter," in *Voices from the Oil Fields*, ed. Paul F. Lambert and Kenny A. Franks (Norman: University of Oklahoma Press, 1976), 100-101.

13. Ned DeWitt, "The Welder," in Lambert and Franks, *Voices from the Oil Fields*, 219-220.
14. C. L. "Lee" McKinney to Samuel D. Myres, Sept. 23, 1971, interview (Archives of the Permian Basin Petroleum Museum, Midland, TX); Diana D. Olien [Hinton] and Roger M. Olien, *Oil in Texas: The Gusher Age, 1895- 1945* (Austin: University of Texas Press, 2002), 79-82.
15. Specialty Shooting Company Nitro Truck Exhibit (Permian Basin Petroleum Museum, Midland, TX); DeWitt, "Shooter," 109; "Thornton, Ward A.," *The Handbook of Texas Online*, http://www.tshaonline.org/handbook/online/articles/TT/fth57.html [accessed Oct. 4, 2007].
16. *Odessa Times*, May 11, 1934.
17. McKinney to Myres, Sept. 23, 1971 (interview); Olien, "Oil Field Shooters."
18. Rison, "Manufacture of Nitroglycerin and Use of High Explosives in Oil and Gas Wells," 263.
19. Cloud, *Petroleum Production*, 412-414.
20. Rison, "Manufacture of Nitroglycerin and Use of High Explosives in Oil and Gas Wells," 265-266.
21. Cloud, *Petroleum Production*, 412; McKinney to Myres, Sept. 23, 1971 (interview).
22. Ibid.
23. Cloud, *Petroleum Production*, 405-409.
24. Rison, "Manufacture of Nitroglycerin and Use of High Explosives in Oil and Gas Wells," 273-279; Cloud, *Petroleum Production*, 405-410.
25. Rison, "Manufacture of Nitroglycerin and Use of High Explosives in Oil and Gas Wells," 271.
26. Paul F. Lewis, "The How and Why of Oil Well Shooting," *The Oil Weekly*, Mar. 7, 1938, p. 50.
27. Rison, "Manufacture of Nitroglycerin and Use of High Explosives in Oil and Gas Wells," 416.
28. Lewis, "How and Why of Oil Well Shooting," 46, 50.
29. Cloud, *Petroleum Production*, 407; "Shorty" Moses to Ned DeWitt [n.d.], in "Shooters Don't Make But One Mistake" in Lambert and Franks. *Voices from the Oil Fields*, 104-105 (quotation).
30. Hinton and Olien, *Oil in Texas*, 185-190; DeWitt, "Shooter," 90, 104-105; Yergin, *Prize*, 251-257.
31. McKinney to Myres, Sept. 23, 1971 (interview); Lewis, "How and Why of Oil Well Shooting," 45.
32. McKinney to Myres, Sept. 23, 1971 (interview); F. Stanley, *The Tex Thornton Story* (Nazareth, TX: n.p., 1971), 11.
33. Lewis, "How and Why of Oil Well Shooting," 46.
34. Ibid., 46-47.
35. Ibid., 52.